HAMLYN ALL COLOUR
CAKES AND BAKING

HAMLYN ALL COLOUR
CAKES AND BAKING

HAMLYN

Front jacket shows, clockwise from top right, *Basic White Bread* (1), *Chocolate Caramel Slices* (233), *Butter Triangles* (21), *Walnut and Chocolate Gâteau* (185)

Title page shows, clockwise from top right, *Iced Fancies* (101), *Aladdin's Cave Gâteau* (207), *Humpty Dumpty* (177), *Bara Brith* (34)

Back jacket shows, clockwise from top right, *Crystallized Fruit Cake* (53), *Summerfruit Ring* (261), *Choux Cream Butterflies* (97), *Valentine Cake* (145)

Published 1989 by
The Hamlyn Publishing Group Limited
a division of the Octopus Publishing Group
Michelin House, 81 Fulham Road,
London SW3 6RB

Reprinted 1990

Taken from The Octopus Publishing Group copyright publications

Special photography by David Jordan: 1, 31, 234, 264, 266
All other photography from the Octopus Picture Library:
James Jackson, Fred Mancini, Roger Phillips, Paul Williams

Line drawings by Rob Shone
except 4, 8, 10, 24, 41, 49, 96 by Roberta Colegate-Stone;
20, 87, 90 by Gay John Galsworthy; 58 by Sandra Pond

ISBN 0 600 56739 7

Set in Linotron Univers
by J&L Composition Ltd, Filey, North Yorkshire
Produced by Mandarin Offset
Printed and bound in Hong Kong

Contents

Introduction

The welcoming and enticing aroma of freshly-baked bread, the crisp and short bite of home-made biscuits and cookies, the singing hiss of griddle scones and the proud presentation, then slicing, of a specially-made birthday or celebration cake are just some of the delights of home baking.

Hamlyn All Colour Cakes and Baking *is a celebration of home baking, providing an invaluable collection of recipes for cakes, biscuits, teabreads, gâteaux, small cakes and pâtisserie. The variety on offer means that there is bound to be a perfect cake, cookie, bread or gâteau in terms of flavour, appearance, degree of preparation complexity and occasion suitability every time you bake. Choosing your cake with care, remembering how much time you have for baking, icing and decorating, ensures success.*

A colour photograph illustrates each recipe, so that you can see the result you are aiming for. Those important decorating and finishing touches are also highlighted in the photographs as well as in the Cook's Tips which appear below each recipe. Attractive colour coding identifies individual chapters as you flick through the book.

Preparation and cooking times are clearly given before the recipe method, so that you can see at a glance whether you have time to cook a particular recipe. And, to save repetition, many of the basic recipes used throughout are grouped together at the front of the book for easy reference.

Choose from nearly 300 appetizing recipes to find the right one for every occasion, be it a bread for breakfast, a family cake for elevenses, a biscuit for a packed lunch box, a tea-time pastry, elegant gâteaux for a special dinner party menu or a novelty cake for a celebratory party.

Basic Fruit Cake

250 g/9 oz butter
275 g/10 oz soft brown sugar
1 tablespoon black treacle
6 eggs
300 g/11 oz plain flour
1½ teaspoons ground mixed spice
¾ teaspoon grated nutmeg
75 g/3 oz ground almonds
grated rind of 2 lemons
grated rind of 2 oranges
100 g/4 oz chopped almonds
100 g/4 oz glacé cherries
175 g/6 oz raisins
300 g/11 oz sultanas
450 g/1 lb currants
100 g/4 oz chopped mixed peel
3 tablespoons brandy
2 tablespoons orange juice

Cream the butter and sugar until light and fluffy. Beat in the treacle. Add the eggs, one at a time, adding a little of the flour with each egg after the first. Mix the flour with all the remaining ingredients except the brandy and orange juice, and gradually fold into the creamed mixture. Stir in the brandy and orange juice. Place in a 23-cm/9-in square or 30-cm/10-in round deep cake tin greased and lined with double greaseproof paper. Protect the outside of the tin with newspaper and bake at 140C, 275F, gas 1 for 3–5 hours, checking after the first 3 hours, then at intervals after that. Allow the cake to cool in the tin for 15 minutes before turning out to cool on a wire rack.

Whisked Sponge

3 eggs
100 g/4 oz caster sugar
75 g/3 oz plain flour, sifted

Place the eggs and sugar in a heatproof bowl over a pan of simmering water and whisk until the mixture is thick and pale. Remove from the heat and whisk until cool. Fold in the flour then turn into a 23-cm/9-in moule à la manqué tin or cake tin. Bake at 190C, 375F, gas 5, for 35–40 minutes. Turn onto a wire rack to cool. Use as required.

Variations
Chocolate: Replace 25 g/1 oz flour with cocoa powder.
Coffee: Add 1 tablespoon instant coffee powder with the flour.

Choux Pastry

150 g/5 oz plain flour
pinch of salt
100 g/4 oz butter
250 ml/8 fl oz water
4 eggs, beaten

Sift the flour and salt together and set aside. Melt the butter in a pan. Add the water and bring to the boil. Add the flour all at once and beat until the mixture leaves the sides of the pan. Cool slightly, then add the eggs a little at a time, beating vigorously. Use as required.

Shortcrust Pastry

225 g/8 oz plain flour
pinch of salt
50 g/2 oz lard
50 g/2 oz butter or margarine
3 tablespoons cold water

Sift the flour and salt into a bowl. Rub in the lard and butter until the mixture resembles fine breadcrumbs. Add the water and bind to a firm but pliable dough. Use as required.

Rich Shortcrust Pastry

275 g/10 oz plain flour
175 g/6 oz butter
2 tablespoons caster sugar
1 egg yolk, beaten with 1 tablespoon cold water

Sift the flour into a bowl and rub in the butter until the mixture resembles fine breadcrumbs. Stir in the sugar and add enough egg yolk mixture to make a firm dough. Knead lightly until smooth, wrap in clingfilm and chill for 30 minutes. Use as required.

Easy Flaky Pastry

350 g/12 oz plain flour
pinch of salt
50 g/2 oz lard, chilled
175 g/6 oz butter, chilled and cut into 5-
    mm/¼-in dice
about 6 tablespoons iced water

Sift the flour and salt into a bowl and rub in the lard. Add the diced butter and rub it until the mixture resembles fine bread-crumbs. Sprinkle on the water and mix with a knife to a smooth dough. Turn onto a flat surface and shape into a flat disc. Wrap in clingfilm and chill for 1 hour. Use as required.

Almond Paste

550 g/1¼ lb ground almonds
275 g/10 oz icing sugar
275 g/10 oz caster sugar
2 teaspoons lemon juice
few drops of almond essence
few drops of orange flower water
2 eggs

Place the ground almonds, icing and caster sugar in a bowl and mix well. Add the lemon juice, almond essence, orange flower water and sufficient egg to form a stiff but manageable paste. Knead together with the fingers until smooth. **Enough to cover a 30-cm/10-in round cake or 23-cm/9-in square cake**.

Apricot Glaze

225 g/8 oz apricot jam
3 tablespoons water
squeeze of lemon juice

Place the jam and water in a pan and heat until dissolved. Add the lemon juice, then sieve and return to the pan. Bring to the boil and simmer until syrupy. Use while still warm.

American Frosting

1 egg white
175 g/6 oz icing sugar
1 tablespoon golden syrup
3 tablespoons water
pinch of salt
1 teaspoon lemon juice

Place all the ingredients in a bowl over a pan of hot water and whisk until the icing stands in peaks. Remove from the heat and continue whisking until cool. Use at once.

Butter Icing

75 g/3 oz butter or margarine
225 g/8 oz icing sugar
2 tablespoons milk

Place all the ingredients in a mixing bowl and beat together with a wooden spoon until creamy.

Variations

Coffee: Replace 1 tablespoon milk with 1 tablespoon coffee essence or 1 tablespoon instant coffee dissolved in 1 tablespoon boiling water. Cool before adding to the icing.
Lemon: Substitute lemon juice for the milk.
Orange: Substitute orange juice for the milk.
Chocolate: Replace 1 tablespoon milk with 1 tablespoon cocoa powder blended with 2 tablespoons hot water.

Chocolate Fudge Icing

50 g/2 oz butter or margarine
1 tablespoon milk
1 tablespoon cocoa powder
2 tablespoons hot water
225 g/8 oz icing sugar, sifted

Place the butter, milk, cocoa powder dissolved in the hot water and icing sugar in a bowl over a pan of hot water. Stir until smooth and glossy. Remove from the heat and allow to cool. Beat well with a wooden spoon until thick enough to spread.

Satin Icing

50 g/2 oz butter or margarine
4 tablespoons lemon juice
about 675 g/1½ lb icing sugar, sifted
few drops of food colouring (optional)

Warm the butter and lemon juice in a pan until melted. Add 225 g/8 oz of the icing sugar and heat gently, stirring, until dissolved. Increase the heat slightly and simmer gently for 2 minutes; do not overboil at this stage or the icing will be too hard. Remove from the heat and add a further 225 g/8 oz of the icing sugar. Beat thoroughly with a wooden spoon, then turn into a mixing bowl. Gradually mix in enough of the remaining icing sugar to give a soft dough. Turn onto a surface dusted with icing sugar and knead until smooth, adding colouring if used. Use to mould decorations or to cover the top and sides of a cake. If wrapped in clingfilm, this icing will keep in the refrigerator for up to 6 weeks.

Royal Icing

4 egg whites
1 kg/2 lb icing sugar, sifted
2 teaspoons glycerine
few drops of rose water

Place the egg whites in a bowl and whisk until frothy. Gradually add the icing sugar, beating well between additions, until the icing is shiny and very white. Finally beat in the glycerine and rose water. **Enough to cover the top and sides of a 30-cm/10-in round cake or 23-cm/9-in square cake**.

Notes for American and Australian users

In America the 8-fl oz measuring cup is used. In Australia metric measures are now used in conjunction with the standard 250-ml measuring cup. The Imperial pint, used in Britain and Australia, is 20 fl oz, while the American pint is 16 fl oz. It is important to remember that the Australian tablespoon differs from both the British and American tablespoons; the table below gives a comparison. The British standard tablespoon, which has been used throughout this book, holds 17.7 ml, the American 14.2 ml, and the Australian 20 ml. A teaspoon holds approximately 5 ml in all three countries.

British	American	Australian
1 teaspoon	1 teaspoon	1 teaspoon
1 tablespoon	1 tablespoon	1 tablespoon
2 tablespoons	3 tablespoons	2 tablespoons
3½ tablespoons	4 tablespoons	3 tablespoons
4 tablespoons	5 tablespoons	3½ tablespoons

An Imperial/American guide to solid and liquid measures

Imperial	American
Solid measures	
1 lb butter or margarine	2 cups
1 lb flour	4 cups
1 lb granulated or caster sugar	2 cups
1 lb icing sugar	3 cups
8 oz rice	1 cup
Liquid measures	
¼ pint liquid	⅔ cup liquid
½ pint	1¼ cups
¾ pint	2 cups
1 pint	2½ cups
1½ pints	3¾ cups
2 pints	5 cups (2½ pints)

Note: When making any of the recipes in this book, only follow one set of measures as they are not interchangeable.

Breads

This chapter offers more than the traditional baker's dozen of breads, from the basic white and wholemeal to the more unusual granary, French, soda, rye, herb, Naan, poppyseed and peanut, together with a good selection of rolls, muffins and small, shaped loaves. Many make delicious breakfast, tea, lunch or anytime eating, while others make tasty lunch box, picnic and snack time fare. When time is plentiful, consider baking in bulk and freeze away a good selection – all can be quickly defrosted, then refreshed in a hot oven for same-day baked freshness.

1 | Basic White Bread

Preparation time
20 minutes, plus about
3 hours to prove

Cooking time
35–40 minutes

Oven temperature
220C, 425F, gas 7

Makes 2
(1-kg/2-lb)
loaves

Calories
2635 per loaf

You will need
25 g/1 oz fresh yeast
1 teaspoon caster sugar
900 ml/1½ pints warm water
1.5 kg/3 lb strong plain white flour
1 tablespoon salt
1 tablespoon oil
flour to sprinkle

Cream the yeast with the sugar and a little of the water and leave for 10 minutes. Sift the flour and salt into a bowl. Pour in the yeast, remaining water and oil. Mix to a smooth dough.

Turn onto a floured surface and knead for 8–10 minutes until smooth and elastic. Place in a clean, warmed bowl, cover with a damp cloth and leave to rise in a warm place for 2 hours until doubled in size.

Knead on a floured surface for a few minutes, divide in half and place in two greased 1-kg/2-lb loaf tins. Cover and leave in a warm place for 30 minutes until risen to the tops of the tins.

Sprinkle with flour and bake for 35–40 minutes. Cool on a wire rack.

2 | Crusty French Loaves

Preparation time
20 minutes, plus about
2 hours to prove

Cooking time
22–25 minutes

Oven temperature
220C, 425F, gas 7

Makes 2 loaves

Calories
785 per loaf

You will need
2 teaspoons dried yeast
300 ml/½ pint warm water
1 teaspoon caster sugar
400 g/14 oz plain flour
50 g/2 oz cornflour
1 teaspoon salt
beaten egg to glaze
poppy seeds (optional)

Mix the yeast, water and sugar and leave for 10 minutes. Sift the flours and salt into a bowl. Gradually add the yeast liquid and mix to a dough. Turn onto a floured surface and knead for 5–10 minutes until smooth and elastic. Place in a clean, oiled bowl, cover and leave to rise in a warm place for 1 hour.

Knead for a few minutes, divide in half and roll each piece to a 35 × 15-cm/14 × 6-in oblong with rounded ends. Roll up from the long side like a Swiss roll and place, seam-side down, on a floured baking tray. Slash with a sharp knife at regular intervals. Mix a pinch of salt with the egg and glaze the loaves. Leave in a warm place for 30 minutes until doubled in size.

Sprinkle with poppyseeds if liked and bake for 22–25 minutes until crisp and brown. Cool on a wire rack.

Cook's Tip

Glaze bread according to whether you want it gold-crusted, floury-soft or crunchy-crisp. Glazing with beaten egg gives a golden look and brushing with milk or dusting with flour gives a soft bap-like appearance.

Brush lightly with vegetable oil for a crunchy crust.

Cook's Tip

If a softer French loaf is liked, place a roasting tin of hot water in the bottom of the oven during baking. The steam produced will help to keep the loaves a little softer in crust.

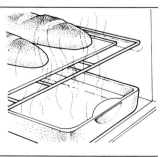

3 | Granary Bread

Preparation time
20 minutes, plus about
2 hours to prove

Cooking time
35–40 minutes

Oven temperature
220 C, 425 F, gas 7
190 C, 375 F, gas 5

**Makes 2 round
loaves**

Calories
1430 per loaf

You will need
1 tablespoon dried yeast
1 teaspoon caster sugar
450 ml/¾ pint warm water and milk
   mixed
275 g/10 oz plain wholewheat
   flour
275 g/10 oz strong plain white
   flour
1 tablespoon salt
15 g/½ oz butter or margarine
150 g/5 oz cracked wheat
50 g/2 oz wheatgerm
2 tablespoons malt extract

Mix the yeast, sugar, water and milk mixture and leave
for 10 minutes. Sift the flours and salt into a bowl. Rub
in the butter or margarine. Mix in 100 g/4 oz of the
cracked wheat and the wheatgerm. Add the yeast liquid
and malt and mix to a smooth dough.

Turn onto a floured surface and knead for 5 minutes
until smooth and elastic. Place in a clean, oiled bowl,
cover and leave to rise in a warm place for 1 hour.

Knead for a few minutes, divide in half and shape into
rounds. Place on greased baking trays. Cover and leave
in a warm place for 30 minutes until doubled in size,
then sprinkle with the remaining cracked wheat.

Bake at the hotter temperature for 15 minutes then
the lower for 20–25 minutes. Cool on a wire rack.

Cook's Tip

*Granary bread freezes
successfully for up to 3
months. Open freeze until
firm then wrap in foil or
freezer film. Remove, unwrap
and defrost slowly at cool
room temperature, then
refresh the loaf or loaves in a*
*hot oven for same-day baked
freshness.*

4 | Wholemeal Bread

Preparation time
20 minutes, plus about
3 hours to prove

Cooking time
30–40 minutes

Oven temperature
220 C, 425 F, gas 7

**Makes 4
(450-g/1-lb)
loaves**

Calories
1210 per loaf

You will need
1.5 kg/3 lb wholemeal flour
1 tablespoon salt
25 g/1 oz butter
25 g/1 oz fresh yeast
900 ml–1.15 litres/1½–2 pints
   warm water
2 tablespoons malt extract
cracked wheat to sprinkle

Mix the flour and salt and rub in the butter. Mix the
yeast with a little of the water and leave for 10 minutes.
Mix the malt extract with the remaining water, add to
the flour with the yeast and mix to a dough.

Knead for 8–10 minutes until smooth and elastic.
Place in a clean, warmed bowl, cover with a damp cloth
and leave to rise in a warm place for 2 hours until
doubled in size.

Knead for a few minutes, divide into 4 pieces and
place in greased 450-g/1-lb loaf tins or clay flowerpots. Brush with water and sprinkle with cracked wheat.
Cover and leave in a warm place for 30 minutes until
risen to the top of the tins.

Bake for 30–40 minutes. Cool on a wire rack.

Cook's Tip

*Season a new clay flowerpot
before use by brushing the
inside very thoroughly with
oil. Place the empty pot in a
moderately hot oven (200 C,
400 F, gas 6) for 15 minutes.
Allow to cool completely
before use.*

5 | *Savoury Soda Bread*

Preparation time
20 minutes

Cooking time
35 minutes

Oven temperature
220 C, 425 F, gas 7

Makes 1 round loaf

Total calories
1840

You will need
450 g / 1 lb plain flour
½ teaspoon cream of tartar
1 teaspoon salt
1½ teaspoons bicarbonate of soda
1 teaspoon dried mixed herbs
100 g / 4 oz cooked ham, chopped
300 ml / ½ pint milk
beaten egg to glaze

Sift the flour, cream of tartar, salt and bicarbonate of soda into a bowl. Add the herbs and ham and mix well. Add the milk and mix to a smooth dough.

Knead gently on a lightly floured surface, then shape into a round. Place on a greased baking tray and mark the top into four sections with a sharp knife.

Glaze with beaten egg and bake for 35 minutes until golden. Cool on a wire rack. Serve sliced, with butter if liked.

Cook's Tip

This delicious bread has its own baked-in filling and can be simply eaten plain, buttered or spread with a light cream cheese. It makes a tasty lunch box treat to serve with a crisp salad or with soup.

6 | *Wholemeal Soda Bread*

Preparation Time
20 minutes

Cooking time
25–30 minutes

Oven temperature
220 C, 425 F, gas 7

Makes 1 (675-g/ 1½-lb) loaf

Total calories
1995

You will need
225 g / 8 oz plain flour
1 teaspoon bicarbonate of soda
2 teaspoons cream of tartar
2 teaspoons salt
350 g / 12 oz wholemeal flour
300 ml / ½ pint milk
4 tablespoons water
flour to sprinkle

Sift the plain flour, soda, cream of tartar and salt into a mixing bowl. Stir in the wholemeal flour then add the milk and water and mix to a soft dough.

Turn onto a floured surface, knead lightly, then shape into a large round about 5 cm / 2 in thick.

Place on a floured baking tray, cut a deep cross on the top of the loaf and sprinkle with flour. Bake for 25–30 minutes. Transfer to a wire rack to cool.

Cook's Tip

To cook in the microwave, place on a large greased plate. Microwave on Medium (50%) power for 5 minutes, giving the plate a half turn twice. Increase the power setting to Full (100%) and microwave for a further 3 minutes, giving the plate a half turn twice. Allow to stand for 10 minutes before transferring to a wire rack to cool.

7 | Light Rye Bread

Preparation time
20 minutes, plus about
3½ hours to prove

Cooking time
50 minutes

Oven temperature
180 C, 350 F, gas 4

**Makes 2 (450-g/
1-lb) loaves**

Calories
1210 per loaf

You will need
675 g/1½ lb white rye flour
2 teaspoons caster sugar
2 (25-mg) ascorbic acid tablets,
   crushed
450 ml/¾ pint warm water
1 tablespoon dried yeast
2 teaspoons salt
2 tablespoons caraway seeds
knob of butter
1 teaspoon cornflour mixed with a
   little water to glaze

Sift 225 g/8 oz of the flour and the sugar into a bowl. Add the ascorbic acid tablets, water and yeast and mix until smooth. Leave in a warm place for 1 hour.

Sift the remaining flour and the salt into another bowl. Add the caraway seeds and rub in the butter. Add the risen yeast batter and mix to a soft dough. Knead on a floured surface for 5 minutes until smooth and elastic. Place in a clean, warmed bowl, cover and leave to rise in a warm place for 1–1½ hours until doubled in size.

Knead for a few minutes, divide in half and shape into smooth balls. Place on greased baking trays, cover and leave in a warm place until doubled in size.

Bake for 30 minutes, brush with the cornflour glaze and bake for a further 20 minutes. Cool on a wire rack.

Cook's Tip

Ascorbic acid tablets can be bought from chemists or can occasionally be purchased from supermarkets.

8 | Poppyseed Loaves

Preparation time
20 minutes

Cooking time
1¼ hours

Oven temperature
160 C, 325 F, gas 3

**Makes 2 (1-kg/
2-lb) loaves**

Calories
4225 per loaf

You will need
4 eggs, beaten
450 g/1 lb sugar
300 ml/½ pint corn oil
675 g/1½ lb plain flour
1 (397-g/14-oz) can condensed
   milk
1 teaspoon vanilla essence
1½ teaspoons bicarbonate of soda
1 teaspoon salt
5 tablespoons poppyseeds

Mix the eggs with the sugar, corn oil, flour, condensed milk, vanilla essence, bicarbonate of soda, salt and half of the poppyseeds. Divide the mixture evenly between two greased and floured 1-kg/2-lb loaf tins. Sprinkle with the remaining poppyseeds.

Bake for 1¼ hours until well risen and golden. Remove from the tins and allow to cool on a wire rack.

This is a rich and sweet bread that is ideal to serve lightly buttered or toasted at teatime.

Cook's Tip

If a loaf such as this one begins to brown too much before it is fully cooked, then cover with a piece of foil for the remainder of the cooking time.

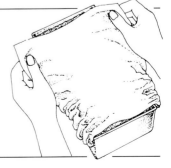

9 | Quick and Easy Celery Lunch Loaf

Preparation time
20 minutes

Cooking time
45–50 minutes

Oven temperature
190 C, 375 F, gas 5

Makes 1 cob loaf

Total calories
1295

You will need
225 g/8 oz self-raising flour
½ teaspoon salt
¼ teaspoon cayenne pepper
25 g/1 oz butter or margarine
100 g/4 oz celery heart, finely
  chopped
100 g/4 oz Edam cheese, grated
1 tablespoon snipped chives
150 ml/¼ pint milk

Sift the flour, salt and cayenne pepper into a bowl. Rub in the butter then stir in the celery, Edam and chives. Add the milk and mix to a soft dough. Turn onto a lightly floured surface and knead until smooth.

Shape into a cob by drawing the dough upwards and into the centre. Place tucks side down on a greased baking tray and slash the top with a sharp knife.

Bake for 45–50 minutes. Cover the loaf with a little foil towards the end of the cooking time if the crust is browning too much. Cool on a wire rack. Serve sliced while still warm.

Cook's Tip

This versatile lunch loaf can also be made with a little bacon. Add 25 g/1 oz cooked, chopped bacon with the celery.

10 | Crunchy Peanut Bread

Preparation time
20 minutes

Cooking time
1–1¼ hours

Oven temperature
180 C, 350 F, gas 4

**Makes 1 (1-kg/
2-lb) loaf**

Total calories
4205

You will need
300 ml/½ pint milk
4 tablespoons smooth peanut
  butter
100 g/4 oz soft brown sugar
450 g/1 lb plain flour
1 tablespoon baking powder
100 g/4 oz unsalted butter
1 egg, beaten
100 g/4 oz salted peanuts,
  coarsely chopped

For the topping
50 g/2 oz Gouda cheese, grated
25 g/1 oz salted peanuts, coarsely
  chopped

Place the milk, peanut butter and sugar in a pan and heat until the sugar has dissolved and the mixture is smooth. Allow to cool.

Sift the flour and baking powder into a bowl. Rub in the butter until the mixture resembles fine breadcrumbs. Add the egg, peanuts and cooled peanut butter mixture, mixing well. Spoon into a well-greased 1-kg/2-lb loaf tin and level the surface. Sprinkle with the cheese and peanuts.

Bake for 1–1¼ hours or until golden and cooked through. Cool on a wire rack. Serve sliced and buttered with extra slices of cheese if liked.

Cook's Tip

Baking powder loses its potency if stored for a long time. To test, sprinkle 1 teaspoon into a little hot water. If it fizzes enthusiastically then it is good for use.

11 | Herb Bread

Preparation time
20 minutes, plus 30
minutes to prove

Cooking time
25–30 minutes

Oven temperature
200 C, 400 F, gas 6

**Makes 1 (450-g/
1-lb) loaf**

Total calories
1615

You will need
25 g / 1 oz fresh yeast
250 ml / 8 fl oz warm milk
1 egg, beaten
2 teaspoons dried tarragon
2 teaspoons caster sugar
2 teaspoons salt
350 g / 12 oz strong plain white
    flour, sifted
1 tablespoon oil
2 teaspoons fennel seeds

Cream the yeast with half the milk. Put the remaining milk in a large bowl and mix in the egg, tarragon, sugar and salt. Add the yeast mixture and 275 g / 10 oz of the flour. Beat well to form a creamy dough. Add the remaining flour and oil and beat until thoroughly blended.

Place the mixture in a well-greased 450-g / 1-lb loaf tin, brush with water and sprinkle with the fennel seeds. Cover with cling film and leave in a warm place for 30 minutes to rise.

Bake for 25–30 minutes until golden brown and the bread sounds hollow when tapped. Cool on a wire rack.

Cook's Tip

You can make this herb bread with fresh tarragon when available but use 4 teaspoons of the chopped herb. It is delicious toasted and served with pâté.

12 | Ploughman's Pinwheel Loaf

Preparation time
20 minutes, plus about
2–2½ hours to prove

Cooking time
30 minutes

Oven temperature
220 C, 425 F, gas 7

**Makes 1 (450-g/
1-lb) loaf**

Total calories
1345

You will need
½ tablespoon dried yeast
1 teaspoon caster sugar
100 ml / 4 fl oz warm milk
225 g / 8 oz strong plain white flour
½ teaspoon salt
25 g / 1 oz butter or margarine
1 egg, beaten
½ onion, grated
50 g / 2 oz Cheddar cheese, grated
1 tablespoon sweet pickle or
    chutney

Mix the yeast with the sugar and milk and leave for 10 minutes. Sift the flour and salt into a bowl and rub in the butter. Add the yeast and half of the egg and mix to a smooth dough. Knead for 10 minutes until smooth and elastic. Place in an oiled bowl, cover and leave to rise in a warm place until doubled in size.

Knead on a floured surface for a few minutes then roll out to a 23 × 13-cm/9 × 5-in rectangle.

Mix the onion with three-quarters of the cheese and pickle. Spread over the dough, almost to the edges. Roll up from a long side like a Swiss roll. Place, seam-side down, in a greased 450-g/1-lb loaf tin. Cover and leave in a warm place until doubled in size.

Glaze with the remaining egg and sprinkle with the remaining cheese. Bake for 30 minutes until golden.

Cook's Tip

This bread is best served warm straight from the oven. Serve with soups, salads and savoury dishes, remembering to choose a complementary pickle or chutney for the filling.

13 | Naan Bread

Preparation time
20 minutes, plus about
4 hours to prove

Cooking time
about 30 minutes

**Makes 12 oval
breads**

Calories
180 per bread

You will need
1 tablespoon dried yeast
150 ml/$\frac{1}{4}$ pint warm milk
1$\frac{1}{2}$ teaspoons caster sugar
350 g/12 oz plain flour
1 teaspoon salt
$\frac{1}{2}$ teaspoon baking powder
150 ml/$\frac{1}{4}$ pint natural yogurt
oil to grease
butter to spread

Mix the yeast with the milk and sugar and leave for 10 minutes. Sift the flour, salt and baking powder into a bowl. Add the yeast liquid and yogurt and mix to a soft dough. Knead on a floured surface for 10 minutes until smooth and elastic. Place in a clean, oiled bowl, cover and leave to rise in a warm place for 3$\frac{1}{2}$–4 hours.

Knead on a floured surface for a few minutes, divide into 12 pieces, roll into balls, then flatten into large oval shapes.

Lightly oil a griddle or heavy-based frying pan and heat until very hot. Cook the bread ovals, one or two at a time, until golden on the underside. Remove from the pan and spread the uncooked side with a little butter. Cook under a hot grill until golden.

Cook's Tip

Naan bread is an Indian bread that is traditionally cooked on the walls of a clay oven called a tandoor. The oven is very hot and cooks the bread quickly with its fierce heat. This version however works just as well. Serve warm or hot with Indian or spicy dishes.

14 | Savoury Sausage Bread Ring

Preparation time
30 minutes, plus about
2 hours to prove

Cooking time
30–40 minutes

Oven temperature
200 C, 400 F, gas 6

Serves 6–8

Calories
415–310 per portion

You will need
150 ml/$\frac{1}{4}$ pint warm water
1 teaspoon caster sugar
1 teaspoon dried yeast
100 g/4 oz strong plain white flour
100 g/4 oz plain wheatmeal flour
salt and pepper
7 g/$\frac{1}{4}$ oz lard
450 g/1 lb sausagemeat
2 tablespoons sweet pickle or
  chutney
1 small onion, grated
beaten egg to glaze
75–100 g/3–4 oz Cheddar
  cheese, grated

Mix the water with the sugar and yeast and leave for 10 minutes. Sift the flours and 1 teaspoon salt into a bowl then rub in the lard. Add the yeast and mix to a smooth dough. Knead on a floured surface for 10 minutes. Place in an oiled bowl, cover and leave to rise in a warm place for 1$\frac{1}{2}$–2 hours until doubled in size.

Knead on a floured surface for a few minutes. Roll out to a 40 × 15-cm/16 × 6-in rectangle.

Mix the sausagemeat with the pickle, onion and salt and pepper to taste. Spread over the dough almost to the edges. Fold and roll over the edges to make a sausage shape, sealing the edges with water. Place, seam-side down, on a greased baking tray and shape into a ring. Slash the top at regular intervals, glaze with egg and top with cheese. Bake for 30–40 minutes.

Cook's Tip

You can ring the changes with the filling in this savoury bread ring by mixing the sausagemeat with a few chopped herbs, curry powder or chopped apple, if liked.

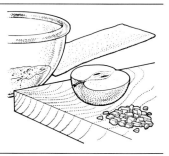

15 | Kentish Huffkins

Preparation time
20 minutes, plus about
2 hours to prove

Cooking time
20 minutes

Oven temperature
230 C, 450 F, gas 8

Makes 8

Calories
385 per huffkin

You will need
1 tablespoon dried yeast
1 teaspoon caster sugar
450 ml/¾ pint warm water and milk
   mixed
675 g/1½ lb strong plain white flour
1½ teaspoons salt
50 g/2 oz lard

Mix the yeast with the sugar and half the water and milk mixture and leave for 10 minutes. Sift the flour and salt into a bowl then rub in the lard. Add the yeast and remaining milk mixture and mix to a soft dough. Knead on a lightly floured surface for 5–10 minutes until smooth and elastic. Place in a bowl, cover and leave to rise in a warm place for 1 hour until doubled in size.

Knead on a floured surface for a few minutes, divide into 8 pieces and shape each into a smooth ball. Flatten to 2.5 cm/1 in thick with a rolling pin and place on greased baking trays. Cover and leave in a warm place for 45–50 minutes until doubled in size.

Bake for 10 minutes then turn over with a spatula and bake for a further 10 minutes. Remove and leave to cool on a wire rack, covered with a clean teatowel.

16 | Light Brown Baps

Preparation time
20 minutes, plus about
2 hours to prove

Cooking time
15–20 minutes

Oven temperature
200 C, 400 F, gas 6

Makes 12

Calories
180 per bap

You will need
350 ml/12 fl oz milk
1 teaspoon caster sugar
2 teaspoons dried yeast
225 g/8 oz strong plain white flour
225 g/8 oz plain wholewheat flour
1 teaspoon salt
50 g/2 oz lard
flour to dust

Mix the milk with the sugar and yeast and leave for 10 minutes. Sift the flours and salt into a bowl then rub in the lard. Add the yeast and mix to a soft dough.

Turn onto a floured surface and knead for 5–10 minutes until smooth and elastic. Place in an oiled bowl, cover and leave to rise in a warm place for 1 hour until doubled in size.

Knead for a few minutes then divide and shape into 12 baps, floured on all sides. Place, well apart, on greased baking trays, cover and leave in a warm place to rise until doubled in size.

Dust with extra flour and slash the top of each bap. Bake for 15–20 minutes. Cool on a wire rack.

Cook's Tip

Covering the huffkins with a teatowel after cooking helps to achieve the soft outer crust typical of these bread rolls. Traditionally Kentish Huffkins are split and filled with savoury fillings, usually two fillings in each roll.

Cook's Tip

These baps can be frozen before proving and baking for convenience if liked. Defrost completely, about 1–2 hours, then prove as above before baking.

17 | French Brioches

Preparation time
20 minutes, plus
1½–2 hours to prove

Cooking time
10 minutes

Oven temperature
230 C, 450 F, gas 8

Makes 12

Calories
120 per brioche

You will need
1 tablespoon dried yeast
1½ tablespoons warm water
1 tablespoon caster sugar
225 g/8 oz strong plain white flour
½ teaspoon salt
2 eggs, beaten
50 g/2 oz butter, melted
beaten egg to glaze

Mix the yeast with the water and 1 teaspoon of the sugar and leave for 10 minutes. Sift the flour, salt and remaining sugar into a bowl. Add the yeast, eggs and butter and mix to a smooth dough. Knead on a floured surface for 5 minutes until smooth and elastic. Place in an oiled bowl, cover and leave to rise in a warm place for 1 hour until doubled in size.

Knead for a few minutes then divide into 12 pieces. Shape three-quarters of each into a round and place in an oiled 7.5-cm/3-in fluted patty tin. Press a hole in the centre. Shape the remaining one-quarter into a ball and place on top. Cover and leave in a warm place to rise until the dough reaches the top of the tins.

Glaze with egg and bake for 10 minutes. Cool on a wire rack. Best eaten on day of making.

Cook's Tip

Brioches freeze beautifully for up to 3 months and so are worth making in bulk. Open freeze until firm then wrap in foil or freezer film or place in a freezer box. Defrost at room temperature then reheat in a moderate oven (180 C, 350 F, gas 4) for a few minutes to refresh.

18 | Bacon Supper Rolls

Preparation time
30 minutes, plus about
3 hours to prove

Cooking time
25–30 minutes

Oven temperature
220 C, 425 F, gas 7

Makes 8

Calories
255 per roll

You will need
250 ml/8 fl oz warm water
1 teaspoon sugar
½ tablespoon dried yeast
450 g/1 lb stoneground 100% wholewheat flour
1 teaspoon salt
½ teaspoon black pepper
25 g/1 oz butter
beaten egg to glaze

For the filling
15 g/½ oz butter
6 rashers lean bacon, chopped
1 onion, sliced
4 teaspoons prepared English mustard
2 tomatoes, peeled and sliced

Prepare the bread dough and leave to rise as for Savoury Sausage Bread Ring (recipe 14).

To make the filling, melt the butter and fry the bacon and onion until crisp. Drain well.

Divide the dough into 8 pieces. Cut one-fifth of the dough off each piece and roll into a 30-cm/12-in strip. Fold in half crossways and twist together. Roll out the remaining dough to make 8 (13-cm/5-in) rounds. Spread with mustard and top with an equal quantity of the bacon mixture then a tomato slice. Fold over the edges to make turnovers, sealing the edges, and place on greased baking trays. Place a dough twist across the centre of each, cover and leave in a warm place for about 1 hour until doubled in size.

Glaze with beaten egg and bake for 25–30 minutes.

Cook's Tip

These rolls are best served warm. If wrapped in foil they will keep warm for about 30 minutes. Alternatively, make ahead and reheat in a moderate oven for 15–20 minutes – ideally serve on the same day of making.

19 | English Muffins

Preparation time
20 minutes, plus about 1½ hours to prove

Cooking time
15–16 minutes

Oven temperature
230C, 450F, gas 8

Makes 8–10

Calories
245–200 per muffin

You will need
1 tablespoon dried yeast
½ teaspoon caster sugar
300 ml/½ pint warm milk
1 egg, beaten
25 g/1 oz butter, melted
450 g/1 lb plain flour
1 teaspoon salt

Mix the yeast with the sugar and half of the milk and leave for 10 minutes.

Mix the egg with the remaining milk and butter. Sift the flour and salt into a bowl. Add the yeast and egg mixtures and mix to a soft dough. Knead on a lightly floured surface for about 5 minutes until smooth and elastic. Place in an oiled bowl, cover and leave to rise for about 1½ hours in a warm place until doubled in size.

Roll out the dough on a floured surface and stamp out 8–10 rounds with a 7.5-cm/3-in scone or biscuit cutter. Place on greased baking trays and bake for 8 minutes. Turn over with a spatula and bake for a further 7–8 minutes. Cool on a wire rack. Serve split and toasted, with butter.

Cook's Tip

Dried yeast, unlike fresh yeast, will keep for many months but needs to be activated with sugar and water before use. Both types can be used in all recipes but remember when using dried yeast to use only half the quantity specified for fresh.

20 | Mustard, Walnut and Bacon Flowerpots

Preparation time
20 minutes, plus about 2–3 hours to prove

Cooking time
35 minutes

Oven temperature
220C, 425F, gas 7

Makes 4

Calories
970 per flowerpot

You will need
550 ml/18 fl oz warm water
4 tablespoons Dijon mustard
1 tablespoon plus pinch of caster sugar
1 tablespoon dried yeast
750 g/1 lb 10 oz wheatmeal flour
2 teaspoons salt
25 g/1 oz lard
100 g/4 oz walnuts, chopped
100 g/4 oz bacon, cooked and chopped
beaten egg to glaze
toasted barley flakes to sprinkle

Mix the water with the mustard. Mix half the mustard water with the pinch of sugar and yeast and leave for 10 minutes. Sift the flour, remaining sugar and salt into a bowl. Rub in the lard then stir in the walnuts and bacon. Add the yeast and remaining mustard water and mix to a smooth dough. Knead on a floured surface for 10 minutes until smooth. Place in a bowl, cover and leave in a warm place until doubled in size.

Knead on a floured surface for a few minutes, divide into 4 pieces and shape to fit 4 (750-ml/1¼-pint) tall well-greased clay flowerpots. Cover and leave in a warm place until the dough almost fills the pots.

Slash the tops with a sharp knife, glaze with egg and sprinkle with barley flakes. Bake for 35 minutes.

Cook's Tip

You may substitute pecans for the walnuts in this recipe. They have a milder yet equally nutty flavour.

Scones and Teabreads

Plain, wholemeal, herbed, spiced or fruited – the variety seems endless. Best served on the day of making, they can be split and buttered, halved then piled high with jam and cream, or served plain and savoury with cheese or salad. Serve plain, sweet scones with their culinary cousins, teabreads, for high tea. The range here is extensive with a choice of sugar-crusted Lardy Cake, fruity Bara Brith, iced Swedish Tea Ring, sticky and rum-laden Fruit Savarin and Spicy Chelsea Buns, not forgetting Hot Cross Buns.

21 | Butter Triangles

Preparation time
20 minutes, plus about 2 hours to prove

Cooking time
10 minutes

Oven temperature
220 C, 425 F, gas 7

Makes 15

Calories
225 per triangle

You will need

For the dough
25 g/1 oz fresh yeast
225 ml/7½ fl oz warm water
1 egg, beaten
75 g/3 oz caster sugar
450 g/1 lb strong plain white flour
½ teaspoon salt
50 g/2 oz butter, softened

For the filling
100 g/4 oz butter, melted
100 g/4 oz lemon curd
beaten egg to glaze
sugar to sprinkle

Cream the yeast with the water, egg, 1 teaspoon sugar and 4 tablespoons flour. Leave to stand for 30 minutes.

Sift the remaining flour and salt into a bowl. Add the remaining sugar and yeast liquid and mix to a soft dough. Knead the butter into the dough until smooth. Place in a warmed greased bowl, cover and leave to rise in a warm place for 30 minutes.

Cut the dough into 15 pieces and shape into balls. Leave for 5 minutes then roll into 10-cm/4-in rounds. Brush with melted butter and place ½ teaspoon lemon curd in the centre of each. Fold in half, brush with butter and fold in half again to make quarter circles. Place on greased baking trays, glaze with egg and sprinkle with sugar. Cover and leave to rise for 20–25 minutes.

Bake for 10 minutes then cool on a wire rack.

22 | Bath Buns

Preparation time
20 minutes, plus about 1 hour to prove

Cooking time
10–12 minutes

Oven temperature
230 C, 450 F, gas 8

Makes 16

Calories
150 per bun

You will need
1 recipe rich fermented dough (see Sally Lunns recipe 23)

For the filling
100 g/4 oz sultanas
thinly pared rind of 2 lemons, shredded
25 g/1 oz cubed sugar, crushed

For the topping
beaten egg
crushed cube sugar

Make up the dough and leave to rise as for Sally Lunns. Sprinkle the sultanas, lemon rind shreds and crushed sugar onto the dough and knead until well distributed.

Shape roughly into 16 buns and place on greased baking trays, spacing well apart. Cover and leave to rise in a warm place for about 20 minutes.

Brush with beaten egg to glaze and sprinkle with more crushed cube sugar.

Bake for 10–12 minutes until golden. Cool on a wire rack.

Cook's Tip

These delicious lemon flavoured buns are a favourite at teatime but they will also make a welcome appearance at coffee time or even breakfast and brunch.

Cook's Tip

Bath Buns, originally created in Bath, were originally not a fruited bun but a bun flavoured with caraway. Whilst not true to the original, today's favourite bun has a rich fruit filling and sticky sugary top.

23 | Sally Lunns

Preparation time
20 minutes, plus about
1 hour to prove

Cooking time
15–20 minutes

Oven temperature
220 C, 425 F, gas 7

**Makes 2 (15-cm/
6-in) cakes**

Calories
995 per sally lunn

You will need
20 g/¾ oz fresh yeast
150 ml/¼ pint warm milk
50 g/2 oz caster sugar
350 g/12 oz strong plain white
   flour
1 egg, beaten
finely grated rind of 1 lemon
50 g/2 oz butter, softened
beaten egg to glaze

Cream the yeast with the milk, 1 teaspoon sugar and 2 tablespoons flour until smooth. Leave to stand for 20 minutes.

Sift the remaining flour into a bowl, add the remaining sugar, egg, lemon rind and yeast mixture. Mix to a soft dough. Knead in the butter until the dough is smooth. Shape into a ball, place in a warm, greased bowl, cover and leave to rise in a warm place for 30 minutes.

Divide in half and shape each into a ball and place in 2 greased 15-cm/6-in round cake tins. Cover and leave in a warm place for 30 minutes then glaze with egg.

Bake for 15–20 minutes or until golden brown. Turn out to cool on a wire rack.

24 | Rum Babas

Preparation time
20 minutes, plus about
1 hour to prove

Cooking time
12–15 minutes

Oven temperature
200 C, 400 F, gas 6

Serves 16

Calories
240 per rum baba

You will need
25 g/1 oz fresh yeast
6 tablespoons warm milk
225 g/8 oz strong plain white flour
½ teaspoon salt
25 g/1 oz caster sugar
4 eggs, beaten
100 g/4 oz butter, softened
4 tablespoons clear honey
2 tablespoons dark rum
300 ml/½ pint double cream
glacé cherries to decorate

Cream the yeast with the milk and mix in 50 g/2 oz of the flour. Leave to stand for 20 minutes.

Mix the yeast liquid with the flour, salt, sugar, eggs and butter, beating well for about 3–4 minutes. Half-fill 16 lightly greased small ring moulds with the batter. Cover and leave in a warm-place to rise until the batter two-thirds fills the moulds.

Bake for 12–15 minutes then turn out to cool on a wire rack.

To make the syrup, heat the honey with 4 tablespoons water and the rum. Stir over a low heat until well mixed. Spoon over the warm babas and leave to cool.

To serve, whip the cream and pipe or spoon into the centres of the babas. Decorate with glacé cherries.

Cook's Tip

This famous teacake was supposed to have originated in Bath but seems to take its name from the French soleil lune 'sun and moon' – a good description since the top is golden like the sun and the inside is pale like the moon.

Today it is often topped with icing but traditionally it was served plain. It makes a splendid bread for toasting especially since it stales quickly.

Cook's Tip

It helps if you warm the spoon before measuring out honey from a jar. The warmed honey dribbles from the spoon more readily giving a more accurate and speedy measurement.

25 | Basic Scones

Preparation time
10–15 minutes

Cooking time
10 minutes

Oven temperature
220C, 425F, gas 7

Makes about 10

Calories
130 per scone

You will need
225 g/8 oz plain flour
1 teaspoon cream of tartar
½ teaspoon bicarbonate of soda
pinch of salt
50 g/2 oz butter or margarine
25 g/1 oz caster sugar
about 100 ml/4 fl oz milk
milk to glaze

Sift the flour, cream of tartar, soda and salt into a bowl. Rub in the butter until the mixture resembles fine bread-crumbs. Stir in the sugar and enough milk to mix to a soft dough.

Turn onto a floured surface, knead lightly and roll out to 2 cm/¾ in thickness. Cut into 5-cm/2-in rounds and place on a floured baking tray. Brush with milk to glaze.

Bake for 10 minutes then transfer to a wire rack to cool. Serve with butter or cream, and jam.

Cook's Tip

Wholemeal scones can be made using the above method and ingredients, simply substitute 100 g/4 oz plain wholemeal flour for 100 g/4 oz plain white flour.

26 | Fruit Scones

Preparation time
10–15 minutes

Cooking time
10 minutes

Oven temperature
220C, 425F, gas 7

Makes about 12

Calories
120 per scone

You will need
225 g/8 oz self-raising flour
½ teaspoon baking powder
50 g/2 oz butter or margarine
2 tablespoons caster sugar
75 g/3 oz mixed dried fruit
about 150 ml/¼ pint milk
milk to glaze

Sift the flour and baking powder into a bowl. Rub in the butter until the mixture resembles fine breadcrumbs. Stir in the sugar and fruit and add enough milk to mix to a soft dough.

Turn onto a floured surface, knead lightly and roll out to 2 cm/¾ in thickness. Cut into 5-cm/2-in rounds and place on a lightly floured baking tray. Brush with milk to glaze.

Bake for 10 minutes then cool on a wire rack. Serve with butter and jam.

Cook's Tip

Most scones will keep for a day or two if stored in an airtight tin but are always best refreshed in the oven for a few minutes before serving.

27 | Drop Scones

Preparation time
10 minutes

Cooking time
about 15–20 minutes

Makes about 14

Calories
90 per scone

You will need
225 g/8 oz plain flour
1 teaspoon cream of tartar
½ teaspoon bicarbonate of soda
½ teaspoon salt
25 g/1 oz caster sugar
1 large egg
250 ml/8 fl oz milk
1 tablespoon oil

Sift the dry ingredients together into a mixing bowl and make a well in the centre. Add the egg and half the milk and mix to a smooth batter. Gradually beat in the remaining milk with the oil.

Heat a heavy frying pan or griddle and grease lightly. Drop tablespoons of the batter onto the hot surface and cook until the top is blistered. Turn with a palette knife and cook until the underside is golden brown.

Serve with butter.

28 | Yeasty Scones

Preparation time
10 minutes, plus about
1¼ hours to prove

Cooking time
12–15 minutes

Oven temperature
230 C, 450 F, gas 8

Makes about 20

Calories
160 per scone

You will need
25 g/1 oz fresh yeast
150 ml/¼ pint warm water
550 g/1¼ lb strong plain white
flour
2 teaspoons baking powder
75 g/3 oz butter
1 egg
100 g/4 oz caster sugar
150 ml/¼ pint milk
100 g/4 oz sultanas
milk to glaze

Mix the yeast with the warm water and 50 g/2 oz of the flour. Leave to stand for 30 minutes.

Sift the remaining flour and the baking powder into a bowl and rub in the butter. Beat together the egg, sugar and milk and add to the flour with the yeast mixture. Mix vigorously to a smooth dough. Knead in the sultanas.

Knead and shape the dough into a ball. Turn onto a floured surface and roll out to 2.5 cm/1 in thickness. Cut into 5-cm/2-in rounds and place on greased baking trays. Cover and leave to rise in a warm place for 40 minutes, brushing with milk to glaze after 30 minutes.

Bake for 12–15 minutes then cool on a wire rack.

Cook's Tip

Keep the scones warm for serving by wrapping in a clean folded tea towel – this way they will keep moist and warm until they are all cooked.

Cook's Tip

These scones while a little more lengthy to prepare are delicious. They are well worth making in bulk for the freezer. They will freeze for up to 4 months and can be refreshed quickly in the oven after defrosting for eating.

29 | Savoury Scones

Preparation time
10 minutes

Cooking time
10 minutes

Oven temperature
220 C, 425 F, gas 7

Makes about 12

Calories
130 per scone

You will need
225 g/8 oz self-raising flour
½ teaspoon baking powder
pinch of salt
1 teaspoon dry mustard powder
50 g/2 oz butter or margarine
75 g/3 oz Cheddar cheese, grated
50 g/2 oz cooked sliced ham, diced
about 150 ml/¼ pint milk
milk to glaze

Sift the flour, baking powder, salt and mustard into a bowl. Rub in the butter until the mixture resembles fine breadcrumbs. Stir in the cheese and ham and enough milk to mix to a soft dough.

Turn onto a floured surface, knead lightly and roll out to 2 cm/¾ in thickness. Cut into 5-cm/2-in rounds and place on a lightly floured baking tray. Brush with milk to glaze.

Bake for 10 minutes then cool on a wire rack. Serve with butter.

30 | Cheesy Herb Scones

Preparation time
10 minutes

Cooking time
15–20 minutes

Oven temperature
220 C, 425 F, gas 7

Makes 9

Calories
170 per scone

You will need
225 g/8 oz self-raising flour
pinch of salt
1 teaspoon mustard powder
40 g/1½ oz butter or margarine
1 onion, chopped
100 g/4 oz Cheddar cheese, grated
1½ teaspoons dried mixed herbs
about 150 ml/¼ pint milk
nibbed wheat to sprinkle (optional)

Sift the flour, salt and mustard into a bowl. Rub in the butter until the mixture resembles fine breadcrumbs. Stir in the onion, cheese and herbs, mixing well. Add enough milk to bind to a soft dough.

Roll out on a lightly floured surface to about 2.5 cm/1 in thickness. Stamp out 9 rounds with a 6-cm/2½-in cutter, re-rolling as necessary. Place on a floured baking tray and brush with a little water or extra milk. Sprinkle with nibbed wheat, if used.

Bake for 15–20 minutes or until well risen and golden. Cool on a wire rack. Serve warm or cold with butter.

Cook's Tip

Brown scones, rather like brown bread, are becoming more favoured for good health. The above recipe can also be made with wholemeal flour but substitute only half of the flour. Serve with soups, salads and other cold fare.

Cook's Tip

Judge carefully the amount of milk to add to a scone mixture to make a soft dough. Too much liquid, resulting in a sticky dough, will produce hard brittle scones; too little and the scones will be dry and crumbly.

31 | Cotswold Scone Ring

Preparation time
10–15 minutes

Cooking time
15–20 minutes

Oven temperature
220C, 425F, gas 7

Makes 8

Calories
265 per scone

You will need
225 g/8 oz self-raising flour
1 teaspoon baking powder
pinch of salt
1 teaspoon mustard powder
40 g/1½ oz butter or margarine
100 g/4 oz Cotswold cheese with
   chives, grated
about 150 ml/¼ pint milk
beaten egg to glaze

For the filling
2 (62.5-g/2.2-oz) packets soft
   cream cheese
2 tablespoons snipped chives
½ teaspoon garlic granules

Sift the flour, baking powder, salt and mustard into a bowl. Rub in the butter until the mixture resembles fine breadcrumbs. Stir in the cheese and add enough milk to mix to a soft dough.

Turn onto a floured surface and knead until smooth. Roll out to 1 cm/½ in thickness. Using a 7.5-cm/3-in plain cutter, cut out 8 scones. Arrange them in a circle, overlapping slightly, on a greased baking tray. Brush with egg to glaze. Bake for 15–20 minutes, or until firm and golden. Cool on a wire rack.

To make the filling, mix the cream cheese with the chives and garlic granules. Break the scones apart while still warm, split each one and spread with the cheese mixture. Serve immediately.

32 | Fruit Scone Round

Preparation time
15 minutes

Cooking time
15–20 minutes

Oven temperature
200C, 400F, gas 6

**Makes 1 (18-cm/
7-in) round**

Total calories
1455

You will need
225 g/8 oz self-raising flour
1 teaspoon baking powder
50 g/2 oz butter or margarine
25 g/1 oz caster sugar
75 g/3 oz mixed dried fruit
about 150 ml/¼ pint milk
milk to glaze

Sift the flour and baking powder into a bowl and rub in the butter until the mixture resembles fine breadcrumbs. Stir in the sugar and fruit and add enough milk to mix to a soft dough.

Turn onto a floured surface, knead lightly then form into an 18-cm/7-in round and place on a floured baking tray.

Score the round into 8 sections, then brush with milk to glaze.

Bake for 15–20 minutes until golden brown. Cool on a wire rack. Serve with butter and jam.

Cook's Tip

This savoury scone is a boon for packed lunches, picnics or buffet lunches. Vary the topping occasionally by sprinkling with grated cheese, poppyseeds, sesame seeds or coarse sea salt, instead of the plain egg glaze.

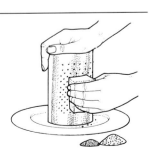

Cook's Tip

It is thought that scones probably originated in Scotland, forming part of the traditional high tea. The recipe above is a good basic fruit mixture baked in a round ready for pulling or slicing apart for serving.

33 | Chelsea Buns

Preparation time
20 minutes, plus about
2 hours to prove

Cooking time
12–15 minutes

Oven temperature
220 C, 425 F, gas 7

Makes about 20

Calories
200 per bun

You will need
1 recipe basic plain dough (see
    Butter Triangles recipe 21)

For the filling
150 g/5 oz butter, melted
75 g/3 oz caster sugar
100 g/4 oz sultanas
1 teaspoon ground mixed spice
caster sugar to sprinkle

Make up the dough and leave to rise as for Butter Triangles. Roll out the dough on a floured surface to a 45 × 30-cm/18 × 12-in rectangle. Brush all but 2 tablespoons of the butter over the dough, leaving a 2.5-cm/1-in border along one long side; brush this with water. Sprinkle with sugar, sultanas and spice then roll up widthways, sealing along the dampened edge. Coat the roll with the remaining butter and cut into 2-cm/¾-in slices. Place on greased baking trays, about 1 cm/½ in apart. Cover and leave to rise in a warm place for 40 minutes; they will spread until touching each other.

Bake for 12–15 minutes. Sprinkle with caster sugar then cool on a wire rack.

34 | Bara Brith

Preparation time
20 minutes, plus about
1½–2 hours to prove

Cooking time
35 minutes

Oven temperature
190 C, 375 F, gas 5

**Makes 1 large
round loaf**

Total calories
2365

You will need
225 g/8 oz currants
150 g/5 oz sultanas
25 g/1 oz chopped mixed peel
275 g/10 oz strong plain white
    flour
1 teaspoon salt
15 g/½ oz lard
25 g/1 oz caster sugar
½ teaspoon ground mixed spice
1 egg
150 ml/¼ pint warm milk
15 g/½ oz fresh yeast
clear honey to glaze

Rinse the currants, sultanas and peel in warm water then drain and dry well. Sift the flour and salt into a bowl then rub in the lard. Mix the sugar and spice and add to the flour.

Beat the egg and milk together, add the yeast and leave for 15 minutes. Pour into the flour mixture and mix, drawing in the flour, to make a smooth dough.

Knead the fruit and peel into the dough and shape into a ball. Cover and leave for 10 minutes.

Shape the dough into a round loaf and place on a greased baking tray. Cover and leave in a warm place to rise for 1½ hours.

Bake for 35 minutes until golden. Turn out to cool on a wire rack and brush with honey immediately. Serve with butter.

Cook's Tip

Chelsea Buns are so called because they originated at the old Chelsea Bun House where thousands of the buns were baked everyday. These buns are baked close together so that they can be pulled apart for eating, revealing their soft doughy sides.

Cook's Tip

Washing the fruit and peel in warm water before adding to the dough helps to soften the ingredients and makes a moister cake that does not crumble too much when sliced. Drain and dry on absorbent kitchen paper.

35 | Selkirk Bannock

Preparation time
20 minutes, plus about
2 hours to prove

Cooking time
20 minutes

Oven temperature
220 C, 425 F, gas 7

**Makes 1 large
round teabread**

Total calories
1930

You will need
225 g/8 oz strong plain white flour
½ teaspoon salt
40 g/1½ oz butter
40 g/1½ oz caster sugar
150 ml/¼ pint warm milk
15 g/½ oz fresh yeast
225 g/8 oz sultanas
beaten egg to glaze

Sift the flour and salt into a bowl and rub in the butter.

Dissolve the sugar in the milk, add the yeast and leave for 15 minutes. Pour into the dry ingredients and mix well to a smooth dough. Knead for 5 minutes until smooth and elastic then shape into a round. Place in a clean, warm bowl, cover and leave to rise in a warm place for 30 minutes.

Add the sultanas and knead until well distributed. Cover and leave to rise again for 15 minutes.

Shape into a ball, place on a greased baking tray, cover and leave to rise in a warm place for 1 hour. After 15 minutes flatten slightly and brush with egg.

Bake for about 20 minutes until golden. Cool on a wire rack. Serve with butter.

Cook's Tip

Cover yeasted breads like this one with cling film or a damp clean teacloth during proving. This ensures that the bread does not dry out and develop a crust before further kneading.

36 | Raisin, Almond and Grapefruit Loaf

Preparation time
20 minutes

Cooking time
1 hour

Oven temperature
180 C, 350 F, gas 4

**Makes 1 (1-kg/
2-lb) loaf**

Total calories
3660

You will need
450 g/1 lb raisins, coarsely
    chopped
5 tablespoons water
350 g/12 oz self-raising flour
1 teaspoon baking powder
50 g/2 oz butter
50 g/2 oz caster sugar
100 g/4 oz blanched almonds,
    coarsely chopped
3 tablespoons milk
5 tablespoons frozen concentrated
    grapefruit juice, defrosted
2 eggs, beaten
1 grapefruit

Place the raisins in a saucepan with the water and bring slowly to the boil. Remove from the heat.

Sift the flour with the baking powder into a bowl. Rub in the butter, then stir in the sugar and almonds. Add the milk, grapefruit juice, eggs and raisin mixture and mix well.

Grate the rind from the grapefruit and remove the segments of flesh. Fold the rind and flesh into the cake mixture. Pour into a greased 1-kg/2-lb loaf tin.

Bake for 1 hour or until golden brown. Turn out to cool on a wire rack.

Cook's Tip

To ensure that you get all the grated grapefruit rind for the cake, brush the pieces of grated rind from the grater with a dry pastry brush.

37 | Farmhouse Loaf

Preparation time
15 minutes

Cooking time
50–60 minutes

Oven temperature
180C, 350F, gas 4

**Makes 1 (450-g/
1-lb) loaf**

Total calories
2025

You will need
100 g/4 oz self-raising flour
100 g/4 oz plain wholemeal flour
pinch of grated nutmeg
½ teaspoon bicarbonate of soda
75 g/3 oz butter or margarine
100 g/4 oz caster sugar
50 g/2 oz raisins
25 g/1 oz glacé cherries
25 g/1 oz sultanas
25 g/1 oz chopped mixed peel
grated rind of 1 lemon
1 egg, beaten
6 tablespoons milk

Place the flours, nutmeg and bicarbonate of soda in a mixing bowl and rub in the butter. Add the sugar, fruits, peel and lemon rind. Mix in the egg and milk to produce a mixture with a soft dropping consistency. Spoon into a greased and lined 450-g/1-lb loaf tin.

Bake for 50–60 minutes. Turn out to cool on a wire rack. Serve sliced and spread with butter.

38 | Chocolate Pistachio Loaf

Preparation time
10–15 minutes

Cooking time
1¼–1½ hours

Oven temperature
180C, 350F, gas 4

**Makes 1 (450-g/
1-lb) loaf cake**

Total calories
3240

You will need
100 g/4 oz self-raising flour
100 g/4 oz butter or margarine
50 g/2 oz caster sugar
25 g/1 oz ground almonds
50 g/2 oz cocoa powder
50 g/2 oz plain chocolate, chopped
50 g/2 oz pistachio nuts, chopped
2 eggs
2 tablespoons milk

For the icing and decoration
175 g/6 oz plain chocolate
knob of butter
few pistachio nuts, chopped

Place all the cake ingredients in a mixing bowl and beat with a wooden spoon until well mixed, about 2–3 minutes. Spoon the mixture into a greased and lined 450-g/1-lb loaf tin and level the surface.

Bake for 1¼–1½ hours then turn out to cool on a wire rack.

To make the icing, melt the chocolate in a bowl over a saucepan of hot water. Beat in the knob of butter to keep the chocolate shiny. Pour all over the cool loaf and sprinkle with chopped pistachio nuts.

Cook's Tip

A soft dropping consistency is achieved when a spoonful of mixture, when raised up from the bowl, drops slowly and easily from the spoon.

Cook's Tip

If pistachio nuts are not available, nibbed almonds coloured with green food colouring can be substituted.

39 | Cherry Madeira Cake

Preparation time
15 minutes

Cooking time
1¼–1½ hours

Oven temperature
160 C, 325 F, gas 3

Makes 1 (1-kg/ 2-lb) loaf cake

Total calories
3340

You will need
175 g/6 oz butter or margarine
175 g/6 oz caster sugar
3 eggs
225 g/8 oz plain flour
½ teaspoon baking powder
175 g/6 oz glacé cherries, chopped
2 thin strips citron peel (optional)

Cream the butter and sugar together until light and fluffy. Beat in the eggs, one at a time, adding a little of the flour with each egg after the first. Fold in the rest of the flour with the baking powder and cherries.

Place in a greased and lined 1-kg/2-lb loaf tin, and arrange the peel, if used, over the centre. Bake for 1¼–1½ hours. Turn out to cool on a wire rack.

40 | Spiced Coffee Teabread

Preparation time
15 minutes

Cooking time
1–1¼ hours

Oven temperature
180 C, 350 F, gas 4

Makes 1 (1-kg/ 2-lb) loaf

Total calories
2605

You will need
225 g/8 oz self-raising flour
100 g/4 oz butter or margarine
100 g/4 oz soft dark brown sugar
3 tablespoons black coffee
75 g/3 oz walnuts, chopped
2 eggs
100 g/4 oz glacé cherries, chopped
½ teaspoon ground cinnamon
¼ teaspoon ground mixed spice
grated rind of 1 lemon

Place the flour in a mixing bowl and rub in the butter. Stir in the sugar, coffee, walnuts, eggs, cherries, cinnamon, spice and lemon rind and mix well. Spoon into a greased and base-lined 1-kg/2-lb loaf tin.

Bake for 1–1¼ hours then turn out to cool on a wire rack. Serve sliced and spread with butter.

Cook's Tip

This cake can also be made in an 18-cm/7-in deep round cake tin and baked as above. You can also vary the flavour by adding 2 teaspoons ground ginger and 50 g/2 oz chopped crystallized ginger to the mixture.

Cook's Tip

When rubbing in the flour and butter, allow only the tips of the fingers and thumbs to come in contact with the mixture. Lift the mixture high from the bowl to trap plenty of air.

41 | Date and Pineapple Loaf

Preparation time
15–20 minutes

Cooking time
1¼–1½ hours

Oven temperature
160 C, 325 F, gas 3

Makes 1 (1-kg/ 2-lb) loaf

Total calories
2180

You will need
50 g/2 oz butter or margarine
225 g/8 oz stoned dates, chopped
50 g/2 oz soft light brown sugar
150 ml/¼ pint water
1 teaspoon bicarbonate of soda
50 g/2 oz glacé pineapple, chopped
1 egg, beaten
225 g/8 oz self-raising flour

For the topping
2 tablespoons honey
25 g/1 oz glacé pineapple, chopped

Place the butter, dates, sugar and water in a saucepan and bring to the boil. Remove from the heat and allow to cool.

Add the remaining ingredients and mix well together. Place in a greased and lined 1-kg/2-lb loaf tin.

Bake for 1¼–1½ hours then turn out to cool on a wire rack.

To make the topping, melt the honey and brush over the top of the loaf. Sprinkle with glacé pineapple to decorate.

42 | Date and Walnut Bread

Preparation time
20–25 minutes

Cooking time
45 minutes

Oven temperature
180 C, 350 F, gas 4

Makes 1 (450-g/ 1-lb) loaf

Total calories
2490

You will need
225 g/8 oz self-raising flour
½ teaspoon salt
1 teaspoon bicarbonate of soda
175 g/6 oz dates, stoned and chopped
100 g/4 oz walnuts, coarsely chopped
250 ml/8 fl oz boiling water
50 g/2 oz butter or margarine
100 g/4 oz brown sugar
1 egg, beaten
5 tablespoons milk

Sift the flour with the salt and bicarbonate of soda.

Place the dates and walnuts in a bowl and pour over the boiling water. Cool to lukewarm.

Cream the butter with the sugar until light and fluffy. Add the egg and mix well. Add the flour mixture and date and walnut mixture and blend well. Finally stir in the milk. Spoon into a greased and floured 450-g/1-lb loaf tin.

Bake for 45 minutes or until a skewer inserted into the centre of the cake comes out clean. Turn out to cool on a wire rack. Serve sliced, and buttered if liked.

Cook's Tip

If glacé pineapple is not available then crystallized ginger may be used instead.

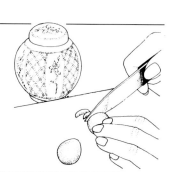

Cook's Tip

It is important to preheat the oven for at least 15 minutes before baking a cake (unless your oven manufacturer specifies otherwise). If the temperature is too low, the texture of the cake is liable to be coarse.

43 | Yorkshire Parkin

Preparation time
15 minutes

Cooking time
1 hour

Oven temperature
180 C, 350 F, gas 4

**Makes 1 (18-cm/
7-in) square
cake**

Total calories
3795

You will need
225 g/8 oz plain flour
½ teaspoon salt
1 teaspoon ground mixed spice
1 teaspoon ground cinnamon
1 teaspoon ground ginger
1 teaspoon bicarbonate of soda
225 g/8 oz medium oatmeal
175 g/6 oz black treacle
150 g/5 oz butter or margarine
100 g/4 oz soft brown sugar
150 ml/¼ pint milk
1 egg, beaten

Sift the flour, salt, spice, cinnamon, ginger and bicarbonate of soda into a bowl. Mix in the oatmeal.

Place the treacle, butter, sugar and milk in a saucepan and heat gently until well combined and the butter has melted. Add to the dry ingredients and mix well. Stir in the egg, then spoon into a greased and lined 18-cm/7-in deep, square cake tin.

Bake for 1 hour then turn out to cool on a wire rack. Store, wrapped in foil, for about 1 week before cutting into squares to serve.

44 | Traditional Parkin

Preparation time
15–20 minutes

Cooking time
1¼–1½ hours

Oven temperature
180 C, 350 F, gas 4

**Makes 1 (23-cm/
9-in) square cake**

Total calories
3985

You will need
175 g/6 oz black treacle
175 g/6 oz butter or margarine
100 g/4 oz soft brown sugar
225 g/8 oz plain flour
2 teaspoons ground ginger
½ teaspoon grated nutmeg
¼ teaspoon ground cinnamon
1 teaspoon bicarbonate of soda
225 g/8 oz oatmeal
1 egg, beaten
150 ml/¼ pint milk

Place the treacle, butter and sugar in a saucepan and melt over a low heat. Allow to cool slightly.

Sift the flour with the spices and bicarbonate of soda. Stir in the oatmeal. Pour in the melted mixture with the egg and milk and mix well until smooth. Pour into a greased and lined 23-cm/9-in square cake tin.

Bake for 1¼–1½ hours. Leave to cool in the tin for a few minutes before turning out to cool on a wire rack. Serve sliced and spread with butter.

Cook's Tip

To weigh the treacle without making a mess, first weigh the saucepan that it is to be cooked in, then weigh the treacle in it.

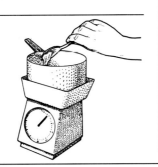

Cook's Tip

This cake is best stored for a few days before eating so that the flavours will develop. Store wrapped in foil or in an airtight tin.

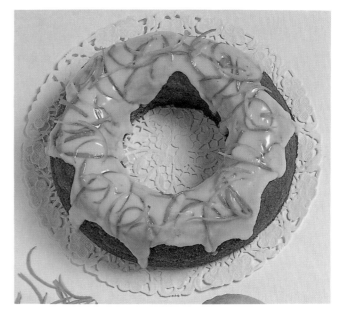

45 | Lardy Cake

Preparation time
20 minutes, plus about
3 hours to prove

Cooking time
30 minutes

Oven temperature
220 C, 425 F, gas 7

**Makes 1 (30 ×
25-cm/12 × 10-in)
cake**

Total calories
3375

You will need
⅓ recipe Basic White Bread dough
   (see recipe 1)
100 g/4 oz lard
100 g/4 oz caster sugar
1 teaspoon ground mixed spice
½ teaspoon grated nutmeg
100 g/4 oz mixed dried fruit
2 teaspoons oil

Knead the risen dough for a few minutes then roll out to a rectangle about 5 mm/¼ in thick. Dot with half of the lard. Mix the sugar with the spice and nutmeg. Sprinkle half over the dough with half of the dried fruit. Roll up like a Swiss roll, then roll out again as before. Dot with lard and sprinkle with sugar, spice and fruit as before. Roll up and roll out again as before. Repeat the rolling up and rolling out process twice as before without any additions. Finally roll out to a rectangle large enough to line the base of a 30 × 25-cm/12 × 10-in tin. Cover and leave in a warm place for about 1 hour until doubled in size.

Brush with oil, sprinkle with any remaining sugar mixture and score deeply into diamond shapes. Bake for 30 minutes. Serve cut into squares while still warm.

Cook's Tip

If you have run out of the basic ready prepared mixed spice then remember it usually contains ground cinnamon, cloves and nutmeg so mix up your own. Sometimes a little Jamaica pepper and ground *coriander may also be added.*

46 | St Clement's Ring Cake

Preparation time
15 minutes

Cooking time
40–45 minutes

Oven temperature
160 C, 325 F, gas 3

**Makes 1 (20-cm/
8-in) ring cake**

Total calories
3720

You will need
175 g/6 oz butter or margarine
175 g/6 oz caster sugar
3 eggs
100 g/4 oz self-raising flour
50 g/2 oz ground almonds
grated rind of 1 orange
grated rind of 1 lemon

For the icing and decoration
225 g/8 oz icing sugar, sifted
2–3 tablespoons lemon juice or
   squash
shredded orange and lemon rind

Cream the butter with the sugar until light and fluffy. Beat in the eggs, one at a time, adding a little of the sifted flour with each egg after the first. Fold in the remaining flour with the almonds and fruit rinds. Spoon into a greased and floured 20-cm/8-in ring tin.

Bake for 40–45 minutes then turn out to cool on a wire rack.

To make the icing, mix the icing sugar with the lemon juice or squash until smooth. Pour over the cool cake, allowing it to run down the sides. Decorate with shredded orange and lemon rind.

Cook's Tip

This cake freezes well un-iced. Place the cooled cake in a polythene bag, press out the air and secure with a twist tie. Label and freeze for up to 3 months. Thaw at room temperature for 3–4 hours.

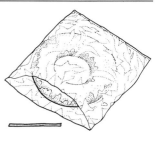

47 | Swedish Tea Ring

Preparation time
20 minutes, plus about
2½ hours to prove

Cooking time
30 minutes

Oven temperature
200 C, 400 F, gas 6

**Makes 1 (15-cm/
6-in) ring
teabread**

Total calories
2895

You will need
1 recipe rich dough (see Selkirk
  Bannock recipe 35, without
  sultanas)

For the filling
50 g/2 oz butter, softened
75 g/3 oz demerara sugar
50 g/2 oz glacé cherries, chopped
50 g/2 oz raisins
1 teaspoon ground cinnamon

For the topping
100 g/4 oz icing sugar, sifted
1 tablespoon lemon juice
25 g/1 oz glacé cherries
25 g/1 oz walnut halves
15 g/½ oz angelica

Make up the dough and leave to rise in a warm place for 2 hours or until doubled in size. Knead on a floured surface for 5 minutes, then roll into a 45 × 25-cm/18 × 10-in oblong. Spread with the butter, leaving a 2.5-cm/1-in border on one long side; brush this with water. Sprinkle with the sugar, fruit and cinnamon. Roll up widthways and seal along the dampened edge.

Place on a greased baking tray and form into a ring, joining the ends together. Using scissors, make slanting cuts two-thirds through the ring at 2.5-cm/1-in intervals and turn each section on its side. Cover and leave to rise in a warm place for 30 minutes.

Bake for 30 minutes then cool on a wire rack. Mix the icing sugar with the lemon juice and pour over the ring. Decorate with cherries, nuts and angelica.

48 | Fluted Lemon Caraway Cake

Preparation time
15 minutes

Cooking time
1 – 1¼ hours

Oven temperature
160 C, 325 F, gas 3

**Makes 1 (19-cm/
7½-in) fluted cake**

Total calories
3800

You will need
175 g/6 oz butter or margarine
100 g/4 oz caster sugar
4 eggs
225 g/8 oz self-raising flour
1 teaspoon caraway seeds
grated rind of 1 lemon
3 tablespoons lemon curd

For the icing and decoration
225 g/8 oz icing sugar, sifted
2–3 tablespoons water
glacé cherries
angelica leaves

Cream the butter with the sugar until light and fluffy. Beat in the eggs, one at a time, adding a little flour with each egg after the first. Fold in the remaining flour, caraway seeds, lemon rind and lemon curd. Spoon into a greased and lined 19-cm/7½-in fluted mould.

Bake for 1–1¼ hours then turn out to cool on a wire rack.

To make the icing, mix the icing sugar with the water until smooth. Pour over the cool cake, allowing it to run down the sides. Decorate with whole glacé chrries and angelica leaves.

Cook's Tip

*Vary the iced fruited topping
to this teabread to ring the
changes. Try using other
glacé fruits like pineapple or
apricots. Vary the nuts and
chop for sprinkling rather
than leaving them whole.*

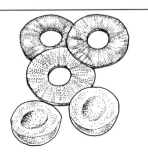

Cook's Tip

*Rinse the angelica in hot
water to soften it and to
remove the sugar. This will
make it a better colour and
easier to cut.*

49 | Gingerbread Ring Cake

Preparation time
15 minutes

Cooking time
1–1¼ hours

Oven temperature
160 C, 325 F, gas 3

Makes 1 (20-cm/ 8-in) ring cake

Total calories
2895

You will need
100 g/4 oz butter or margarine
100 g/4 oz soft brown sugar
175 g/6 oz black treacle
225 g/8 oz plain flour
3–4 teaspoons ground ginger
½ teaspoon ground cinnamon
1 egg, beaten
½ teaspoon bicarbonate of soda
6 tablespoons milk

For the icing and decoration
100 g/4 oz icing sugar, sifted
5 teaspoons water
crystallized ginger

Melt the butter, sugar and treacle over a low heat until dissolved. Sift the flour and spices into a bowl and pour in the melted mixture and egg. Dissolve the bicarbonate of soda in the milk and stir into the flour mixture, mixing well. Pour quickly into a greased and floured 20-cm/8-in ring tin.

Bake for 1–1¼ hours. Leave in the tin for a few minutes before turning out to cool on a wire rack.

To make the icing, mix the icing sugar with the water until smooth. Pour over the cake, allowing it to run down the sides. Decorate with crystallized ginger.

Cook's Tip

This is a good basic recipe that lends itself to variations. For a fruity gingerbread ring add 75 g/3 oz raisins with the dry ingredients. For an orange gingerbread ring add the coarsely grated rind of 2 oranges instead.

50 | Quick Orange and Walnut Tea Ring

Preparation time
20 minutes, plus
1–1½ hours to prove

Cooking time
30 minutes

Oven temperature
220 C, 425 F, gas 7
180 C, 350 F, gas 4

Makes 1 large ring teabread

Total calories
1605

You will need
1 (280-g/10-oz) packet brown
   bread mix
185 ml/6½ fl oz warm water
25 g/1 oz butter, melted
50 g/2 oz walnuts, finely chopped
25 g/1 oz sugar
grated rind of 1 orange

For the icing and decoration
100 g/4 oz icing sugar, sifted
5 teaspoons frozen concentrated
   orange juice, defrosted
whole or chopped walnuts

Place the bread mix in a bowl and add the water. Mix to a firm dough. Knead on a floured surface for 5 minutes until smooth and elastic. Roll out to a 35 × 20-cm/14 × 8-in rectangle. Brush with butter and sprinkle with the walnuts, sugar and orange rind. Roll up from a long end. Dampen the ends and press together to make a ring. Place on a greased baking tray. Cover and leave in a warm place for 1–1½ hours to rise until doubled in size.

Bake at the hotter temperature for 15 minutes, reduce to the lower temperature and bake for a further 15 minutes. Cool on a wire rack.

To make the icing, mix the icing sugar with the orange juice until smooth. Pour over the cooled teabread, allowing it to run down the sides. Top with walnuts.

Cook's Tip

This is a splendid yeasted tea-bread to freeze. Freeze the un-iced ring for up to 3 months. Defrost at room temperature for 2–3 hours then ice and decorate as above.

51 | Fruit Savarin

Preparation time
20 minutes, plus 1–2 hours to prove

Cooking time
40 minutes

Oven temperature
200 C, 400 F, gas 6

Serves 8–10

Calories
355–285 per portion

You will need
1 teaspoon caster sugar
175 ml/6 fl oz warm milk
15 g/½ oz dried yeast
225 g/8 oz plain flour, sifted
pinch of salt
3 eggs, beaten
100 g/4 oz butter, melted

For the glaze
150 g/5 oz granulated sugar
250 ml/8 fl oz water
juice of 1 lemon
5 tablespoons dark rum

For the filling
45 g/1 lb mixed fresh fruit salad

Mix the sugar with the milk and yeast and leave for 10 minutes. Mix the flour with the salt. Add the yeast liquid, eggs and butter and beat to make a smooth batter. Pour into a greased 23-cm/9-in plain ring mould. Cover and leave to rise in a warm place until the mixture has risen to the top of the tin.

Bake for 40 minutes until golden and cooked through. Turn out to cool on a wire rack.

To make the glaze, mix the sugar with the water. Bring to the boil and boil for 5 minutes to reduce by half. Add the lemon juice and rum. Prick the savarin all over then spoon over the warm glaze and leave to soak in.

Cool completely then fill the centre with fresh fruit salad to serve.

Cook's Tip

Make up a colourful seasonal fruit salad for this savarin. Soft fruits like strawberries are especially good with grapes, orange segments and diced apple. Decorate the edge with a little piped cream if liked.

52 | Honey Fruit Savarin

Preparation time
20 minutes, plus rising time

Cooking time
35–40 minutes

Oven temperature
200 C, 400 F, gas 6

Makes 1 (20-cm/ 8-in) savarin

Total calories
2665

You will need
225 g/8 oz strong plain flour
½ teaspoon salt
250 ml/8 fl oz milk
2 tablespoons clear honey
15 g/½ oz dried yeast
4 eggs
100 g/4 oz butter, melted

For the glaze and filling
4 tablespoons clear honey
4 tablespoons white rum
2 tablespoons boiling water
2 tablespoons apricot jam, warmed and sieved
350 g/12 oz prepared strawberries
whipped cream (optional)

Sift the flour with the salt. Heat the milk with the honey until lukewarm. Sprinkle over the yeast and leave in a warm place until frothy.

Add the yeast to the flour with the eggs and butter and beat to a smooth batter. Beat for a further 5 minutes. Cover and leave in a warm place until doubled in size. Pour into a greased 20-cm/9-in ring tin. Cover and leave in a warm place until risen to the top of the tin. Bake for 35–40 minutes then turn out to cool on a wire rack.

Mix the honey with the rum and water and spoon about half over the still warm savarin. Leave to soak in, then brush with the apricot jam. Mix the remaining syrup into the prepared strawberries. Place the cake on a serving plate and fill the centre with the strawberries. Pipe with a little whipped cream to decorate if liked.

Cook's Tip

If the savarin isn't piped with fresh whipped cream for serving then offer it with a bowl of clotted cream for guests to help themselves.

Family Cakes

Here is a chapter simply bursting with ideas for homely cakes for mid-morning and tea-time eating. Cakes stuffed with fruit and spices, studded with nuts and seeds, coated or spread with chocolate or icing and sweetened with fruit juices, honey or sugar. All are simple to make with no elaborate decoration. Many are long-standing family favourites, others are destined to become so. Children and would-be or first-time bakers could do no better than to look here for inspiration for that first baked cake!

53 | Crystallized Fruit Cake

Preparation time
20 minutes

Cooking time
3 hours

Oven temperature
160 C, 325 F, gas 3
150 C, 300 F, gas 2

Makes 1 (18-cm/ 7-in) cake

Total calories
5085

You will need
225 g/8 oz plain flour
1 teaspoon ground mixed spice
175 g/6 oz butter or margarine
175 g/6 oz soft brown sugar
3 eggs
225 g/8 oz raisins
100 g/4 oz sultanas
25 g/1 oz angelica
100 g/4 oz glacé cherries, quartered
25 g/1 oz crystallized ginger
1 tablespoon sherry

For the decoration
75 g/3 oz crystallized fruits
50 g/2 oz walnut halves
½ recipe Apricot Glaze (see Introduction)

Sift the flour with the mixed spice. Cream the butter and sugar until light and fluffy. Beat in the eggs, one at a time, adding a tablespoon of the flour with the last two. Fold in the remaining flour, the fruit, ginger and sherry.

Spoon into a greased and lined 18-cm/7-in deep cake tin and decorate with the crystallized fruits and walnuts. Tie a thick band of brown paper around the tin and stand on a pad of brown paper on a baking tray.

Bake at the higher temperature for 1 hour, then lower the temperature and bake for a further 2 hours, until a skewer inserted into the centre comes out clean. Cool on a wire rack and brush with the glaze before serving.

Cook's Tip

When glazing fruit and nuts as above with apricot glaze, add a little boiling water to the jam to give a smoother consistency if a little too thick.

54 | Victoria Sandwich

Preparation time
15–20 minutes

Cooking time
20–25 minutes

Oven temperature
180 C, 350 F, gas 4

Makes 1 (18-cm/ 7-in) cake

Total calories
1605

You will need
100 g/4 oz butter or margarine
100 g/4 oz caster sugar
2 eggs
100 g/4 oz self-raising flour, sifted
1 tablespoon hot water

Cream the butter and sugar together until light and fluffy. Beat in the eggs, one at a time, adding a tablespoon of the flour with the second egg. Fold in the remaining flour, then the hot water.

Turn the mixture into 2 greased and lined 18-cm/7-in sandwich tins. Bake for 20–25 minutes or until the cakes spring back when lightly pressed. Turn onto a wire rack to cool.

Fill with raspberry jam or use as required.

Cook's Tip

To make a coffee sandwich simply add 1 tablespoon coffee powder with the flour. To make an orange or lemon sandwich cake, add the grated rind of 1 orange or lemon with the butter and sugar.

55 | Ginger Cake

Preparation time
15–20 minutes

Cooking time
1–1¼ hours

Oven temperature
180C, 350F, gas 4

Makes 1 (18-cm/ 7-in) cake

Total calories
3895

You will need
175 g/6 oz butter or margarine
175 g/6 oz caster sugar
3 eggs
225 g/8 oz self-raising flour
½ teaspoon ground ginger
75 g/3 oz preserved ginger, chopped
4 tablespoons ginger syrup
175 g/6 oz icing sugar, sifted
preserved ginger slices to decorate

Cream the butter and sugar until light and fluffy. Add the eggs, one at a time, adding a tablespoon of flour with the last two. Sift and fold in the remaining flour and the ginger. Fold in the preserved ginger and 2 tablespoons of the syrup. Spoon into a greased and lined 18-cm/7-in cake tin.

Bake for 1–1¼ hours then cool on a wire rack.

Beat the icing sugar and remaining syrup together. Pour over the cake and leave to set. Decorate with the slices of preserved ginger.

Cook's Tip

If you have insufficient ginger syrup in your jar of preserved ginger then use ginger wine instead.

56 | Everyday Fruit Cake

Preparation time
20 minutes

Cooking time
1¼–1½ hours

Oven temperature
180C, 350F, gas 4

Makes 1 (15-cm/ 6-in) cake

Total calories
2580

You will need.
225 g/8 oz self-raising flour
½ teaspoon ground mixed spice
½ teaspoon ground cinnamon
100 g/4 oz butter or margarine
100 g/4 oz soft brown sugar
100 g/4 oz sultanas
100 g/4 oz currants
50 g/2 oz glacé cherries, quartered
1 large egg
5 tablespoons milk

Sift the flour and spices into a mixing bowl. Add the butter and rub in until the mixture resembles fine breadcrumbs. Stir in the sugar and fruit. Whisk the egg and milk together, add to the mixture and beat well.

Place in a greased and lined 15-cm/6-in deep cake tin. Bake for 1¼–1½ hours. Leave in the tin for 5 minutes, then turn onto a wire rack to cool.

Cook's Tip

Store fruit cakes in an airtight tin for absolute freshness. Wrap in foil if liked. A piece of apple added to the tin will also ensure that moistness is retained.

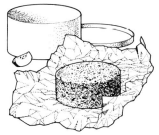

57 | Swiss Roll

Preparation time
20 minutes

Cooking time
10–12 minutes

Oven temperature
200 C, 400 F, gas 6

Makes 1 (20-cm/ 8-in) roll

Total calories
1055

You will need
3 eggs
75 g / 3 oz caster sugar
75 g / 3 oz plain flour, sifted

For the filling and decoration
caster sugar to dredge
about 6 tablespoons raspberry jam

Whisk the eggs and sugar together in a large bowl until the whisk leaves a trail, then fold in the flour. Turn the mixture into a greased and lined 20 × 30-cm/8 × 12-in Swiss roll tin and smooth the surface.

Bake for 10–12 minutes or until pale golden and springy to the touch.

Sprinkle a sheet of greaseproof paper liberally with sugar and place on a slightly damp, clean cloth. Turn the sponge out onto the sugared paper and remove the lining paper. Spread the sponge with jam and carefully roll up from the short edge, using the cloth to help you. Transfer to a wire rack to cool.

Cook's Tip

If the sponge bakes a little crisp around the edges then trim before filling and rolling with a sharp knife.

58 | Battenburg

Preparation time
30–40 minutes

Cooking time
30–35 minutes

Oven temperature
180 C, 350 F, gas 4

Makes 1 (20-cm/ 8-in) oblong cake

Total calories
2775

You will need
100 g / 4 oz butter or margarine
100 g / 4 oz caster sugar
few drops of almond essence
   (optional)
2 large eggs, beaten
50 g / 2 oz plain flour, sifted
50 g / 2 oz self-raising flour, sifted
few drops of pink food colouring
3 tablespoons apricot jam,
   warmed and sieved
225 g / 8 oz almond paste

Cream the butter with the sugar until light and fluffy, adding the almond essence if using. Add the eggs, one at a time, beating well. Fold in the flours. Divide the mixture in half and colour one half pink. Turn the pink mixture into a greased and lined 1-kg/2-lb loaf tin. Cover with a piece of greaseproof paper and spread the plain mixture on top.

Bake for 30–35 minutes or until firm. Turn out onto a wire rack, remove the paper and allow to cool.

Trim the two halves carefully to remove all crust, then cut each in half lengthways. Sandwich the strips together with some of the jam, alternating the colours.

Roll out the almond paste to the same length as the cake and 4 times as wide, spread with the remaining jam. Use to surround the cake completely. Neaten the join cutting off spare paste with a knife.

Cook's Tip

To give the Battenburg a professional finish, crimp the top edges of the cake with the thumb and forefinger and mark the top in a criss-cross pattern with a knife. Add a broad plait and dredge lightly with caster sugar.

59 | Coconut Cake

Preparation time
15 minutes, plus 30 minutes standing time

Cooking time
45–50 minutes

Oven temperature
190 C, 375 F, gas 5

Makes 1 (450-g/ 1-lb) loaf cake

Total calories
2505

You will need
2 eggs
about 6 tablespoons milk
100 g/4 oz caster sugar
75 g/3 oz desiccated coconut
175 g/6 oz plain flour
2 teaspoons baking powder
100 g/4 oz butter or margarine

For the topping
2 tablespoons desiccated coconut
1 tablespoon demerara sugar

Break the eggs into a measuring jug, beat lightly, then add the milk to make up to 150 ml/¼ pint. Mix in half the sugar and the coconut and leave to stand for 30 minutes.

Sift the flour and baking powder together into a bowl, then stir in the remaining sugar. Rub in the butter until the mixture resembles fine breadcrumbs, then add the coconut mixture. Mix gently but thoroughly together.

Turn the mixture into a greased and floured 450-g/ 1-lb loaf tin. Mix together the coconut and sugar for the topping and sprinkle over the top.

Bake for 45–50 minutes or until firm to the touch. Cool on a wire rack.

60 | Cherry and Coconut Cake

Preparation time
15 minutes

Cooking time
45–50 minutes

Oven temperature
180 C, 350 F, gas 4

Makes 1 (450-g/ 1-lb) loaf cake

Total calories
2300

You will need
150 g/5 oz self-raising flour
¼ teaspoon salt
100 g/4 oz caster sugar
75 g/3 oz butter or margarine
1 egg
5 tablespoons milk
175 g/6 oz glacé cherries, halved
50 g/2 oz desiccated coconut
1 tablespoon demerara sugar

Sift the flour and salt into a bowl. Stir in the caster sugar then rub in the butter until the mixture resembles fine breadcrumbs.

Beat the egg and milk together and toss the cherries with the coconut. Add both to the flour mixture and fold in gently.

Place in a greased and floured 450-g/1-lb loaf tin and sprinkle with the demerara sugar. Bake for 45–50 minutes or until firm to the touch. Turn out to cool on a wire rack.

Cook's Tip

If you are unsure about the size or capacity of your baking tins then why not paint the measurement on the base or side with nail varnish so that you needn't check or measure time and time again.

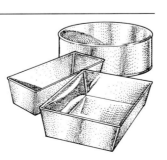

Cook's Tip

Remember when spooning a cake mixture into a baking tin to level the surface with the back of a spoon or palette knife so that the cake rises evenly during baking.

61 | Date and Walnut Cake

Preparation time
15 minutes, plus
soaking time

Cooking time
1–1¼ hours

Oven temperature
180 C, 350 F, gas 4

**Makes 1 (20-cm/
8-in) cake**

Total calories
3170

You will need
150 ml/¼ pint hot water
225 g/8 oz dates, halved and
    stoned
150 g/5 oz butter or margarine
100 g/4 oz soft brown sugar
2 tablespoons golden syrup
2 eggs
250 g/9 oz self-raising flour, sifted
25 g/1 oz walnuts, coarsely
    chopped
walnut halves to decorate

Pour the water onto the dates and leave until cold.

Cream the butter and the sugar together until light and fluffy. Beat in the syrup, then the eggs, one at a time. Fold in the flour then stir in the chopped walnuts with the dates and their soaking water.

Spoon into a greased and lined 20-cm/8-in round cake tin. Decorate with walnut halves and bake for 1–1¼ hours, covering loosely with foil for the last 30 minutes. Turn onto a wire rack to cool.

Cook's Tip

**Store this date and walnut
cake in an airtight tin. Never
store with biscuits – they will
absorb the moisture from the
cake and become soggy.**

62 | Carrot and Fruit Cake

Preparation time
15 minutes, plus cooling
time

Cooking time
55–60 minutes

Oven temperature
180 C, 350 F, gas 4

**Makes 1 (23-cm/
9-in) cake**

Total calories
2515

You will need
100 g/4 oz soft brown sugar
6 tablespoons clear honey
175 g/6 oz carrots, finely grated
100 g/4 oz raisins
50 g/2 oz chopped dates
¾ teaspoon grated nutmeg
100 g/4 oz butter
150 ml/¼ pint water
1 egg, beaten
100 g/4 oz plain wholemeal flour
100 g/4 oz plain white flour, sifted
2 teaspoons baking powder, sifted

Mix the sugar, honey, carrots, raisins, dates, nutmeg, butter and water together in a saucepan. Bring to the boil and simmer for 5 minutes. Turn into a mixing bowl and allow to cool.

Stir in the egg. Mix the flours and the baking powder together and sprinkle over the mixture. Mix thoroughly together.

Turn into a greased and floured 23-cm/9-in deep, round cake tin. Bake for 55–60 minutes or until firm to the touch. Cool on a wire rack.

Cook's Tip

**To smooth the surface of a
heavy cake mixture like this
one, spread the surface with a
metal spoon that has been
dipped in hot water.**

63 | Marbled Almond Cake

Preparation time
20–25 minutes

Cooking time
1¼ hours

Oven temperature
160 C, 325 F, gas 3

Makes 1 (18-cm/7-in) cake

Total calories
3690

You will need
75 g/3 oz ground almonds
200 g/7 oz caster sugar
3 eggs, beaten
150 g/5 oz butter or margarine, softened
150 g/5 oz plain flour, sifted
225 g/8 oz glacé cherries, halved
25 g/1 oz desiccated coconut

Mix the ground almonds with 75 g/3 oz of the sugar. Mix to a paste with 2 tablespoons of the egg and set aside.

Cream the butter and remaining sugar together until light and fluffy. Beat in the remaining egg, a little at a time, adding 2 tablespoons of the flour when half of the egg is used. Fold in the remaining flour.

Mix the cherries with the coconut and fold into the creamed mixture, stirring gently to distribute evenly.

Turn half the mixture into a greased 18-cm/7-in deep, round cake tin. Roll out the almond paste to fit just inside the tin and place on top of the mixture, pressing down gently. Place the remaining cake mixture on top.

Bake for 1¼ hours, covering with foil for the last 30 minutes to prevent over-browning. Leave in the tin for 5 minutes, then cool on a wire rack.

Cook's Tip

You can make your own wonderfully fresh ground almonds if you have a blender or food processor. Simply grind or process a quantity of blanched almonds equal to that which you want ground, using the metal blade, until finely ground, about 20–25 seconds.

64 | Fruit 'n' Nut Cake

Preparation time
20 minutes

Cooking time
1¾–2 hours

Oven temperature
150 C, 300 F, gas 2

Makes 1 (18-cm/7-in) square cake

Total calories
4375

You will need
150 g/5 oz butter or margarine
6 tablespoons golden syrup
100 g/4 oz dried apricots
50 g/2 oz sultanas
225 g/8 oz raisins
100 g/4 oz currants
50 g/2 oz almonds, chopped
10 tablespoons milk
225 g/8 oz plain flour
pinch of grated nutmeg
grated rind of 1 orange
2 eggs, beaten
½ teaspoon bicarbonate of soda

For the topping
50 g/2 oz dried apricots
50 g/2 oz whole almonds
25 g/1 oz glacé cherries
2 tablespoons honey

Place the butter, syrup, fruit, nuts and milk in a pan and melt over a low heat. Simmer gently for 5 minutes. Cool slightly. Place the flour, nutmeg and orange rind in a bowl and add the eggs. Stir the bicarbonate of soda into the cooled fruit mixture and add to the dry ingredients. Mix well and place in a greased and lined 18-cm/7-in deep, square cake tin. Smooth the surface.

Bake for 1¾–2 hours then turn out to cool on a wire rack.

To make the topping, place all the ingredients in a saucepan and heat until thoroughly mixed. Spread on top of the cake.

Cook's Tip

You can test a fruit cake to see if it is cooked by inserting a fine skewer or wooden cocktail stick into the centre of the cake – if the skewer or stick comes out clean of mixture then the cake is cooked – if not, cook longer.

65 | Apple and Blackberry Sponge Cake

Preparation time
25 minutes

Cooking time
25–30 minutes

Oven temperature
190 C, 375 F, gas 5

Makes 1 (20-cm/ 8-in) cake

Total calories
4195

You will need
100 g/4 oz butter or margarine
100 g/4 oz caster sugar
2 large eggs, beaten
100 g/4 oz self-raising flour, sifted

For the filling and topping
675 g/1½ lb cooking apples,
    peeled, cored and sliced
175 g/6 oz sugar
6 tablespoons blackberry jam
300 ml/½ pint double cream,
    whipped
sifted icing sugar to dust

Cream the butter with the sugar until light and fluffy. Add the eggs, a little at a time, with a little flour. Fold in the remaining flour. Spoon into a greased and floured 20-cm/8-in deep, round cake tin. Bake for 25–30 minutes until golden and firm. Cool on a wire rack.

Meanwhile, cook the apples with the sugar until soft and pulpy. Press through a nylon sieve and cool.

Split the sponge into two layers. Spread the bottom layer with half of the jam. Top with half of the cream and the apple mixture. Cover with the second cake layer and sift icing sugar over. Place the remaining cream in a piping bag and pipe swirls around the top edge of the cake. Pipe the remaining jam over the cream swirls.

Serve lightly chilled.

Cook's Tip

An easy way to fill a nylon piping bag is to insert the nozzle in the end and stand the bag in a round grater. Fold the edge back over the top edge of the grater. The cream can then be spooned in easily.

66 | Cherry and Almond Cake

Preparation time
15–20 minutes

Cooking time
1¼–1½ hours

Oven temperature
180 C, 350 F, gas 4

Makes 1 (18-cm/ 7-in) cake

Total calories
3640

You will need
175 g/6 oz butter or margarine
175 g/6 oz caster sugar
3 eggs, beaten
150 g/5 oz self-raising flour
50 g/2 oz plain flour
3 tablespoons cornflour
3 tablespoons ground almonds
175 g/6 oz glacé cherries, halved
50 g/2 oz sultanas
2 tablespoons flaked almonds

Cream the butter and sugar until light and fluffy. Beat in the eggs, a little at a time, mixing well. Sift the flours with the ground almonds and fold into the creamed mixture. Fold in the cherries and sultanas. Spoon into a greased and lined 18-cm/7-in deep, round cake tin. Make a slight hollow in the centre so that the cake will rise evenly.

Sprinkle the cake with flaked almonds and bake for 1¼–1½ hours or until a skewer inserted into the centre comes out clean. Cool on a wire rack.

Cook's Tip

If the creamed mixture begins to curdle a little when adding the eggs, add 1–2 tablespoons flour with each new egg introduced.

67 | Mid-morning Coffee-time Cake

Preparation time
15 minutes

Cooking time
55 minutes

Oven temperature
18i C, 350 F, gas 4

Makes 1 (18-cm/7-in) square cake

Total calories
3165

You will need
100 g / 4 oz butter
200 g / 7 oz caster sugar
2 eggs, beaten
1 teaspoon vanilla essence
300 ml / ½ pint soured cream
175 g / 6 oz self-raising flour
1 teaspoon bicarbonate of soda
75 g / 3 oz hazelnuts or walnuts, coarsely chopped

Cream the butter with the sugar until light and fluffy. Gradually beat in the eggs. Stir in the vanilla essence and soured cream. Sift the flour with the soda and fold into the creamed mixture. Add 50 g / 2 oz of the nuts and mix well. Spoon into a greased and lined 18-cm / 7-in deep, square cake tin.

Bake for 30 minutes or until a skewer inserted into the centre comes out clean. Without removing the cake from the oven, carefully sprinkle the remaining nuts on top. Bake for a further 25 minutes. Turn out and allow to cool on a wire rack. Serve warm or cold.

68 | Passion Cake

Preparation time
20 minutes

Cooking time
1 hour 5 minutes

Oven temperature
180 C, 350 F, gas 4

Makes 1 (23-cm/9-in) cake

Total calories
5430

You will need
50 g / 2 oz walnuts, coarsely chopped
2 ripe bananas, mashed
175 g / 6 oz Muscovado sugar
3 eggs, beaten
275 g / 10 oz plain flour
1 teaspoon salt
1 teaspoon bicarbonate of soda
2 teaspoons baking powder
175 ml / 6 fl oz corn oil
175 g / 6 oz grated carrot
walnut halves to decorate (optional)

For the icing
75 g / 3 oz butter, softened
75 g / 3 oz cream cheese
175 g / 6 oz icing sugar, sifted
½ teaspoon vanilla essence

Mix the walnuts with the banana. Add the sugar and eggs and mix well. Sift the flour with the salt, soda and baking powder. Add to the nut mixture with the oil and beat well. Fold in the carrot. Spoon into a greased and lined 23-cm / 9-in deep, round cake tin.

Bake for about 1 hour 5 minutes until golden and a skewer inserted into the centre comes out clean. Cool on a wire rack.

To prepare the icing, beat the butter with the cream cheese until light. Beat in the icing sugar and vanilla essence. Spread over the cake and mark with a fork to give a rough-textured finish. Decorate with walnut halves, if liked.

Cook's Tip

To prevent the bowl from slipping while the mixture is being creamed, place the bowl on a damp teatowel or sponge.

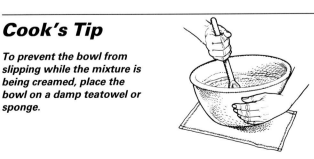

Cook's Tip

It is essential to use ripe bananas for this recipe. Choose bananas without a hint of green and those that have brownish streaks to their skins.

69 | Harlequin Ring

Preparation time
20–25 minutes

Cooking time
40 minutes

Oven temperature
180 C, 350 F, gas 4

Makes 1 large ring cake

Total calories
4050

You will need
175 g/6 oz butter or margarine
175 g/6 oz caster sugar
3 large eggs, beaten
175 g/6 oz self-raising flour
15 g/½ oz cocoa powder, dissolved
  in 3 tablespoons milk
grated rind of ½ lemon
1 tablespoon lemon juice
yellow food colouring

For the topping
225 g/8 oz granulated sugar
4 tablespoons water
1 egg white
50 g/2 oz long-thread coconut,
  toasted

Cream the butter with the sugar until light and fluffy. Add the eggs with a little flour and beat well. Fold in the remaining flour. Remove two-thirds of the mixture and mix with the cocoa. Add the lemon rind, lemon juice and colouring to the remaining one-third.

Spread the cocoa mixture over the bottom and sides of a greased 1.75-litre/3-pint ring mould. Place the lemon mixture in a piping bag fitted with a large plain nozzle and pipe around the centre of the chocolate mixture. Using a palette knife carefully level the surfaces. Bake for 40 minutes, then cool on a wire rack.

To make the topping, dissolve the sugar in the water then boil to 115 C/240 F or the soft ball stage. Whisk the egg white until stiff. Pour the sugar syrup over and whisk until opaque. Quickly swirl over the cake and sprinkle with coconut.

Cook's Tip

To test a syrup for the soft ball stage, drop some of the sugar syrup into a bowl of iced water. The syrup should form a soft ball when squeezed between the fingers.

70 | Coffee and Pear Cake

Preparation time
25–30 minutes

Cooking time
30–40 minutes

Oven temperature
160 C, 325 F, gas 3

Makes 1 (18-cm/7-in) cake

Total calories
4570

You will need
175 g/6 oz butter or margarine
175 g/6 oz soft brown sugar
3 eggs
200 g/7 oz self-raising flour
2 tablespoons coffee essence

For the icing and decoration
350 g/12 oz coffee butter icing
  (see Introduction)
1 (411-g/14½-oz) can pear halves
chopped walnuts
angelica leaves

Cream the butter with the sugar until light and fluffy. Beat in the eggs, one at a time, adding a little flour with each egg after the first. Fold in the remaining flour and coffee essence. Divide the mixture between 2 greased and lined 18-cm/7-in sandwich tins. Bake for 30–40 minutes. Turn out to cool on a wire rack.

To decorate the cake, make the coffee butter icing and mix a little with two of the drained and chopped pears. Use to sandwich the cakes together. Spread some of the remaining icing around the sides, then roll in the chopped walnuts. Spread the remainder over the top of the cake and pipe a decoration around the edges. Slice the remaining pears across very thinly, keeping the pear in shape. Decorate the top with the pear halves, allowing each one to fan out slightly, and the angelica.

Cook's Tip

To cut the pears, place them flat side down and with a sharp knife, make slices across while holding the pear in shape with the other hand.

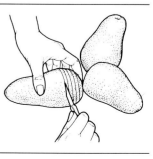

71 | Chocolate Layer Cake

Preparation time
30 minutes

Cooking time
30–40 minutes

Oven temperature
160 C, 325 F, gas 3

**Makes 1 (18-cm/
7-in) cake**

Total calories
3895

You will need
1 tablespoon cocoa powder
1 tablespoon hot water
175 g/6 oz butter or margarine,
    softened
175 g/6 oz caster sugar
3 eggs
175 g/6 oz self-raising flour
1½ teaspoons baking powder

For the icing and decoration
225 g/8 oz chocolate butter icing
    (see Introduction)
brandy (optional)
chocolate vermicelli
chocolate shapes

Mix the cocoa with the hot water and allow to cool. Place all the ingredients for the cake in a bowl and beat with a wooden spoon until well mixed. Divide the mixture between 2 greased and lined 18-cm/7-in sandwich tins. Bake for 30–40 minutes then turn out to cool on a wire rack.

To decorate the cake, make the chocolate icing and mix with a little brandy if liked. Use two-thirds to spread over the top and sides of the cake, using a decorative scraper if liked to give a ridged effect. Roll the sides of the cake in chocolate vermicelli to coat. Place the remainder in a piping bag fitted with a star-shaped nozzle and pipe swirls of icing around the edge of the cake. Decorate with chocolate shapes as shown.

Cook's Tip

**To achieve the decoration
shown on top of the cake,
hold the scraper at an angle of
about 45° to the cake and
press just hard enough to
indent the surface.**

72 | American Carrot Cake

Preparation time
20–25 minutes

Cooking time
1½ hours

Oven temperature
180 C, 350 F, gas 4

**Makes 1 (20-cm/
8-in) cake**

Total calories
5120

You will need
225 g/8 oz butter
225 g/8 oz caster sugar
4 eggs, beaten
225 g/8 oz self-raising flour
grated rind of 1 lemon
2 tablespoons lemon juice
1 tablespoon Kirsch
225 g/8 oz carrots, peeled and
    grated
100 g/4 oz blanched almonds,
    finely chopped

For the lemon icing
225 g/8 oz icing sugar, sifted
5 teaspoons lemon juice
marzipan and angelica to decorate

Cream the butter and sugar together until light and fluffy. Beat in the eggs with a little of the flour, then fold in the remaining flour with the lemon rind, lemon juice and Kirsch. Add the carrots and almonds and mix well. Spoon into a greased and lined 20-cm/8-in deep, round cake tin.

Bake for 1½ hours until well-risen, golden and firm to the touch. Turn out to cool on a wire rack.

To make the icing, mix the icing sugar with the lemon juice until smooth and glossy. Pour over the top of the cooled cake, allowing it to run down the sides. Decorate with marzipan (coloured orange if liked) shaped into carrots with green angelica tops.

Cook's Tip

**To make coloured marzipan,
simply add a few drops of the
chosen colour to the
marzipan ball and knead
until the colour is uniformly
mixed into the paste. Leave
shapes to dry a little before
adding to the cake so that**
**colours do not run into the
icing.**

73 | Yogurt Cake

Preparation time
30 minutes

Cooking time
40–45 minutes

Oven temperature
160 C, 325 F, gas 3

**Makes 1 (20-cm/
8-in) cake**

Total calories
4055

You will need
100 g/4 oz butter or margarine
100 g/4 oz caster sugar
3 eggs
2 teaspoons orange juice
150 ml/¼ pint natural yogurt
100 g/4 oz ground almonds
150 g/5 oz self-raising flour
1 teaspoon baking powder
3 tablespoons cocoa powder
grated rind of 1 orange

For the icing and decoration
350 g/12 oz orange butter icing
   (see Introduction)
chocolate vermicelli
chocolate leaves
orange rind

Place all the cake ingredients in a mixing bowl and beat with a wooden spoon until well mixed. Divide between 2 greased and lined 20-cm/8-in sandwich tins. Bake for 40–45 minutes then turn out to cool on a wire rack.

   To decorate the cake, make up the orange butter icing and use some to sandwich the cakes together. Spread some around the sides of the cake and roll in chocolate vermicelli. Spread a little of the remaining icing on top and pipe a border around the edge. Decorate with chocolate leaves and orange rind.

74 | Olde-fashioned Madeira Cake

Preparation time
15–20 minutes

Cooking time
1¼–1½ hours

Oven temperature
160 C, 325 F, gas 3

**Makes 1 (18-cm/
7-in) cake**

Total calories
2975

You will need
175 g/6 oz butter
175 g/6 oz caster sugar
grated rind of 1 lemon
3 eggs
225 g/8 oz plain flour
1½ teaspoons baking powder
2 tablespoons warm water
piece of candied peel

Cream the butter, sugar and lemon rind together until light and fluffy. Beat in the eggs, one at a time, adding a little of the flour with each egg after the first. Fold in the remaining flour and baking powder using a metal spoon. Gently fold in the water to give a soft, dropping consistency. Place in a greased and base-lined 18-cm/7-in deep cake tin. Place the candied peel in the centre of the cake.

   Bake for 1¼–1½ hours. Allow to cool slightly in the tin before turning out to cool on a wire rack.

Cook's Tip

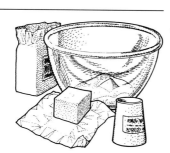

If a strong orangey flavour is liked then make the cake using an orange or mandarin-flavoured fruit yogurt instead of natural.

Cook's Tip

Cakes are called rich, plain or sponge depending upon how much fat, flour, sugar and eggs they have. This is a rich cake, made by the creaming method; it has almost equal quantities of fat and flour, and is rich in eggs and sugar.

75 | Lemon Curd Cake

Preparation time
25 minutes

Cooking time
25–35 minutes

Oven temperature
160 C, 325 F, gas 3

Makes 1 (20-cm/ 8-in) cake

Total calories
3875

You will need
175 g/6 oz butter or margarine
175 g/6 oz caster sugar
3 eggs
175 g/6 oz self-raising flour
grated rind of 1 lemon
2 tablespoons lemon juice

For the icing and decoration
225 g/8 oz lemon butter icing (see Introduction)
4 tablespoons lemon curd
shredded lemon rind

Cream the butter and sugar together until light and fluffy. Add the eggs, one at a time, adding a little of the flour with each egg after the first. Fold in the remaining flour with the lemon rind and juice. Divide between 2 greased and lined 20-cm/8-in sandwich tins. Bake for 25–35 minutes then turn out to cool on a wire rack.

To decorate the cake, make the butter icing and use a little to sandwich the cakes together, Spread the remainder over the top of the cake and using a piping bag fitted with a star-shaped nozzle, pipe a border of icing around the top edge. Heat the lemon curd until runny then pour over the top of the cake, smoothing it out evenly to the edge of the piped border. Sprinkle with the shredded lemon rind.

76 | Cider Apple Cake

Preparation time
25 minutes

Cooking time
45–50 minutes

Oven temperature
180 C, 350 F, gas 4

Makes 1 large rectangular cake

Total calories
2885

You will need
150 g/5 oz butter or margarine
150 g/5 oz caster sugar
2 eggs
225 g/8 oz plain flour
150 ml/$\frac{1}{4}$ pint sweet cider
1 teaspoon baking powder
pinch of grated nutmeg
1 (35-g/1$\frac{1}{4}$-oz) packet dehydrated apple flakes

For the topping
2 red-skinned dessert apples
sieved apricot jam

Cream the butter and sugar together until light and fluffy. Beat in the eggs, one at a time, adding a little flour with the second. Gradually mix in the cider, alternating with the dry ingredients. Finaly add the apple flakes. Place in a greased and lined 28 × 18-cm/11 × 7-in Swiss roll tin and level the surface.

Bake for 45–50 minutes then turn out to cool on a wire rack.

To decorate the cake, core and slice the apples very thinly and overlap in rows on top of the cake. Brush with the sieved apricot jam.

Cook's Tip

Always follow the guidelines in recipes for timings but do also rely upon your own good judgement, since ovens do vary slightly. Remember a sponge cake, like this one, will be cooked when well-risen, golden brown and **springy to the touch – press lightly with the fingertips and the cake will spring back under light pressure.**

Cook's Tip

Dip the apple slices in a little lemon juice to stop them turning brown before placing on top of the cake.

77 | Devil's Food Cake

Preparation time
20–30 minutes

Cooking time
1¾–2 hours

Oven temperature
150C, 300F, gas 2

Makes 1 (20-cm/8-in) cake

Total calories
4565

You will need
175 g/6 oz butter or margarine
175 g/6 oz soft brown sugar
2 eggs
175 g/6 oz golden syrup
50 g/2 oz ground almonds
175 g/6 oz plain flour
50 g/2 oz cocoa powder
175 ml/6 fl oz milk
¼ teaspoon bicarbonate of soda

For the icing and decoration
1 recipe American frosting (see
Introduction)
chocolate curls

Cream the butter and sugar together until light and fluffy. Add the remaining cake ingredients and beat well with a wooden spoon. Pour into a greased and lined 20-cm/8-in deep round cake tin.

Bake for 1¾–2 hours then turn out to cool on a wire rack.

To decorate the cake, make the frosting and spread over the cake, making deep swirls with a palette knife. Decorate with chocolate curls.

78 | Chocolate Fudge Cake

Preparation time
30–40 minutes

Cooking time
40 minutes

Oven temperature
180C, 350F, gas 4

Makes 1 (20-cm/8-in) cake

Total calories
4392

You will need
100 g/4 oz plain chocolate, broken
into pieces
300 ml/½ pint milk
225 g/8 oz self-raising flour
½ teaspoon baking powder
100 g/4 oz butter or margarine
100 g/4 oz soft brown sugar
2 eggs, separated

For the icing and decoration
1 recipe Chocolate Fudge Icing
(see Introduction), cooled and
beaten
toasted hazelnuts

Place the chocolate and the milk in a pan and heat gently, stirring, until melted.

Sift the flour and baking powder together. Cream the fat and sugar until light and fluffy, then beat in the egg yolks one at a time. Fold in the flour mixture, then add three-quarters of the chocolate milk and beat until smooth. Stir in the remaining chocolate milk.

Whisk the egg whites until fairly stiff, then fold 1 tablespoon into the chocolate mixture to lighten it. Carefully fold in the rest. Turn into two lined and greased 20-cm/8-in sandwich tins and bake for 40 minutes, or until the cakes spring back when lightly pressed. Cool on a wire rack. Use one-third of the icing to sandwich the cakes together. Reheat the remaining icing, then pour over the cake to coat completely. Add the hazelnuts before the icing sets.

Cook's Tip

If you do not intend to eat this cake immediately, it will keep well un-iced in an airtight container. Once the cake is iced, it should be eaten as soon as possible.

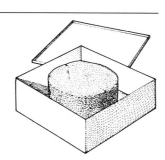

Cook's Tip

If you are in a hurry, a simpler form of chocolate fudge icing can be made quite easily with a microwave. Put the butter in a medium-sized bowl, cook for 30 seconds on Full to melt and stir in the remaining ingredients, using just one tablespoon of boiling water in place of the hot water and milk. Beat well until you have a smooth paste.

79 | Chocolate Minstrel Cake

Preparation time
25 minutes

Cooking time
30–35 minutes

Oven temperature
200 C, 400 F, gas 6

Makes 1 large ring cake

Total calories
3600

You will need
115 g/4½ oz butter
150 g/5 oz caster sugar
5 eggs, separated
225 g/8 oz plain dessert chocolate
75 g/3 oz toasted hazelnuts, ground
4 tablespoons dry brown breadcrumbs
25 g/1 oz plain flour, sifted
2 tablespoons water
50 g/2 oz white chocolate

Cream 90 g/3½ oz of the butter with the sugar until light and fluffy. Beat in the egg yolks. Melt 90 g/3½ oz of the plain chocolate over a pan of hot water. Allow to cool slightly then beat into the creamed mixture. Fold in the nuts, breadcrumbs and flour. Whisk the egg whites until stiff then fold in with a metal spoon.

Spoon into a greased and floured 1.75-litre/3-pint ring mould. Bake for 30–35 minutes then turn out to cool on a wire rack.

To decorate the cake, melt the remaining plain chocolate with the water and remaining butter. Spread over the cake with a palette knife and allow to dribble down the sides. Melt the white chocolate, place in a piping bag fitted with a small plain nozzle and pipe zig-zags over the chocolate. Leave to set.

Cook's Tip

If you do not have a ring mould then use an upturned heatproof glass or beaker in the centre of a deep round baking dish. Hold the glass down firmly while adding the mixture to keep it in the middle of the dish.

80 | Minted Chocolate Marble Loaf

Preparation time
25 minutes

Cooking time
1¼–1½ hours

Oven temperature
160 C, 325 F, gas 3

Makes 1 (1-kg/2-lb) loaf cake

Total calories
3395

You will need
100 g/4 oz butter or margarine
100 g/4 oz caster sugar
3 eggs
225 g/8 oz self-raising flour
2 tablespoons cocoa powder
1 tablespoon hot water
few drops of green food colouring
few drops of peppermint essence

For the icing and decoration
225 g/8 oz chocolate fudge icing (see Introduction)
minted chocolate sticks

Cream the butter and the sugar together until light and fluffy. Beat in the eggs, one at a time, adding a little flour with every egg after the first. Fold in the remaining flour. Divide the mixture in half. Blend the cocoa powder with the hot water and add to one half. Colour the other half of the mixture green and flavour with peppermint essence. Place alternate spoonfuls of the mixtures into a greased and lined 1-kg/2-lb loaf tin. Bang the tin sharply on the table to level out the mixture.

Bake for 1¼–1½ hours then turn out to cool on a wire rack.

To decorate the cake, make up the chocolate fudge icing and spread over the cold loaf. Decorate with the chocolate sticks.

Cook's Tip

To obtain the marbled effect, place spoonfuls of the mixtures at random into the loaf tin and bang the tin sharply on the table to level out the mixture.

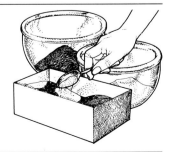

81 | Spicy Pear Surprise

Preparation time
25–30 minutes

Cooking time
35–40 minutes

Oven temperature
160 C, 325 F, gas 3

Makes 1 (20-cm/ 8-in) cake

Total calories
3340

You will need
100 g/4 oz butter or margarine
100 g/4 oz caster sugar
½ teaspoon ground cinnamon
grated rind of 1 orange
2 eggs
100 g/4 oz self-raising flour

For the filling and decoration
300 ml/½ pint double cream
2 tablespoons dark rum
1 tablespoon caster sugar
1 (411-g/14½-oz) can pear halves
1 orange, thinly sliced and
    quartered

Cream the butter with the sugar, cinnamon and orange rind until light and fluffy. Gradually beat in the eggs then fold in the sifted flour with a metal spoon. Divide the mixture between a greased and lined 20-cm/8-in sponge flan tin and a 20-cm/8-in sandwich tin. Bake for 35–40 minutes then turn out to cool on a wire rack.

   To fill and decorate the cake, whip the cream with the rum and sugar until thick. Drain the pears thoroughly and arrange in the flan. Spread some cream over them and place the sandwich cake on top. Spread half of the remaining cream over the top of the cake. Using a large star-shaped nozzle, pipe a cream edging around the top of the cake. Decorate with the quartered orange slices.

82 | Apple and Cinnamon Cake

Preparation time
15 minutes

Cooking time
1–1¼ hours

Oven temperature
180 C, 350 F, gas 4

Makes 1 (20-cm/ 8-in) square cake

Total calories
2965

You will need
275 g/10 oz self-raising flour
1½ teaspoons ground cinnamon
225 g/8 oz demerara sugar
50 g/2 oz raisins
100 g/4 oz butter, melted
2 large eggs, beaten
175 ml/6 fl oz milk
225 g/8 oz dessert apples, peeled,
    cored and chopped
icing sugar to dust

Sift the flour and cinnamon into a bowl and stir in the sugar and raisins. Mix in the melted butter, eggs, milk and apples and beat until smooth. Turn into a greased and lined 20-cm/8-in square cake tin.

   Bake for 1–1¼ hours until the cake springs back when lightly pressed with the fingertips. Turn onto a wire rack to cool. Dust with icing sugar before serving.

Cook's Tip

This cake can also be made with fresh pears. They should be peeled, cored and halved then poached gently in a little syrup until just soft before using to fill the flan.

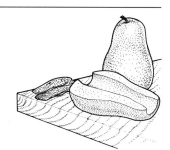

Cook's Tip

Unless you can be sure that your cinnamon is absolutely fresh then grind your own for this recipe. Grind 1–2 cinnamon sticks, depending upon size, in a blender, food processor, herb mill or coffee grinder for best results.

83 | Banana Cake

Preparation time
15–20 minutes

Cooking time
20–25 minutes

Oven temperature
180 C, 350 F, gas 4

Makes 1 (18-cm/7-in) cake

Total calories
2300

You will need
100 g/4 oz butter or margarine
100 g/4 oz caster sugar
2 eggs
100 g/4 oz self-raising flour, sifted
2 bananas, mashed

For the filling
50 g/2 oz ground almonds
50 g/2 oz icing sugar, sifted
1 small banana, mashed
½ teaspoon lemon juice
icing sugar to dust

Cream the butter and sugar together until light and fluffy. Add the eggs, one at a time, adding a little flour with the second egg. Fold in the remaining flour with the bananas. Divide the mixture between 2 greased and lined 18-cm/7-in sandwich tins.

Bake for 20–25 minutes until the cakes spring back when lightly pressed with the fingertips. Turn out to cool on a wire rack.

To make the filling, mix the ground almonds with the icing sugar, then add the banana and lemon juice and mix to a smooth paste. Sandwich the cakes together with the filling and dust with icing sugar.

Cook's Tip

This is the perfect cake to make with those less than perfect or special offer bananas that are just past their peak and are very ripe.

84 | Walnut and Banana Galette

Preparation time
30 minutes

Cooking time
20–25 minutes

Oven temperature
180 C, 350 F, gas 4

Makes 1 (18-cm/7-in) galette

Total calories
4565

You will need
175 g/6 oz butter or margarine
100 g/4 oz caster sugar
grated rind of ½ lemon
175 g/6 oz plain flour
100 g/4 oz walnuts, chopped

For the filling and decoration
300 ml/½ pint double cream
2 tablespoons icing sugar
4 bananas
lemon juice to sprinkle

Cream the butter, sugar and lemon rind until light and fluffy. Fold in the flour and knead together into a soft dough. Place in a polythene bag and chill for 30 minutes.

Divide the dough into three. Grease and flour three baking trays and mark an 18-cm/7-in circle on each. Place a piece of dough in each circle and press out flat to fill the circle. Sprinkle the tops with the walnuts.

Bake for 20–25 minutes then allow to cool before turning out onto a wire rack.

To decorate, whip the cream and fold in the icing sugar. Slice the bananas and sprinkle with a little lemon juice. Sandwich the layers together with some cream and bananas. Pipe cream on the top and decorate with the remaining banana slices. Stand for 30 minutes before serving.

Cook's Tip

To make circles on the floured baking trays, use a saucepan lid of the correct size as a guide.

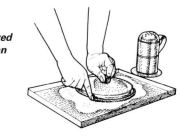

85 | Dundee Cake

Preparation time
20 minutes

Cooking time
3½–4 hours

Oven temperature
150 C, 300 F, gas 2

**Makes 1 (20-cm/
8-in) cake**

Total calories
6285

You will need
225 g/8 oz butter or margarine
225 g/8 oz caster sugar
grated rind of 1 orange
5 eggs
300 g/11 oz plain flour
½ teaspoon baking powder
1 teaspoon ground mixed spice
pinch of grated nutmeg
225 g/8 oz currants
225 g/8 oz sultanas
225 g/8 oz raisins
50 g/2 oz glacé cherries, chopped
100 g/4 oz chopped mixed peel
50 g/2 oz whole blanched almonds
to decorate

Place all the ingredients except the almonds in a mixing bowl and beat with a wooden spoon until well mixed. Place in a greased and lined 20-cm/8-in deep, round cake tin and smooth the top with a hot, wet metal spoon. Arrange the almonds in circles over the top.

Bake for 3½–4 hours, leave to cool in the tin for 5 minutes, then turn out to cool on a wire rack.

86 | Chequered Chocolate Cake

Preparation time
30–40 minutes

Cooking time
45–55 minutes

Oven temperature
160 C, 325 F, gas 3

**Makes 1 (18-cm/
7-in) cake**

Total calories
4470

You will need
175 g/6 oz butter or margarine
175 g/6 oz caster sugar
3 eggs
175 g/6 oz self-raising flour
1½ teaspoons baking powder
2 tablespoons cocoa powder
2 tablespoons hot water

For the filling, icing and decoration
3 tablespoons apricot jam, sieved
350 g/12 oz coffee butter icing
 (see Introduction)
toasted hazelnuts, chopped

Place all the cake ingredients except the cocoa powder and water in a mixing bowl and beat with a wooden spoon until well mixed. Divide the mixture in half. Blend the cocoa powder with the hot water and stir into one half of the cake mixture. Place each mixture into a greased and lined 18-cm/7-in sandwich tin. Bake for 45–55 minutes then turn out to cool on a wire rack.

To assemble the cake, using a 10-cm/4-in cutter and a 6-cm/2½-in cutter, placed inside it, cut out a ring from each cake about 4 cm/1½ in wide. Reassemble the cakes, putting the chocolate ring in the plain cake and the plain ring in the chocolate cake to give a chequered effect. Sandwich together with apricot jam. Spread some of the icing around the cake and roll in hazelnuts. Spread and pipe the rest on top and sprinkle with nuts.

Cook's Tip

Unblanched almonds are normally a little less expensive to purchase. To blanch them, place in a small bowl and pour over some boiling water. Leave for 2–3 minutes then take out one at a time and peel off the skins, which should come away easily.

Cook's Tip

A quick and easy way to put the nuts on the side of the cake is to spread the sides with icing, then roll the cake over the nuts spread on a sheet of greaseproof paper.

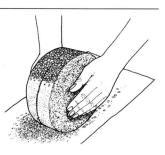

87 | *Walnut Cake*

Preparation time
20 minutes

Cooking time
30–35 minutes

Oven temperature
160 C, 325 F, gas 3

**Makes 1 (18-cm/
7-in) cake**

Total calories
2865

You will need
100 g/4 oz butter or margarine
100 g/4 oz caster sugar
2 eggs
75 g/3 oz self-raising flour
100 g/4 oz walnuts, finely chopped
1 tablespoon milk

For the filling and decoration
1 recipe American frosting (see
   Introduction)
halved walnuts

Cream the butter and sugar together until light and fluffy. Beat in the eggs, one at a time, adding a little flour with the second egg. Fold in the remaining flour, chopped nuts and milk. Divide the mixture between 2 greased and lined 18-cm/7-in sandwich tins.

Bake for 30–35 minutes then turn out to cool on a wire rack.

To fill and decorate the cake, make the American frosting and use a little to sandwich the cakes together. Pour the remainder over the cake, swirling with a palette knife in decorative patterns. Sprinkle with a few walnut halves.

88 | *Mandarin Cloud*

Preparation time
25 minutes

Cooking time
25–30 minutes

Oven temperature
190 C, 375 F, gas 5

**Makes 1 (20-cm/
8-in) cake**

Total calories
4385

You will need
150 g/5 oz plain flour
25 g/1 oz cornflour
2 teaspoons baking powder
150 g/5 oz icing sugar
5 tablespoons oil
6 tablespoons water
3 eggs, separated
finely grated rind and juice of 1
   orange

For the filling and decoration
3 tablespoons ground almonds
2 tablespoons icing sugar, sifted
1 tablespoon orange juice
450 ml/¾ pint double cream
1 (212-g/7½-oz) can mandarin
   oranges, drained

Sift the flour with the cornflour, baking powder and icing sugar. Lightly beat the oil, water and egg yolks together and beat into the dry ingredients. Stir in the orange rind and juice. Whisk the egg whites until stiff and fold into the cake mixture. Pour into 2 greased and lined 20-cm/8-in sandwich tins.

Bake for 25–30 minutes until well risen and just firm. Leave in the tins for 10 minutes then cool on a wire rack.

To make the filling, whisk the ground almonds, icing sugar and orange juice into two-thirds of the whipped cream. Sandwich the cakes together with half of this and use the rest to cover the cake. Pipe the remaining whipped cream around the top edge of the cake and decorate with the mandarins.

Cook's Tip

**When folding ingredients into
a creamed mixture, use a
metal tablespoon and work
quickly and lightly into and
across the mixture to retain
as much air as possible.**

Cook's Tip

**You may use fresh mandarins
or tangerines for this cake.
You will need the segmented
flesh of about 4–5 fruit,
depending upon size.**

89 | Almond Cake

Preparation time
15 minutes

Cooking time
45–50 minutes

Oven temperature
180 C, 350 F, gas 4

Makes 1 (15-cm/ 6-in) cake

Total calories
2625

You will need
150 g/5 oz butter
150 g/5 oz caster sugar
2 drops almond essence
50 g/2 oz ground almonds
finely grated rind of ½ lemon
2 large eggs, beaten
100 g/4 oz plain flour, sifted
15 g/½ oz flaked almonds
2 teaspoons icing sugar, sifted

Cream the butter with the caster sugar and almond essence until light and fluffy. Beat in the ground almonds and lemon rind. Add the eggs, a little at a time, then fold in the flour. Spoon into a greased and floured 15-cm/ 6-in deep, round cake tin, smooth the top and sprinkle with the flaked almonds and icing sugar.

Bake for 45–50 minutes or until firm to the touch. Leave in the tin for 5 minutes, then turn out to cool on a wire rack.

90 | Chocolate and Date Meringue

Preparation time
20–25 minutes

Cooking time
35–40 minutes

Oven temperature
180 C, 350 F, gas 4

Makes 1 (23-cm/ 9-in) gâteau

Total calories
3210

You will need
3 egg whites
100 g/4 oz caster sugar
90 g/3½ oz ground almonds
100 g/4 oz plain chocolate, grated
100 g/4 oz chopped dates
100 g/4 oz walnuts, chopped

For the decoration
150 ml/¼ pint double cream, whipped
50 g/2 oz flaked almonds, toasted

Whisk the egg whites until stiff. Gradually whisk in the sugar until the mixture stands in firm peaks. Fold in the almonds, chocolate, dates and walnuts. Spoon into a greased and lined 23-cm/9-in round, loose-bottomed cake tin.

Bake for 35–40 minutes until golden. Leave in the tin until cool.

To decorate, place the meringue on a serving plate and decorate with whipped cream and almonds.

Cook's Tip

If you are a cake-making enthusiast then you will appreciate a good range of light to medium-weight cake tins. Best gauge is light to medium because it ensures good heat conduction over short cooking times. Most will only require a light greasing or lining with paper to ensure good release properties. If you do not wish to risk the problem of sticking then consider non-stick coatings to such bakeware.

Cook's Tip

Toast almonds under the grill or in the oven but remember to stir from time to time to ensure that they brown evenly.

91 | *Chocolate and Ginger Ring*

Preparation time
20 minutes

Cooking time
1–1¼ hours

Oven temperature
140C, 275F, gas 1

Makes 1 (23-cm/ 9-in) gâteau

Total calories
2630

You will need
4 eggs, separated
250 g/9 oz caster sugar
25 g/1 oz cocoa powder
½ teaspoon cornflour
1–2 tablespoons brandy
150 ml/¼ pint milk
50 g/2 oz plain chocolate, chopped

For the decoration
150 ml/¼ pint double cream, whipped
2–3 pieces preserved ginger, finely sliced

Whisk the egg whites until stiff, then whisk in 2 tablespoons of the sugar. Sift all but 2 tablespoons of the sugar with the cocoa powder and fold in. Spread or pipe the mixture into two 23-cm/9-in rounds on baking trays lined with silicone paper.

Bake for 1–1¼ hours or until dry and crisp. Cool and remove the paper.

Put the egg yolks, cornflour, reserved sugar, brandy and milk in a heatproof bowl over a pan of simmering water and cook, stirring constantly, until thickened. Stir in the chocolate until melted then allow to cool.

Place one of the meringue discs on a plate. Cover with the chocolate filling. Top with the second meringue disc. Decorate with whipped cream and ginger.

92 | *Orange Crisp*

Preparation time
20 minutes

Cooking time
1½–2 hours

Oven temperature
140C, 275F, gas 1

Makes 1 (23-cm/ 9-in) gâteau

Total calories
2870

You will need

For the meringue
4 egg whites
225 g/8 oz caster sugar

For the filling and topping
300 ml/½ pint double cream
150 ml/¼ pint single cream
finely grated rind and juice of 1 orange
1 tablespoon icing sugar, sifted
1 (212-g/7½-oz) can mandarin oranges, drained

To make the meringue discs, whisk the egg whites until stiff, then add 2 tablespoons of the sugar and continue whisking until the mixture is very stiff. Carefully fold in the remaining sugar. Spoon or pipe into two 20–23-cm/8–9-in rounds on baking trays lined with silicone paper. Bake for 1½–2 hours until crisp. Peel off the paper and leave to cool on a wire rack.

Whip the creams, orange rind, orange juice and icing sugar together until thick. Mix the mandarins, reserving some for decoration, with three-quarters of the orange cream, and use to sandwich the meringues together. Pipe the remaining cream around the edge and decorate with the reserved mandarins.

Cook's Tip

It is essential to use fresh eggs in baking, especially for making meringues. To test if an egg is fresh place in a glass of water. If it sinks it is very fresh, if it hovers in the water halfway up the glass it is fresh. If it floats then it is stale.

Cook's Tip

Remember in order to get the greatest volume when whisking egg whites they must be beaten in a clean grease-free bowl. Rub the inside with the cut piece of a lemon to ensure this.

93 | Honey Walnut Roulade

Preparation time
20–25 minutes

Cooking time
12–14 minutes

Oven temperature
200 C, 400 F, gas 6

Serves 4–6

Calories
595–395 per portion

You will need
3 large eggs, separated
2 teaspoons water
75 g/3 oz caster sugar
2 tablespoons clear honey
100 g/4 oz self-raising flour
75 g/3 oz ground walnuts
caster sugar to sprinkle

For the filling
150 ml/¼ pint double cream
25 g/1 oz walnut pieces
1 tablespoon clear honey
whipped cream and walnut halves
   to decorate

Whisk the egg whites with the water until very stiff. Gradually add the sugar, a spoonful at a time, and whisk until thick and glossy. Whisk in the egg yolks and honey, then fold in the flour and ground walnuts with a metal spoon. Turn into a greased, lined and floured 24 × 28-cm/9½ × 11-in Swiss roll tin and level the surface.

Bake for 12–14 minutes then turn out quickly onto a sheet of greaseproof paper sprinkled with caster sugar. Trim the edges with a sharp knife then roll up like a Swiss roll, enclosing the paper. Leave until cold.

To make the filling, whip the cream then fold in the walnut pieces and honey. Unroll the roulade and remove the paper. Spread with the filling and re-roll. Decorate with whipped cream and walnut halves.

94 | Chocolate Almond Torte

Preparation time
20 minutes

Cooking time
35 minutes

Oven temperature
190 C, 375 F, gas 5

Makes 1 (20-cm/ 8-in) cake

Total calories
3760

You will need
100 g/4 oz plain flour
¾ teaspoon baking powder
¼ teaspoon bicarbonate of soda
40 g/1½ oz cocoa powder
75 g/3 oz butter
150 g/5 oz soft brown sugar
2 eggs
3 tablespoons soured cream
¼ teaspoon almond essence
300 ml/½ pint double cream
100 g/4 oz chocolate caraque (see
   Cook's Tip 197)

Sift together the flour, baking powder, soda and cocoa. Cream the butter and sugar together until light, then gradually beat in the eggs, soured cream and almond essence. Fold in the dry ingredients.

Turn into a greased and lined 20-cm/8-in cake tin and level the surface. Bake for about 35 minutes, until firm. Leave the cake in the tin to cool, then turn out.

Whip the cream then swirl over the cake. Top with the chocolate caraque.

Cook's Tip

Ground walnuts are rarely sold but you can easily make your own in a food processor or blender. Simply grind using the metal blade for a few seconds until just powdery.

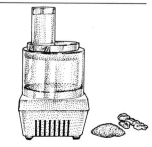

Cook's Tip

During folding, care must be taken not to disturb all the air that has been introduced during the creaming process – a simple stir or worse still beating, would break or burst the bubbles and let out the air. Fold mixtures with a metal spoon that will cut neatly and efficiently through the mixture disturbing the air bubbles as little as possible – a wooden spoon is too thick and clumsy an instrument for this purpose.

95 | Chocolate Freezer Cake

Preparation time
30 minutes, plus cooling
and freezing time

Cooking time
30 minutes

Oven temperature
190 C, 375 F, gas 5

**Makes 1 (20-cm/
8-in) cake**

Total calories
3870

You will need
⅔ recipe coffee-flavoured
  whisked sponge (see
  Introduction)

For the filling and decoration
225 g/8 oz plain chocolate, broken
  into pieces
3 tablespoons black coffee
2 eggs, separated
2 tablespoons dark rum
100 g/4 oz caster sugar
300 ml/½ pint double cream,
  whipped
25 g/1 oz plain chocolate, melted

Make the sponge and place in a greased, lined and
floured 20-cm/8-in deep cake tin. Bake for 25–30
minutes then turn out to cool on a wire rack.

Place the chocolate and coffee in a small pan and heat
to melt. Stir in the egg yolks and rum and leave to cool.
Whisk the egg whites until stiff then whisk in the sugar.
Whisk the chocolate mixture into half of the cream, then
carefully fold in the egg whites.

Split the cake in half horizontally and place the bottom
half back in the cleaned tin. Spoon over the filling. Cover
with the remaining sponge and press down. Cover with
foil and freeze overnight.

Dip the tin in hot water to release the cake and turn
out onto a chilled plate. Spread and pipe decoratively
with the remaining cream and with the chocolate.

Cook's Tip

**To pipe with the chocolate,
place in a greaseproof paper
bag. Snip off the end of the
bag and drizzle the chocolate
across the top of the cake.**

96 | Sponge Finger Pavé

Preparation time
20 minutes, plus 6
hours chilling time

Cooking time
about 10–15 minutes

Serves 4—6

Calories
665–445 per portion

You will need
50 g/2 oz caster sugar
3 tablespoons dark rum
18 sponge fingers
100 g/4 oz butter
100 g/4 oz icing sugar, sifted
4 egg yolks
100 g/4 oz plain chocolate, melted

For the decoration
chocolate curls (see Cook's Tip
  193)
desiccated coconut

Dissolve the sugar in 3 tablespoons water and bring to
the boil in a heavy-based pan. Remove from the heat
and add the rum. Dip the sponge fingers lightly in the
syrup, set aside then reduce any syrup remaining over a
high heat until thick.

Cream the butter and icing sugar together. Beat in the
egg yolks and melted chocolate. Beat in the cool syrup.

To assemble, divide the sponge fingers into three.
Arrange a neat row of six on the base of a serving dish.
Spread with some of the chocolate mixture. Cover with
a second layer of six and cover again with chocolate.
Finally top with the remaining sponge fingers. Cover the
top and sides with any remaining chocolate mixture.
Decorate with chocolate curls and desiccated coconut.
Chill for 6 hours or overnight before serving.

Cook's Tip

**To soften refrigerator-hard fat
for creaming for cakes or for
spreading, heat in the
microwave for 1–2 minutes.**

Small Cakes and Pâtisserie

Dainty, elegant and irresistible small cakes and pâtisserie make splendid tea-time treats, party-time goodies and dessert specialities. Pâtisserie made from a whole host of differing doughs – some short, crisp and sweet, others flaky and highly-risen, seem difficult to make – yet, with the all-essential time and care, prove rewarding.

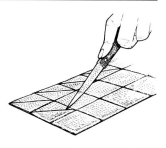

97 | Choux Cream Butterflies

Preparation time
20–25 minutes

Cooking time
20–30 minutes

Oven temperature
220 C, 425 F, gas 7

Makes 6

Calories
415 per cake

You will need
½ recipe choux pastry (see Introduction)
1 tablespoon flaked almonds
3 tablespoons chocolate hazelnut spread
300 ml/½ pint double cream, whipped
icing sugar to dust

Put the choux pastry in a piping bag fitted with a 1-cm/½-in plain nozzle and pipe six (7.5-cm/3-in) circles on a dampened baking tray, leaving plenty of space for them to spread. Sprinkle with the flaked almonds.

Bake for 20–30 minutes or until well risen and golden. Cool on a wire rack.

Slice each choux bun horizontally in half, then cut the top circle vertically in half.

Spread the bases with the chocolate hazelnut spread then pipe with cream. Dust the semi-circles of pastry with icing sugar and press the cut edges firmly into the cream, tilting the outer edges upwards.

Cook's Tip

Choux pastry shapes rise and bake superbly well if cooked on slightly wet or dampened baking trays. The steam produced helps the pastry to rise to unrivalled heights.

98 | Chestnut Tulips

Preparation time
30 minutes

Cooking time
about 20 minutes

Oven temperature
200 C, 400 F, gas 6

Makes 8

Calories
305 per tulip

You will need

For the tulip baskets
40 g/1½ oz plain flour, sifted
75 g/3 oz caster sugar
3 egg whites
25 g/1 oz butter, melted

For the chestnut cream
100 g/4 oz plain chocolate, chopped
150 ml/¼ pint double cream
1 (227-g/8-oz) can unsweetened chestnut purée
1 tablespoon caster sugar
2 tablespoons brandy
8 chocolate triangles to decorate

Mix the flour and sugar in a bowl. Add the egg whites and butter and beat until smooth. Place 3 tablespoons of this mixture on a greased baking tray and spread to form a 13-cm/5-in round. Repeat with another 3 tablespoons of the mixture.

Bake for 4–5 minutes, until golden. Leave to cool slightly, then remove with a plastic spatula and place each one top side down over the base of an inverted and oiled glass, moulding to give wavy edges. Leave to set. Repeat with the remaining mixture to make a total of 8.

To make the filling, heat the chocolate and cream in a pan until melted, then cool. Blend the chestnut purée, sugar, chocolate and brandy in a blender or food processor until smooth. Pipe into the tulip cases. Decorate each with a chocolate triangle.

Cook's Tip

To make chocolate triangles, spread a thin, even layer of melted chocolate onto a piece of greaseproof paper. Leave until just set but not too hard. Cut into squares, then triangles. Carefully lift the tip of the paper and peel away.

99 | Sponge Bites

Preparation time
15 minutes

Cooking time
10 minutes

Oven temperature
190 C, 375 F, gas 5

Makes about 24

Calories
100 per cake

You will need
3 eggs
100 g/4 oz caster sugar
100 g/4 oz plain flour
caster sugar to dust

For the filling
2 tablespoons raspberry jam
300 ml/½ pint double cream,
  whipped

Whisk the eggs with the sugar until pale and thick. Gently fold in the flour.

Place the mixture in a piping bag fitted with a 1-cm/½-in plain nozzle. Pipe into discs, 4 cm/1½ in in diameter, on lined baking trays, 5 cm/2 in apart. There should be enough mixture for 48 discs. Sift over a little sugar.

Bake for 10 minutes or until light golden brown. Allow to cool on the baking trays. When cold, dampen the underside of the paper and carefully peel off the discs.

Sandwich together in pairs with the jam and cream.

100 | Maids of Honour

Preparation time
20 minutes

Cooking time
15–20 minutes

Oven temperature
190 C, 375 F, gas 5

Makes 12

Calories
200 per cake

You will need
½ recipe easy flaky pastry (see
  Introduction)
40 g/1½ oz butter, softened
50 g/2 oz caster sugar
finely grated rind of 1 lemon
1 egg, lightly beaten
50 g/2 oz ground almonds
1 tablespoon double cream
1 tablespoon raspberry jam

Roll out the pastry thinly on a floured surface and use to line 12 (6-cm/2½-in) patty tins.

Cream the butter and sugar together, without beating. Add the lemon rind and egg, then the almonds and cream. Stir gently until smooth.

Place about ¼ teaspoon jam in each pastry case. Cover with the filling to three-quarters fill the cases.

Bake for 15–20 minutes or until golden. Cool on a wire rack.

Cook's Tip

These tempting little bites can be frozen without their filling. Open freeze until firm then place in a rigid box. Freeze for up to 3 months. Defrost at room temperature for about 1 hour before filling as above.

Cook's Tip

These small cakes were first made during Henry VIII's reign and were popular at Hampton Court Palace. The story goes that they were popular with the Queen's maids of honour and so were named after them.

101 | Iced Fancies

Preparation time	**You will need**
40–45 minutes	3 eggs
	75 g/3 oz caster sugar
Cooking time	75 g/3 oz plain flour
15–20 minutes	50 g/2 oz butter, melted
Oven temperature	**For the decoration**
180 C, 350 F, gas 4	apricot jam to brush
	40 chocolate squares
Makes about 24	100 g/4 oz butter icing (see Introduction)
	few crystallized violets
Calories	225 g/8 oz marzipan
165 per cake	angelica leaves
	175 g/6 oz nuts, chopped
	4 glacé cherries, halved

Whisk the eggs with the sugar until very thick. Fold in the flour, then the melted butter. Pour into a greased and lined 30 × 20-cm/12 × 8-in Swiss roll tin. Bake for 15–20 minutes until firm. Cool on a wire rack.

Cut out about eight 2.5-cm/1-in squares, eight 3.5-cm/1½-in rounds and eight triangles whose sides measure 3.5 cm/1½ in. To make chocolate boxes, coat the sides with jam and secure a chocolate square on each side. Top with a swirl of butter icing and a final chocolate square. Decorate with crystallized violets. To make tulip rounds, brush with jam, roll out the marzipan and cut out 24 (3.5-cm/1½-in) rounds and position three around the sides of each to make a flower. Top with a swirl of butter icing and decorate with angelica. For nutty triangles, coat with jam, roll in nuts, pipe with a swirl of butter icing and finish with a cherry.

102 | American Apple Cakes

Preparation time	**You will need**
20 minutes	100 g/4 oz butter
	350 g/12 oz caster sugar
Cooking time	2 eggs, beaten
1¾ hours	225 g/8 oz plain flour
	1 teaspoon bicarbonate of soda
Oven temperature	1½ teaspoons ground cinnamon
180 C, 350 F, gas 4	1½ teaspoons grated nutmeg
150 C, 300 F, gas 2	pinch of salt
	675 g/1½ lb dessert apples, peeled, cored and finely chopped
Makes 24	100 g/4 oz chopped mixed nuts
Calories	
160 per cake	

Cream the butter and sugar together until light and fluffy. Gradually beat in the eggs, mixing well. Sift the flour, soda, spices and salt together and fold into the creamed mixture, then fold in the apples and nuts. Turn into a greased 23 × 33-cm/9 × 13-in tin.

Bake for 1¼ hours at the higher temperature, then lower the temperature and cook for a further 45 minutes. Cool in the tin, then turn out and cut into squares.

Cook's Tip

You can really let your imagination run wild with these little iced cakes – decorate with chocolate, marzipan fruits, fondant icing, nuts, hundreds and thousands and dragees.

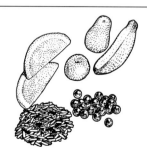

Cook's Tip

This is a rich, moist apple cake that can be frozen. Cut into squares then freeze for up to 3 months in a rigid container. Defrost at room temperature for about 2–3 hours.

103 | Date Buns

Preparation time
10 minutes

Cooking time
15 minutes

Oven temperature
190 C, 375 F, gas 5

Makes 18

Calories
95 per bun

You will need
175 g/6 oz self-raising flour
pinch of salt
1 teaspoon ground ginger
75 g/3 oz butter or margarine
75 g/3 oz soft brown sugar
75 g/3 oz stoned dates, chopped
1 egg, beaten
1–2 tablespoons milk

Sift the flour, salt and ginger into a bowl. Rub in the butter until the mixture resembles breadcrumbs. Stir in the sugar and dates, then mix in the egg and enough milk to give a dropping consistency. Divide between 18 greased and floured bun tins.

Bake for 15 minutes until golden and firm to the touch. Turn onto a wire rack to cool.

104 | Raspberry Viennese Swirls

Preparation time
20 minutes

Cooking time
20–25 minutes

Oven temperature
180 C, 350 F, gas 4

Makes 12

Calories
240 per cake

You will need
225 g/8 oz butter, softened
50 g/2 oz icing sugar, sifted
$\frac{1}{4}$ teaspoon vanilla essence
225 g/8 oz plain flour
50 g/2 oz cornflour
icing sugar to dust
2 tablespoons seedless raspberry
    jam

Cream the butter with the sugar until light and fluffy. Beat in the vanilla essence. Sift the flour with the cornflour and gradually beat into the creamed mixture. Place in a piping bag fitted with a large star-shaped nozzle. Pipe swirls of the mixture into 12 paper bun cases set in bun tins.

Bake for 20–25 minutes or until light golden brown. Cool on a wire rack.

Dust the tops with icing sugar and place a small spoonful of jam in the centre of each.

Cook's Tip

These little buns can also be made with chocolate chips. Use 75 g/3 oz but omit the ground ginger.

Cook's Tip

If you heat the jam a little first before spooning into the centre of the swirls you will achieve a more professional finish.

105 | Coconut Crisps

Preparation time
15 minutes

You will need
1 egg white
50 g/2 oz caster sugar
100 g/4 oz desiccated coconut
few glacé cherries, sliced

Cooking time
15–20 minutes

Oven temperature
180 C, 350 F, gas 4

Makes 12

Calories
70 per crisp

Whisk the egg white until stiff then gradually whisk in all the sugar until thick and glossy. Stir in the coconut to give a stiff mixture. Using wet hands, shape into 12 balls about the size of walnuts and place on greased baking trays.

Bake for 15–20 minutes, until golden in colour and firm to the touch. Remove and cool on a wire rack. Decorate each cake with a slice of glacé cherry.

106 | Lemon Maids

Preparation time
20–25 minutes

Cooking time
20 minutes

Oven temperature
180 C, 350 F, gas 4

Makes 18

Calories
225 per cake

You will need

For the pastry
225 g/8 oz plain flour
100 g/4 oz butter or margarine
grated rind of 2 lemons
40 g/1½ oz caster sugar
1 tablespoon cold water
4 tablespoons lemon curd

For the sponge topping
75 g/3 oz butter, softened
75 g/3 oz caster sugar
75 g/3 oz self-raising flour
25 g/1 oz ground almonds
1 egg, lightly beaten
3 tablespoons lemon juice

For the icing and decoration
175 g/6 oz lemon curd
75 g/3 oz ground almonds
coarsely grated lemon rind

To make the pastry, sift the flour into a bowl, rub in the butter, then add the lemon rind and sugar. Add the water and mix to a smooth dough. Roll out thinly and cut out 18 (6–7.5-cm/2½–3-in) rounds and use to line patty tins. Place a little lemon curd in each case.

To make the sponge topping, place all the ingredients in a bowl and beat until pale and fluffy. Spoon over the lemon curd. Bake for 20 minutes, until well risen and golden. Turn out to cool on a wire rack.

To ice and decorate the cakes, mix the lemon curd with the ground almonds and spread over the cooled cakes. Decorate with lemon rind.

Cook's Tip

These little cakes make an attractive present. Place them in small paper cases and arrange in a box or tray. Tie a ribbon around the box before presenting the gift.

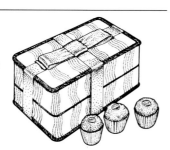

Cook's Tip

These cakes can also be made with an orange flavouring. Use the grated rind of 1 large orange and 4 tablespoons orange curd for the bases; 3 tablespoons orange juice for the sponge topping; and 175 g/6 oz orange curd with grated orange rind for the decoration.

107 | Minty Chocolate Cups

Preparation time
15 minutes

Cooking time
20 minutes

Oven temperature
190C, 375F, gas 5

Makes 24

Calories
140 per cup

You will need
100 g/4 oz butter or margarine
100 g/4 oz caster sugar
¼ teaspoon peppermint essence
2 eggs, lightly beaten
100 g/4 oz self-raising flour
100 g/4 oz plain chocolate, grated

For the icing and decoration
225 g/8 oz plain chocolate, melted
crystallized mint leaves

Cream the butter with the sugar until light and fluffy. Gradually beat in the peppermint essence and eggs. Sift the flour over the mixture and fold in using a metal spoon. Finally fold in the grated chocolate. Divide the mixture between 24 bun cases placed on a baking tray or set in bun tins.

Bake for 20 minutes then turn out to cool on a wire rack.

When cold, spread the tops of the cakes with melted chocolate and decorate with a few crystallized mint leaves. The cakes can be served in their paper cases or with the cases removed.

108 | Apple and Ginger Rings

Preparation time
15–20 minutes

Cooking time
20–25 minutes

Oven temperature
190C, 375F, gas 5

Makes 9

Calories
145 per ring

You will need
2 eggs
100 g/4 oz golden syrup
1 medium cooking apple, about
    175 g/6 oz
juice of 1 lemon
1 piece preserved ginger, chopped
100 g/4 oz self-raising flour
¼ teaspoon ground ginger

For the icing and decoration
100 g/4 oz icing sugar
1–2 tablespoons ginger wine
crystallized ginger
few slices of apple, dipped in
    lemon juice

Whisk the eggs with the syrup until pale and thick. Peel, core and grate the apple, sprinkle with the lemon juice and mix with the preserved ginger. Fold the apple mixture into the eggs. Sift the flour with the ground ginger and fold into the egg mixture. Divide the mixture between nine well-greased 11-cm/4½-in ring tins.

Bake for 20–25 minutes then turn out to cool on a wire rack.

To ice and decorate the rings, sift the icing sugar into a bowl and mix to a smooth consistency with the ginger wine. Drizzle the icing over the cooled cakes and decorate with crystallized ginger and small pieces of apple.

Cook's Tip

To make crystallized mint leaves, mix 15 g/½ oz gum arabic with 2 tablespoons rose water and shake well in a jar. Leave for 2 hours. Using a fine paintbrush, paint mint leaves with the solution then sprinkle with caster sugar to **coat. Leave to dry until hard before using.**

Cook's Tip

To prevent fruit from discolouring, slice with a stainless steel knife and sprinkle with lemon juice.

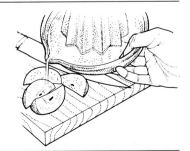

109 | Nutty Angelica Fancies

Preparation time
15–20 minutes

Cooking time
25–30 minutes

Oven temperature
180 C, 350 F, gas 4

Makes 12

Calories
295 per cake

You will need
100 g/4 oz butter or margarine
100 g/4 oz caster sugar
2 eggs, lightly beaten
100 g/4 oz self-raising flour
100 g/4 oz walnuts, chopped
75 g/3 oz angelica, chopped

For the icing and decoration
225 g/8 oz icing sugar, sifted
2 tablespoons water
25 g/1 oz walnuts, chopped
50 g/2 oz angelica, chopped

Cream the butter with the sugar until light and fluffy. Gradually beat in the eggs and fold in the flour, using a metal spoon. Mix together the walnuts and angelica and fold into the cake mixture. Divide the mixture between 12 greased dariole moulds.

Bake for 25–30 minutes then turn out to cool on a wire rack.

To make the icing, mix the icing sugar with the water until thick and smooth. Drizzle over the top of each cake and sprinkle with a mixture of the chopped walnuts and angelica.

110 | Almond Clusters

Preparation time
10 minutes

Cooking time
35 minutes

Oven temperature
160 C, 325 F, gas 3

Makes 24

Calories
95 per meringue

You will need
3 egg whites
175 g/6 oz caster sugar
225 g/8 oz flaked almonds
few drops of almond essence
50 g/2 oz plain chocolate, melted

Whisk the egg whites until stiff then gradually whisk in all the sugar until thick and glossy. Fold in the almonds and a few drops of almond essence. Place small mounds of the mixture on a baking tray lined with non-stick cooking parchment.

Bake for 35 minutes then remove and cool on a wire rack.

Place the melted chocolate in a small greaseproof piping bag, cut a tiny hole in the point of the bag and pipe swirls of chocolate over the tops of the cakes.

Cook's Tip

Place the filled dariole moulds on a baking tray for cooking to ease the lifting in and out of the oven.

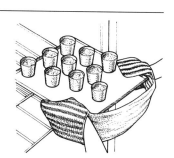

Cook's Tip

These little cakes make an ideal base for a dessert. They may be served in individual dishes with scoops of ice cream and topped with a light fruit sauce.

111 | Nectarine Meringues Chantilly

Preparation time
20 minutes

Cooking time
1 hour

Oven temperature
140 C, 275 F, gas 1

Makes 6

Calories
420 per meringue

You will need
4 egg whites
250 g/9 oz caster sugar
pink food colouring or coffee
    essence (optional)

For the crème chantilly
300 ml/½ pint double cream
2 teaspoons caster sugar
½ teaspoon vanilla essence
2 ripe nectarines, sliced

Whisk the egg whites until stiff then gradually whisk in half of the sugar until thick and glossy. Fold in all but 1 tablespoon of the remaining sugar then leave plain, or colour pink or coffee with the colouring or essence, if liked. Spoon or pipe 12 mounds or swirls onto a baking tray lined with rice paper. Sprinkle with the reserved sugar.

Bake for 1 hour until firm, remove from the oven, turn over with a palette knife and gently press the soft centres to make a shallow hollow for the crème chantilly. Cool on a wire rack.

To make the filling, whip the cream until thick. Add the sugar and vanilla. Sandwich the meringues together in pairs with the cream and sliced nectarines.

Cook's Tip

When fresh nectarines are not available, these meringues can be sandwiched together with cream and sliced fresh or canned peaches, sliced strawberries, cooked pears or hulled raspberries.

112 | Nutty Fruit Round

Preparation time
20 minutes

Cooking time
30–40 minutes

Oven temperature
180 C, 350 F, gas 4

Makes 8

Calories
240 per wedge

You will need
50 g/2 oz sultanas
50 g/2 oz raisins
25 g/1 oz currants
25 g/1 oz chopped mixed peel
50 g/2 oz glacé cherries, chopped
grated rind and juice of 1 orange
2 tablespoons dark rum
75 g/3 oz golden syrup
75 g/3 oz walnuts, chopped
1 egg
50 g/2 oz wheatgerm
75 g/3 oz plain wholewheat flour
½ teaspoon baking powder

For the icing and decoration
100 g/4 oz icing sugar
1–2 tablespoons dark rum

Mix the sultanas with the raisins, currants, peel and cherries. Add the orange rind and juice, rum and syrup then heat slowly until boiling. Allow to cool slightly then add the nuts and beat in the egg. Mix the wheatgerm with the flour and baking powder and beat into the fruit mixture. Spread evenly into a greased and lined 23-cm/9-in sandwich tin.

Bake for 30–40 minutes then allow to cool in the tin.

When cold, carefully turn out onto a plate and remove the greaseproof paper. Invert the cake onto a serving plate.

To make the icing, sift the icing sugar into a bowl and beat in the rum to make a smooth icing. Drizzle over the top of the cake and cut into eight wedges to serve.

Cook's Tip

Cut the cake into wedges just before the icing sets to give a clean cut that does not break the icing.

113 | Danish Spiced Apricot Whirls

Preparation time
20 minutes

Cooking time
45 minutes

Oven temperature
220C, 425F, gas 7

Makes 6

Calories
495 per whirl

You will need
1 (411-g/14½-oz) can apricot halves, drained and chopped
75 g/3 oz dried figs, chopped
75 g/3 oz raisins
50 g/2 oz walnuts, chopped
3 tablespoons chopped mixed peel
50 g/2 oz soft light brown sugar
1 teaspoon ground ginger
½ teaspoon ground cloves
1 tablespoon lemon juice
1 (368-g/13-oz) packet frozen puff pastry, defrosted
caster sugar to dust

Mix the apricots with the figs, raisins, walnuts, peel, sugar, ginger, cloves and lemon juice, mixing well.

Roll out the pastry on a lightly floured surface to a 30 × 60-cm/12 × 24-in rectangle. Cut into six equal strips crossways. Divide the filling into six portions and spread down the centre of each pastry strip. Dampen the edges with water and roll up from the short end to make pinwheels, sealing the edges carefully. Place in a greased and lined 20-cm/8-in round cake tin. Brush with a little water and dust with caster sugar.

Bake for about 45 minutes, remove from the tin, then carefully separate the six pinwheels for serving.

114 | Apple Crescents

Preparation time
20 minutes

Cooking time
15 minutes

Oven temperature
220C, 425F, gas 7

Makes about 10

Calories
185 per crescent

You will need
1 (215-g/7½-oz) packet frozen puff pastry, defrosted
275 g/10 oz cooking apples, peeled, cored and finely chopped
1 tablespoon caster sugar

For the decoration
caster sugar
175 ml/6 fl oz double cream, whipped

Roll out the pastry on a floured surface to 3 mm/⅛ in thickness. Cut out as many 10-cm/4-in rounds as possible, re-rolling as necessary. Roll the rounds across the centre to make them slightly oval.

Mix the apple and sugar together, and place a tablespoon of the mixture in the centre of each pastry round. Dampen the edges with water and fold to make half moons, sealing the edges. Brush with water and sprinkle with sugar. Place on baking trays.

Bake for 15 minutes or until golden brown. Transfer to a wire rack and leave until cold.

Carefully split the crescents along the join and pipe in whipped cream.

Cook's Tip

These delicious spiced pastry whirls are best served warm. Try them with a little clotted cream for a really sinful treat!

Cook's Tip

Any rounds made from rolled and re-rolled pastry trimmings will not rise quite as well as first rolled ones, so try and cut out as many rounds from the first pastry rolling as possible.

115 | Eccles Cakes

Preparation time
25 minutes

Cooking time
15–20 minutes

Oven temperature
220 C, 425 F, gas 7

Makes about 10

Calories
145 per cake

You will need
1 (215-g/7½-oz) packet frozen puff
    pastry, defrosted
100 g/4 oz currants
25 g/1 oz demerara sugar
25 g/1 oz butter, melted
caster sugar to dust

Roll out the pastry on a floured surface to a 3 mm/⅛ in thickness and cut out as many 10-cm/4-in rounds as possible, re-rolling as necessary.

Mix the currants, demerara sugar and butter together and place a heaped teaspoon of the mixture in the middle of each pastry round. Fold the edges in towards the centre, pinch them together and flatten slightly. Turn the rounds over. Fit each one into a 6-cm/2½-in pastry cutter, forming a neat round shape. Make 3 small cuts in the top of each round. Brush the tops lightly with water and dust with caster sugar.

Bake for 15–20 minutes or until golden brown. Cool on a wire rack.

116 | Brownies

Preparation time
15 minutes

Cooking time
50–55 minutes

Oven temperature
160 C, 325 F, gas 3

Makes 16–18

Calories
200–180 per brownie

You will need
50 g/2 oz self-raising flour
½ teaspoon baking powder
40 g/1½ oz cocoa powder
25 g/1 oz ground almonds
225 g/8 oz soft brown sugar
grated rind of 1 orange
100 g/4 oz butter or margarine
2 eggs, lightly beaten

For the icing
100 g/4 oz plain chocolate
25 g/1 oz butter or margarine
50 g/2 oz blanched almonds,
    chopped

Sift the flour with the baking powder and cocoa into a bowl. Add the ground almonds, sugar and orange rind and mix well. Beat the butter and eggs into the dry ingredients until smooth. Spread evenly into a greased and lined 18-cm/7-in square, shallow baking tin.

Bake for 50–55 minutes then allow to cool in the tin.

To ice the brownies, melt the chocolate with the butter then stir in the almonds. Spread evenly over the brownies then cut into small squares when half set.

Cook's Tip

The Eccles cakes can be flattened evenly by rolling lightly with a rolling pin using light pressure.

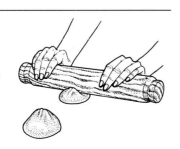

Cook's Tip

Brownies freeze well un-iced. Interleave the squares with waxed paper, wrap, label and freeze for up to 3 months. They make a wonderful emergency pudding too!

117 | Caramel Triangles

Preparation time
20 minutes

Cooking time
30–35 minutes

Oven temperature
180 C, 350 F, gas 4

Makes 18

Calories
200 per triangle

You will need
100 g/4 oz butter or margarine
50 g/2 oz caster sugar
175 g/6 oz wholemeal flour

For the filling and icing
100 g/4 oz butter or margarine
50 g/2 oz soft brown sugar
1 (196-g/6.1-oz) can condensed
   milk
100 g/4 oz plain chocolate, broken
   into pieces
4 teaspoons single cream

Cream the butter and sugar together until light and fluffy. Add the flour and stir until the mixture binds together. Knead until smooth. Roll out to a square and press evenly into a greased 23-cm/9-in shallow, square tin. Prick well with a fork.

Bake for about 25 minutes, then leave to cool in the tin.

Place the butter, sugar and condensed milk in a pan and heat gently, stirring until dissolved. Bring slowly to the boil, then cook, stirring constantly, for 5–7 minutes. Cool slightly then pour over the cold biscuit mixture and leave to set.

Place the chocolate and cream in a pan and heat gently until melted. Spread over the filling, leave to set, then cut into triangles.

118 | Minted Yorkshire Slices

Preparation time
20–25 minutes

Cooking time
20–25 minutes

Oven temperature
200 C, 400 F, gas 6

Makes 8

Calories
400 per slice

You will need
$\frac{2}{3}$ recipe easy flaky pastry (see
   Introduction)
350 g/12 oz sultanas
10 mint leaves
50 g/2 oz sugar
25 g/1 oz butter, melted
caster sugar to dust

Roll out 200 g/7 oz of the pastry on a floured surface and use to line a 20-cm/8-in flan tin. Cover with the sultanas. Chop the mint with a little of the sugar, then mix in the remaining sugar. Sprinkle over the sultanas, then pour over the butter.

Roll out the remaining pastry and place on top; dampen the edges and seal well. Prick all over with a fork, brush lightly with water and dust with caster sugar.

Bake for 20–25 minutes or until golden brown. Cut into slices and serve warm or cold.

Cook's Tip

The recipe for the chocolate icing above is also sufficient to cover a small round cake, say 18 cm/7 in. in diameter.

Cook's Tip

It is essential to use fresh mint for this recipe – dried really doesn't have enough flavour. Chop the mint with a little granulated sugar to begin with, to help to extract the juices, then add the remaining sugar.

119 | Butterfly Cakes

Preparation time
15 minutes

Cooking time
20–25 minutes

Oven temperature
190 C, 375 F, gas 5

Makes 18

Calories
180 per cake

You will need
100 g/4 oz butter or margarine
100 g/4 oz caster sugar
2 eggs, beaten
100 g/4 oz self-raising flour, sifted

For the filling
100 g/4 oz butter
225 g/8 oz icing sugar, sifted
2 tablespoons milk
icing sugar to dust

Cream the butter with the sugar until light and fluffy. Beat in the eggs with a little of the flour, then carefully fold in the remaining flour. Spoon into 18 paper bun cases set in bun tins.

Bake for 20–25 minutes or until well-risen and golden. Cool on a wire rack.

To make the butter icing, beat the butter with the icing sugar and milk until smooth. Cut a slice off the top of each cake and cut the slices in half. Top each cake with a swirl of the buttercream and place the halved slices in the cream to form 'wings'. Dust lightly with a little sifted icing sugar.

Cook's Tip

These delicious little cakes can also be made with a coffee-flavoured sponge. Add 1 tablespoon coffee essence to the basic creamed mixture. Fill with coffee butter icing too if liked.

120 | Chocolate Boxes

Preparation time
30 minutes

Cooking time
35–40 minutes

Oven temperature
190 C, 375 F, gas 5

Makes 16

Calories
185 per box

You will need
1 recipe chocolate whisked
   sponge (see Introduction)
175 g/6 oz plain chocolate, melted

For the meringue buttercream
2 egg whites
100 g/4 oz icing sugar, sifted
100 g/4 oz unsalted butter

Turn the whisked sponge mixture into a greased and lined 20-cm/8-in square cake tin.

Bake for 35–40 minutes until the cake springs back when pressed with the fingertips. Cool in the tin.

Use the melted chocolate to make 68 chocolate squares about 5 cm/2 in square (see Cook's Tip 98).

To make the buttercream, place the egg whites and sugar in a bowl over a pan of simmering water and whisk until the mixture holds its shape. Cool slightly. Cream the butter and beat into the meringue mixture a little at a time.

Split the cake horizontally and sandwich together with one-quarter of the cream. Cut into 16 squares and spread cream on all sides. Press a chocolate square onto each side to form boxes. Decorate with the remaining cream and the remaining squares cut into triangles.

Cook's Tip

To melt the chocolate for the chocolate squares, cut into pieces or break into squares and place in a bowl over a pan of simmering water. Stir from time to time until melted, smooth and shiny.

121 | Greek Baklavas

Preparation time
25 minutes

Cooking time
25 minutes

Oven temperature
200 C, 400 F, gas 6

Makes 8

Calories
370 per baklava

You will need
75 g/3 oz blanched almonds, finely chopped
75 g/3 oz walnuts, finely chopped
$\frac{1}{2}$ teaspoon ground cinnamon
$\frac{1}{2}$ teaspoon ground mixed spice
150 ml/$\frac{1}{4}$ pint clear honey
1 (368-g/13-oz) packet frozen puff pastry, defrosted
20 g/$\frac{3}{4}$ oz butter, melted
juice of $\frac{1}{2}$ lemon

Mix the almonds with the walnuts, cinnamon, spice and 50 ml/2 fl oz of the honey. Roll out the pastry into a 33-cm/13-in square. Cut into four squares. Place one square in a 16.5-cm/6$\frac{1}{2}$-in shallow, square cake tin lined with foil. Brush with a little butter. Cover with another square than spread over the nut filling. Cover with the third square, brush again with butter then cover with the remaining square. Brush with butter and cut through the top two layers to mark out four squares. Cut each in half again to make triangles. Bake for 25 minutes.

Meanwhile, mix the lemon juice with the remaining honey and make up to 150 ml/$\frac{1}{4}$ pint with water. Bring to the boil and simmer for 2 minutes. Spoon over the hot baklava still in its tin and leave to soak for 2 hours before removing from the tin to serve.

Cook's Tip

To serve the baklavas, cut through the bottom two layers of pastry with a sharp knife to make eight triangular baklavas – the typical shape of these sweet Greek pastries.

122 | Citrus Choux Rings

Preparation time
20 minutes

Cooking time
40–45 minutes

Oven temperature
200 C, 400 F, gas 6
180 C, 350 F, gas 4

Makes 10

Calories
240 per cake

You will need
$\frac{1}{2}$ recipe choux pastry (see Introduction)
finely grated rind of 1 orange
25 g/1 oz flaked almonds
25 g/1 oz cornflour
3 tablespoons water
finely grated rind and juice of 2 lemons
juice of 1 orange
4 tablespoons medium dry white wine
100 g/4 oz caster sugar
200 ml/7 fl oz double cream
icing sugar to dust

Make the choux pastry and mix with the orange rind, then place in a piping bag fitted with a 1-cm/$\frac{1}{2}$-in plain nozzle and pipe 10 rings, well apart on dampened baking trays. Sprinkle evenly with the almonds.

Bake at the higher temperature for 20 minutes, then reduce the temperature and bake for a further 20–25 minutes. Remove from the oven, split in half horizontally and cool on a wire rack.

To make the filling, mix the cornflour with the water to a paste. Place the lemon rind and juice in a pan with the orange juice, wine and sugar. Bring to the boil, pour over the cornflour and whisk. Return to the pan and cook, stirring constantly for 1 minute. Allow to cool.

Fold the orange mixture with the whipped cream and use to sandwich the choux rings. Dust with icing sugar.

Cook's Tip

The choux rings are split after cooking and before cooling to allow excess steam to escape that may be trapped inside the buns. If this is not released the buns may have a tendency to become soggy upon cooling.

123 | Lemon Treacle Tarts

Preparation time
20–25 minutes

Cooking time
35 minutes

Oven temperature
180 C, 350 F, gas 4

Makes 6

Calories
585 per tart

You will need
225 g/8 oz plain flour
150 g/5 oz butter
grated rind of 1 small lemon
1 egg yolk
2 tablespoons water
beaten egg to glaze
caster sugar to dust

For the filling
175 g/6 oz fresh white
 breadcrumbs
375 g/13 oz golden syrup
finely grated rind of 1 lemon
1 tablespoon lemon juice

Sift the flour into a bowl. Rub in the butter then stir in the lemon rind. Mix the egg yolk with the water and add to the dry ingredients and bind to a firm dough. Roll out on a floured surface and use to line six greased 10-cm/4-in individual flan cases. Reserve any dough trimmings.

Mix the breadcrumbs with the golden syrup, lemon rind and juice. Spoon into the pastry cases and decorate with pastry leaves made from the trimmings. Glaze the leaves with beaten egg and dust with caster sugar.

Bake for 35 minutes or until golden. Cool on a wire rack.

Cook's Tip

These delicious tarts make a very good pudding too if served with cream, ice-cream or custard.

124 | Festive Mince Pies

Preparation time
20 minutes

Cooking time
20–25 minutes

Oven temperature
200 C, 400 F, gas 6

Makes 24

Calories
140 per pie

You will need

For the pastry
275 g/10 oz plain flour
25 g/1 oz ground almonds
175 g/6 oz butter or margarine
75 g/3 oz icing sugar
grated rind of 1 lemon
1 egg yolk
3 tablespoons milk

For the filling
225 g/8 oz mincemeat
1 tablespoon brandy
grated rind of 1 small orange
icing sugar to dust

Mix the flour with the ground almonds, rub in the butter then mix in the icing sugar and lemon rind. Mix the egg yolk with the milk and stir into the flour mixture, binding to make a firm dough. Chill for 30 minutes.

Roll out two-thirds of the pastry on a floured surface and cut 24 rounds with a 7.5-cm/3-in fluted cutter. Use to line greased tartlet tins. Mix the mincemeat with the brandy and orange rind and spoon into the cases.

Roll out the remaining pastry and, using a star-shaped cutter, cut out 24 stars for the pie lids. Place in position and bake for 20–25 minutes until pale golden. Cool on a wire rack.

Serve warm, dusted with icing sugar.

Cook's Tip

You could top the mince pies with other festive cut-out shapes – bells, reindeer, and Christmas trees, for example.

125 | Strawberry Palmiers

Preparation time
20–25 minutes

Cooking time
20 minutes

Oven temperature
220C, 425F, gas 7

Makes 8

Calories
550 per palmier

You will need
150 g/5 oz caster sugar
1 (368-g/13-oz) packet frozen puff
  pastry, defrosted
225 g/8 oz strawberries
450 ml/¾ pint double cream
2 teaspoons icing sugar, sifted

Sprinkle a board with 25 g/1 oz of the sugar and roll out the pastry to a 30-cm/12-in square. Trim the edges square, brush with water and sprinkle with 50 g/2 oz of the sugar. Fold two opposite sides together to meet in the centre, brush again with water and sprinkle with the remaining sugar. Fold again in the same way and press down lightly. Finally fold the two sides up together to produce a single roll that when cut across will form heart-shaped slices. Cut into 16 (1-cm/½-in) slices and place on a baking tray.

Bake for 10 minutes, turn over with a spatula and bake for a further 10 minutes. Cool on a wire rack.

Halve the strawberries and reserve a few to decorate. Whip the cream with the sugar until thick. Sandwich the palmiers with the cream and strawberries. Decorate the tops with the reserved strawberries.

Cook's Tip

Pastry palmiers will keep fresh in an airtight tin for several days without their filling. For best results fill at the very last moment to appreciate the crisp pastry with the creamy soft and fruity filling.

126 | Blackberry and Apple Jalousie

Preparation time
30 minutes

Cooking time
25–30 minutes

Oven temperature
220C, 425F, gas 7

Serves 6

Calories
385 per portion

You will need
675 g/1½ lb cooking apples,
  peeled, cored and thickly sliced
25 g/1 oz butter
1½ teaspoons ground mace
100 g/4 oz blackberries, hulled
75 g/3 oz demerara sugar
1 (368-g/13-oz) packet frozen puff
  pastry, defrosted
beaten egg to glaze

Place the apples in a pan with the butter and 1 teaspoon of mace and cook until just softened. Add the blackberries and cook for a further 2 minutes. Stir in 50 g/2 oz of the sugar and leave to cool.

Divide the pastry in half and roll out each piece on a floured surface to a 28 × 20-cm/11 × 8-in rectangle. Place one on a dampened baking tray. Fold the second in half lengthways and cut diagonal slits through the folded edge at 1-cm/½-in intervals to within 2.5 cm/1 in of the cut edges. Open out for use.

Place the apple mixture on the pastry, brush the edges with beaten egg and cover with the cut pastry top, sealing the edges well. Glaze with egg and sprinkle with the remaining sugar and mace. Bake for 25–30 minutes until golden. Serve warm or cold.

Cook's Tip

This jalousie is doubly delicious if served with Calvados cream. To prepare this, whip 300 ml/½ pint double cream with 2 tablespoons Calvados until softly stiff. Chill before serving.

127 | Plaited Bavarian Cherry Slice

Preparation time
25–30 minutes

Cooking time
40 minutes

Oven temperature
220 C, 425 F, gas 7

Serves 6

Calories
505 per portion

You will need
675 g/1½ lb ripe cherries, stoned
100 g/4 oz ground almonds
50 g/2 oz caster sugar
1 egg, beaten
1 teaspoon ground mixed spice
1 (368-g/13-oz) packet frozen puff
  pastry, defrosted
4 teaspoons granulated sugar
beaten egg to glaze
15 g/½ oz flaked almonds
icing sugar to dust

Cook the cherries with a little water until tender, about 8–10 minutes. Mix the almonds with the sugar, egg and mixed spice.

Roll out the pastry on a floured surface to a 30 × 35-cm/12 × 14-in rectangle. Place on a dampened baking tray and spread the almond mixture down the centre. Top with the drained cooked cherries and sprinkle over the granulated sugar. Brush the borders with beaten egg and make cuts diagonally on the two long sides at 1.5-cm/¾-in intervals. Fold the short end flaps over the filling, then lift the side strips over the filling to give a plaited effect. Glaze with beaten egg and sprinkle with the almonds.

Bake for 30 minutes until golden. Dust with icing sugar to serve.

Cook's Tip

Serve this plait warm or cold. For special occasions top each slice with a little Kirsch and a spoonful of clotted cream.

128 | Apple Strudel

Preparation time
25 minutes, plus about
20–25 minutes
standing time

Cooking time
20–25 minutes

Oven temperature
200 C, 400 F, gas 6

Serves 6

Calories
205 per portion

You will need

For the strudel pastry
150 g/5 oz plain flour
pinch of salt
2 teaspoons oil
½ egg, beaten
about 100 ml/4 fl oz warm water

For the filling
450 g/1 lb cooking apples, peeled,
  cored and sliced
50 g/2 oz currants
50 g/2 oz sultanas
1 teaspoon ground cinnamon
3 tablespoons breadcrumbs,
  toasted
25 g/1 oz butter, melted
icing sugar to dust

Mix the flour with the salt in a large bowl. Make a well in the centre, add the oil, egg and 2–3 tablespoons of the water. Start to mix, adding more warm water to make a soft paste. Beat, using your hand, until smooth. Cover and leave for 15 minutes, then knead until very smooth.

Mix the apples with the currants, sultanas, cinnamon and 1 tablespoon of the breadcrumbs. Roll out the pastry on a floured surface to 1 cm/½ in thickness. Lift onto a floured teacloth, leave for 8 minutes. Carefully stretch it until very thin. Brush with the butter and sprinkle with the crumbs. Scatter over the fruit and roll up.

Place on a greased baking tray in a horseshoe shape and brush with butter. Bake for 20–25 minutes until golden. Dust with icing sugar and slice to serve.

Cook's Tip

Strudel pastry is a wafer-thin pastry that is popular throughout Europe. Use the fists of the hands to stretch the dough if you have long fingernails that are likely to puncture the dough.

129 | Strawberry Mille Feuilles

Preparation time
25 minutes

Cooking time
20 minutes

Oven temperature
220C, 425F, gas 7

Serves 4–6

Calories
920–615 per portion

You will need
1 (368-g/13-oz) packet frozen puff
   pastry, defrosted
4 tablespoons strawberry jam
1 tablespoon Kirsch or orange juice
300 ml/½ pint double cream
2 teaspoons caster sugar
450 g/1 lb strawberries
75 g/3 oz icing sugar

Roll out the pastry on a floured surface to a 20 × 25-cm/ 8 × 10-in rectangle. Cut lengthways into three equal rectangles and place on dampened baking trays. Bake for 20 minutes until risen and golden. Cool on a wire rack.

Trim the rectangles to the same size, crushing any trimmings to use later. Mix the jam with the Kirsch or orange juice and whip the cream with the caster sugar.

Place one pastry strip on a serving plate. Top with half the jam, half the cream and one-third of the sliced strawberries. Cover with a second pastry strip and repeat the filling. Finish with the third pastry strip.

Mix the icing sugar with a little water to make a paste and spread over the top. Sprinkle with a border of the crushed trimmings. Decorate with the remaining halved strawberries.

Cook's Tip

Mille Feuilles to live up to its name of 'thousand leaves' should have seemingly endless layers of flaky or puff pastry. To ensure that the pastry does rise well and evenly, cut the pastry with a sharp knife in one swift movement – never drag the knife through the pastry during preparation.

130 | Apricot Bourdaloue Tart

Preparation time
40 minutes

Cooking time
25 minutes

Oven temperature
220C, 425F, gas 7

Serves 6

Calories
345 per portion

You will need
½ recipe rich shortcrust pastry
   (see Introduction)
2 egg yolks
50 g/2 oz caster sugar
grated rind of 1 orange
1½ tablespoons cornflour
1½ tablespoons plain flour
300 ml/½ pint milk
1 egg white
675 g/1½ lb halved, stoned and
   poached apricots
2 tablespoons flaked almonds,
   toasted

Roll out the pastry on a floured surface and use to line a 20-cm/8-in flan tin. Bake 'blind' for 15 minutes, remove the foil or beans and bake for a further 10 minutes. Cool on a wire rack.

Whisk the egg yolks and half of the caster sugar together until thick. Beat in the orange rind, cornflour and flour. Scald the milk and pour over the flour mixture, beating constantly. Return to the pan and cook until smooth and thick. Leave to cool.

Whisk the egg white until stiff then whisk in the remaining sugar. Carefully fold through the orange cream. Spoon into the cooked pastry case, creating a small mound in the centre. Top with the apricot halves, cut side down, and spoon over a little of the cooking syrup if liked. Scatter with almonds before serving.

Cook's Tip

To cook the fresh apricots, dissolve 100 g/4 oz sugar in 300 ml/½ pint water and bring to the boil. Add the apricots and simmer for 5 minutes, then remove. Reduce the syrup to a thick glaze by boiling for 5 minutes.

131 | Pear Frangipane Tart

Preparation time
25 minutes

Cooking time
45–50 minutes

Oven temperature
190 C, 375 F, gas 5

Serves 4–6

Calories
1080–720 per portion

You will need
⅔ recipe rich shortcrust pastry
  (see Introduction)
3–4 firm dessert pears
100 g/4 oz sugar
300 ml/½ pint water
few drops of vanilla essence

For the frangipane
100 g/4 oz butter
100 g/4 oz caster sugar
2 eggs
100 g/4 oz ground almonds
25 g/1 oz flour
almond essence or Kirsch to taste

For the glaze
6 tablespoons apricot jam
2 tablespoons water

Roll out the pastry on a floured surface to line a 20-cm/ 8-in flan tin. Prick the base with a fork. Meanwhile, peel, halve and core the pears. Boil the sugar in a pan with the water and vanilla. Add the pears and poach until tender, about 20–25 minutes. Remove and cool.

Prepare the frangipane by beating the butter with the sugar. Beat in the eggs, one at a time, then stir in the almonds and flour and flavour with almond essence or Kirsch. Fill the flan with the frangipane and bake for 25 minutes. Allow to cool. Heat the apricot jam with the water and brush a little over the tart. Top with the poached pears and brush with the remaining glaze.

132 | Golden Treacle Tart

Preparation time
20 minutes

Cooking time
40 minutes

Oven temperature
180 C, 350 F, gas 4

Serves 4–6

Calories
845–565 per portion

You will need
⅔ recipe rich shortcrust pastry
  (see Introduction)
450 g/1 lb golden syrup
2 teaspoons finely grated lemon
  rind
25 g/1 oz butter
4 tablespoons single cream
2 eggs, beaten
whipped cream to decorate or
  serve

Roll out the pastry on a floured surface and use to line a 20-cm/8-in flan ring set on a baking tray.

Gently heat the syrup with the lemon rind until hand hot. Chop the butter and add to the mixture and stir to melt. Leave until almost cold.

Beat the cream and eggs together and fold into the cooled syrup. Mix well and pour into the flan case.

Bake for 40 minutes or until the pastry is crisp and the filling is set. Serve hot or cold with whipped cream.

Cook's Tip

When time is really short you can of course use canned pear halves for this recipe but ensure that they have been well drained and dried on absorbent kitchen paper.

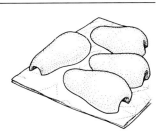

Cook's Tip

Lining a flan ring without stretching the pastry is quite an art but can prove much simpler if you lift the pastry loosely onto a rolling pin then lay it over the flan ring to gently unroll. Remember to ease carefully into the corners **then roll the rolling pin over the edge of the flan to cut off any excess pastry and leave a neat edge. Pinch the pastry slightly at the top, raising it above the edge to allow for shrinkage during cooking.**

133 | Walnut and Strawberry Galette

Preparation time
25 minutes, plus 30
minutes chilling time

Cooking time
20–25 minutes

Oven temperature
180 C, 350 F, gas 4

Serves 6

Calories
670 per portion

You will need

For the pastry galette
175 g/6 oz butter or margarine
100 g/4 oz caster sugar
grated rind of ½ lemon
175 g/6 oz plain flour
100 g/4 oz walnuts, roughly
  chopped

For the filling
300 ml/½ pint whipping cream
1 tablespoon icing sugar
675 g/1½ lb strawberries, hulled

Cream the butter and sugar together until light and fluffy. Beat in the lemon rind and fold in the flour. Knead until smooth then chill for 30 minutes.

Divide into three portions and roll each out on a floured surface to an 18-cm/7-in circle. Crimp the edges then place each on a greased baking tray. Sprinkle the tops with the walnuts. Bake for 20–25 minutes until golden. Allow to cool slightly on the trays then cool on a wire rack.

Whip the cream with the icing sugar until thick. Slice two-thirds of the strawberries and fold into two-thirds of the cream. Use to sandwich the galettes together. Use the remaining cream and strawberries to decorate the top of the galette.

Cook's Tip

After preparing allow the galette to chill for 30 minutes before serving. This will help to soften the pastry rounds slightly (but not make them soggy) so that they are easier to slice.

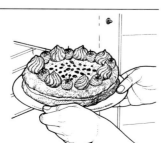

134 | Chocolate Profiteroles

Preparation time
25 minutes

Cooking time
15–20 minutes

Oven temperature
220 C, 425 F, gas 7

Serves 4–6

Calories
785–525 per portion

You will need

For the choux pastry
50 g/2 oz butter
150 ml/¼ pint water
pinch of salt
1 teaspoon caster sugar
100 g/4 oz plain flour
4 eggs, beaten

For the filling
300 ml/½ pint double cream

For the sauce
125 g/4½ oz plain chocolate
450 ml/¾ pint water
25 g/1 oz caster sugar

Place the butter, water, salt and sugar in a pan and bring slowly to the boil. Add the flour and stir quickly to make a paste. Cool slightly then beat in the eggs, one at a time. Place in a piping bag fitted with a large plain nozzle and pipe small rounds on lightly greased baking trays. Bake for 15–20 minutes until crisp. Remove and slit each with a knife to release the steam. Cool.

Fill the profiteroles with the whipped cream and place in a dish. To make the sauce, melt the chocolate in a bowl over a pan of water. Boil the water and sugar together for about 5 minutes then add, spoon by spoon, to the chocolate. Simmer for a further 10 minutes or until the sauce coats the back of a spoon. Spoon over the profiteroles to serve.

Cook's Tip

When making choux pastry allow the fat to melt in the liquid slowly before bringing to the boil – if you don't, the water will evaporate and the proportions of ingredients will change, producing a poor end result.

135 | Peach Cream Kuchen

Preparation time
20 minutes

Cooking time
30 minutes

Oven temperature
200 C, 400 F, gas 6

Serves 8

Calories
400 per portion

You will need
225 g/8 oz plain flour
pinch of baking powder
pinch of salt
100 g/4 oz butter
75 g/3 oz caster sugar

For the filling
2 (411-g/14½-oz) cans peach
    halves, drained
1 teaspoon ground cinnamon
2 large egg yolks
300 ml/½ pint soured cream

Sift the flour, baking powder and salt into a bowl. Rub in the butter, then stir in 2 tablespoons of the sugar. Press onto the base and sides of a 25-cm/10-in loose-bottomed flan tin.

Arrange the peach halves in the case. Mix together the cinnamon and remaining sugar and sprinkle over the fruit. Beat the egg yolks and soured cream together and pour over the peaches.

Bake for about 30 minutes. Leave in the tin to cool, then transfer to a serving plate.

136 | Almond Chocolate Flan

Preparation time
30 minutes, plus
overnight chilling

Cooking time
35 minutes

Oven temperature
180 C, 350 F, gas 4

Serves 6

Calories
665 per portion

You will need

For the pastry
175 g/6 oz ground almonds
50 g/2 oz caster sugar
1 large egg white, lightly beaten

For the filling
300 ml/½ pint double cream
225 g/8 oz plain chocolate

For the decoration
whipped cream
chocolate curls
hazelnuts

Mix the almonds with the sugar, add the egg white and mix to a stiff dough. Chill for 1 hour then roll out on a floured surface to line a 23-cm/9-in fluted metal flan tin. Bake for 35 minutes and allow to cool in the tin.

To make the filling, gently heat the cream in a pan, add the chocolate, broken into pieces and stir until melted. Remove from the heat and beat until cold. Pour into the flan case and chill for at least 24 hours.

Decorate with swirls of whipped cream, chocolate curls and whole hazelnuts.

Cook's Tip

To ensure that you get an even spread of pastry mixture over the base and sides of the flan tin, press and level with the back of a metal spoon using gentle pressure.

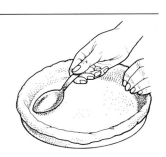

Cook's Tip

The pastry for this flan is very fragile so it may be necessary to patch up any areas that have become damaged while you line the flan tin.

This is a rich flan worthy of the 24 hours chilling time required for making. For best results make up to 2–3 days ahead.

137 | Apple Cream Slice

Preparation time
20 minutes

Cooking time
1 hour

Oven temperature
160 C, 325 F, gas 3

Serves 10

Calories
315 per portion

You will need
½ recipe rich shortcrust pastry
  (see Introduction)
2 eggs
100 g/4 oz sugar
2 tablespoons plain flour, sifted
2 teaspoons finely grated lemon
  rind
150 ml/¼ pint double cream
200 g/7 oz curd cheese
1 tablespoon chunky marmalade
40 g/1½ oz sultanas
pinch of salt
3 green dessert apples

Roll out the pastry on a floured surface and use to line a 20 × 30-cm/8 × 12-in Swiss roll tin.

Beat the eggs and sugar together until pale and thick. Fold in the flour, lemon rind, cream, cheese, marmalade, sultanas and salt.

Peel, core, quarter and thinly slice the apples and arrange over the pastry. Pour over the cream mixture.

Bake for 1 hour then cool in the tin. Serve cold.

Cook's Tip

Apple Cream Slice can also be made with firm cooking pears. Use 3 medium fruit and peel, core and slice thinly for use.

138 | Chocolate Cream Flan

Preparation time
20 minutes

Cooking time
35 minutes

Oven temperature
200 C, 400 F, gas 6
180 C, 350 F, gas 4

Serves 6–8

Calories
690–520 per portion

You will need
½ recipe rich shortcrust pastry
  (see Introduction)

For the filling
100 g/4 oz plain chocolate, broken
  into pieces
100 g/4 oz butter
150 g/5 oz caster sugar
50 g/2 oz plain flour, sifted
3 eggs

For the topping
150 ml/¼ pint double cream,
  whipped
flaked almonds, toasted

Roll out the pastry on a floured surface and use to line a 25-cm/10-in loose-bottomed flan tin. Bake 'blind' at the higher temperature for 20 minutes, removing the paper and beans after 15 minutes.

To make the filling, melt the chocolate and butter in a bowl over a pan of hot water. Beat together the sugar, flour and eggs, then beat into the chocolate. Pour into the pastry case.

Reduce the oven temperature and bake the flan for 20 minutes or until the filling has set. Place on a serving plate and leave until cold.

To decorate, cover with whipped cream and sprinkle with the almonds.

Cook's Tip

To bake 'blind' cut a square of foil or greaseproof paper slightly larger than the flan tin or dish. Prick the base of the flan with a fork. Line with the foil or paper and weigh down with dried beans or baking beans.

139 | Chocolate Orange Sandwich

Preparation time
20 minutes

Cooking time
20–25 minutes, plus 3 hours for filling

Oven temperature
220C, 425F, gas 7

Makes 1 (23-cm/ 9-in) gâteau

Total calories
5310

You will need
1 recipe orange pastry (see Citrus Sparkle recipe 140)
1 (397-g/14-oz) can condensed milk
100 g/4 oz plain chocolate, broken into pieces
2 tablespoons hot water
25 g/1 oz cocoa powder
300 ml/½ pint double cream, whipped

Make 2 pastry rounds as for Citrus Sparkle (recipe 140). Leave to cool.

Immerse the can of condensed milk in boiling water. Cover and boil for 3 hours, topping up the water if necessary. Drain and cool.

Melt the chocolate in a bowl over a pan of simmering water. Stir in the water, cocoa and condensed milk. Remove from the heat and beat until smooth.

Sandwich the pastry rounds together with two-thirds of the chocolate cream and two-thirds of the whipped cream. Spread the remaining filling on top and pipe with the remaining cream.

Cook's Tip

Bake the pastry rounds on dampened baking trays – the steam produced will help the pastry to rise during cooking.

140 | Citrus Sparkle

Preparation time
30 minutes, plus standing and chilling times

Cooking time
20–25 minutes

Oven temperature
220C, 425F, gas 7

Makes 1 (23-cm/ 9-in) gâteau

Total calories
4025

You will need

For the orange pastry
225 g/8 oz plain flour
pinch of salt
finely grated rind and juice of 1 orange
175 g/6 oz butter, chilled and grated
1 tablespoon iced water

For the filling and decoration
thinly pared rind and juice of 1 lemon
2 tablespoons brandy
75 g/3 oz caster sugar
300 ml/½ pint double cream, whipped
3 tablespoons lemon curd
sugared lemon slices

Sift the flour with the salt, add the orange rind and butter and mix. Stir in the orange juice and water, knead lightly and chill for 30 minutes.

Meanwhile, mix the lemon rind, juice and brandy and leave to stand for 1 hour. Divide the pastry in half and roll each piece into a 23-cm/9-in round. Prick then place on baking trays. Bake for 20–25 minutes until golden brown. Cool on the tray.

Strain the lemon mixture, add the sugar and stir to dissolve. Whisk into the cream then use half to sandwich the pastry rounds together with the lemon curd. Spread the remainder on top and decorate with sugared lemon slices.

Cook's Tip

This gâteau can also be sandwiched together with 3 tablespoons marmalade instead of the orange curd if liked.

141 | French Pear Tart

Preparation time
30 minutes

Cooking time
20–30 minutes

Oven temperature
200C, 400F, gas 6

Serves 6

Calories
235 per portion

You will need

For the crispy butter pastry
100 g/4 oz plain flour
pinch of salt
65 g/2½ oz butter, chilled
1½ tablespoons iced water

For the filling
½ recipe confectioner's custard
(see Cook's Tip 210)
2 firm pears, peeled and cored
50 g/2 oz caster sugar

Sift the flour and salt into a bowl and rub in the butter. Stir in the water to make a firm dough. Knead lightly until smooth then chill for 30 minutes before using.

Roll out the pastry on a floured surface and use to line a 23-cm/9-in loose-bottomed flan tin. Bake 'blind' for 20 minutes, removing the paper or foil and beans after 15 minutes.

Spread the crème pâtissière evenly in the flan case. Cut the pears lengthways into thin slices. Place neatly in circles on the custard, overlapping slightly. Sprinkle evenly with the sugar and place under a preheated very hot grill until the sugar caramelizes.

142 | Honey and Almond Tarts

Preparation time
20–25 minutes, plus
cooling time for filling

Cooking time
25 minutes

Oven temperature
200C, 400F, gas 6

Makes 18

Calories
165 per tart

You will need
¾ recipe rich shortcrust pastry
(see Introduction)
50 g/2 oz butter
50 g/2 oz granulated sugar
2 tablespoons clear honey
75 g/3 oz flaked almonds
1 tablespoon double cream

Roll out the pastry on a floured surface and use to line 18 (6-cm/2½-in) patty tins.

Place the butter, sugar and honey in a heavy-based pan and heat gently until melted. Bring to the boil, remove from the heat and stir in the almonds and cream. Leave until cold, then divide between the pastry cases.

Bake for 20 minutes then transfer to a wire rack to cool.

Cook's Tip

The grill must be very hot indeed or the operation will take too long and the custard will separate. As an alternative, omit the sugar, place the tart in a preheated moderate oven, 180C, 350F, gas 4 for 5 minutes, then brush the pears with boiled and sieved apricot jam.

Cook's Tip

If you are in a hurry stand the pan in a bowl of crushed ice or cold water so that the filling will cool quickly for use.

143 | Yorkshire Curd Tarts

Preparation time
20 minutes

Cooking time
20–25 minutes

Oven temperature
190 C, 375 F, gas 5

Makes 18

Calories
180 per tart

You will need

For the pastry
1 egg
pinch of salt
150 g/5 oz butter
225 g/8 oz plain flour, sifted

For the filling
50 g/2 oz butter, softened
50 g/2 oz sugar
½ teaspoon grated nutmeg
2 tablespoons fresh white
    breadcrumbs
2 eggs, lightly beaten
225 g/8 oz curd cheese, sieved
juice of ½ lemon
50 g/2 oz currants

To make the pastry, whisk the egg and salt together, then mix into the butter a little at a time. Add the flour and mix to a firm dough. Knead until smooth and chill until required.

Roll out the pastry on a floured surface and use to line 18 (6-cm/2½-in) patty tins.

To make the filling, mix the butter with the sugar, nutmeg and breadcrumbs. Stir in the eggs and cheese, mixing well. Finally stir in the lemon juice and currants. Divide the mixture between the pastry cases.

Bake for 20–25 minutes then turn out to cool on a wire rack.

Cook's Tip

This recipe could also be used to make one large 20-cm/8-in flan – although the cooking time will need to be increased by 5–10 minutes.

144 | Congress Tarts

Preparation time
20 minutes, plus 1 hour standing time

Cooking time
25 minutes

Oven temperature
180 C, 350 F, gas 4

Makes 18

Calories
190 per tart

You will need
¾ recipe easy flaky pastry (see
    Introduction)
1½ tablespoons raspberry jam
75 g/3 oz ground almonds
175 g/6 oz caster sugar
3 egg whites

Roll out the pastry on a floured surface and use to line 18 (6-cm/2½-in) patty tins. Reserve the pastry trimmings. Place about ¼ teaspoon jam in each case.

To make the filling, mix the ground almonds and sugar together. Add the egg whites and beat well with a wooden spoon for 3 minutes. Drop ½ tablespoon of the mixture into each pastry case to three-quarters fill.

Cut the pastry trimmings into 5-mm × 6-cm/¼ × 2½-in strips. Place them crossways on top of the filling. Leave to stand for 1 hour.

Bake for about 25 minutes or until golden. Cool on a wire rack.

Cook's Tip

It is essential to beat the filling very well – the mixture should be the consistency of thick cream for use.

Celebration and Novelty Cakes

A tiered wedding cake for the special day in your life; a rolled and frosted log for Christmas eating alongside the traditional Christmas cake; or a clock, train or drum cake for a children's birthday party treat – whatever the occasion you'll find ideas galore here for festive, celebration and novelty cakes.

145 | Valentine Cake

Preparation time
about 45 minutes

Cooking time
1½–1¾ hours

Oven temperature
180 C, 350 F, gas 4

**Makes 1 (20-cm/
8-in) heart-
shaped cake**

Total calories
3770

You will need
2 recipes plain or pink Victoria Sandwich mixture (see recipe 54)
100 g/4 oz strawberry jam
1 (23-cm/9-in) heart-shaped cake board
1 recipe Apricot Glaze (see Introduction)
⅔ recipe pink Satin Icing (see Introduction)
100 g/4 oz royal icing
3 pink moulded roses

Turn the prepared cake mixture into a greased and lined 20-cm/8-in heart-shaped tin. Bake for 1½–1¾ hours. Cool on a wire rack.

Cut the cake in half horizontally and sandwich together with the jam. Place on the cake board and brush the top and the sides with the apricot glaze.

Roll out the satin icing on a surface dusted with icing sugar until thin then press onto the cake to coat. Cut off any surplus icing.

Put the royal icing in a piping bag fitted with a No 2 writing nozzle and pipe a line 1 cm/½ in. in from the edge of the cake. Pipe dots on each side of the line. Decorate with roses.

146 | Individual Birthday Cake

Preparation time
20 minutes

Cooking time
50–60 minutes

Oven temperature
160 C, 325 F, gas 3

**Makes 1 (9-cm/
3½-in) cake**

Total calories
1090

You will need
50 g/2 oz butter or margarine
50 g/2 oz caster sugar
few drops of vanilla essence
1 egg
75 g/3 oz self-raising flour

For the icing and decoration
1 gold doily
piece of ribbon
50 g/2 oz icing sugar, sifted
2 teaspoons water
slice of citron peel

Cream the butter with the sugar and vanilla essence until pale and fluffy. Gradually beat in the egg then sift the flour over the mixture and fold in gently. Spoon into a greased and lined 9-cm/3½-in round tin, about 10 cm/4 in deep.

Bake for 50–60 minutes, then turn out to cool on a wire rack.

To ice and decorate the cake, fold a doily around the cake and tie a ribbon around it. Mix the icing sugar with the water to give a thick icing. Spoon on top of the cake and decorate with a slice of citron peel. Leave to set.

Cook's Tip

You can achieve a smooth professional finish to the icing of this cake if you dip your hands in icing sugar and press the icing onto the cake, rubbing with a circular motion.

Cook's Tip

To ensure that a white glacé icing does not become grey, sift the icing sugar through a nylon, not metal, sieve.

147 | Rich Celebration Cake

Preparation time
25 minutes

Cooking time
3½ hours

Oven temperature
150C, 300F, gas 2

Makes 1 (20-cm/ 8-in) round or 1 (18-cm/7-in) square cake

Total calories
8255

You will need
275 g/10 oz butter
275 g/10 oz soft brown sugar
grated rind of ½ lemon
5 large eggs, beaten
350 g/12 oz plain flour
½ teaspoon ground mixed spice
½ teaspoon ground cinnamon
450 g/1 lb currants
200 g/7 oz sultanas
200 g/7 oz raisins
150 g/5 oz glacé cherries, halved
75 g/3 oz chopped mixed peel
75 g/3 oz flaked almonds
2 tablespoons brandy

Cream the butter with the sugar until light and fluffy. Beat in the lemon rind and eggs with a little of the flour. Sift the remaining flour with the spice and cinnamon and fold into the creamed mixture. Fold in the fruit, nuts and brandy, mixing well. Spoon into a greased and lined 20-cm/8-in round or 18-cm/7-in square cake tin.

Bake for 3½ hours or until a skewer inserted into the centre comes out clean. Allow to cool slightly in the tin, then transfer to a wire rack to cool completely.

Decorate as liked – for a traditional almond paste and royal icing decoration you will need 550 g/1¼ lb almond paste and 675 g/1½ lb royal icing.

Cook's Tip

When spooning the mixture into the cake tin, make a slight hollow in the centre of the mixture to enable the cake to rise evenly.

148 | Granny Cake

Preparation time
about 45 minutes

Cooking time
1–1¼ hours

Oven temperature
180C, 350F, gas 4

Makes 1 (20-cm/ 8-in) round cake

Total calories
6340

You will need
175 g/6 oz butter or margarine
175 g/6 oz caster sugar
grated rind of 2 oranges
3 eggs
250 g/9 oz self-raising flour
1½ teaspoons baking powder

For the filling and icing
50 g/2 oz butter
75 g/3 oz icing sugar, sifted
grated rind of 1 large orange
100 g/4 oz ground almonds
4 tablespoons orange juice
225 g/8 oz almond paste
red and yellow food colouring
⅔ recipe Fondant Icing (see Fondant-Iced Christmas Cake recipe 154)
2–3 tablespoons apricot jam
moulded leaves and flowers
ribbon

Place all the cake ingredients in a bowl and beat until smooth. Turn into a greased and base-lined 20-cm/8-in round cake tin and bake for 1–1¼ hours. Cool.

Cream the butter with the icing sugar, orange rind, almonds and juice until fluffy. Halve the cake and sandwich together again with this filling. Cover the cake with the almond paste and dry overnight.

Colour and roll out the fondant icing, brush the cake with the jam and then cover the cake with the icing. Leave to dry then decorate with moulded flowers and leaves and the ribbon.

Cook's Tip

To make moulded flowers and leaves, press small pieces of fondant icing between your fingers which have been dipped in cornflour. Shape into individual petals. Roll the first petal to form the centre of the flower. Mould each **petal around the centre and build up to a flower. Cut off the base of the flower if the petals become too thick. Allow to harden. Highlight the centre of the flower with food colouring, using a fine paintbrush, if liked.**

149 | Silver Wedding Cake

Preparation time
Make 2–3 months in advance

Cooking time
3–5 hours

Oven temperature
140 C, 275 F, gas 1

Makes 1 (23-cm/9-in) square cake

Total calories
18280

You will need
1 (23-cm/9-in) square Basic Fruit Cake (see Introduction)

For the icing and decoration
1 recipe Almond Paste (see Introduction)
1 (25-cm/10-in) square silver cake board
1 recipe Royal Icing (see Introduction)
crystallized flowers
silver cake decorations
silver cake board edging

Make the cake as directed and leave to mature for 2–3 months.

Cover the cake with the almond paste 1–2 weeks before icing and place on the silver cake board. Make up the icing and flat ice the cake. Decorate with crystallized flowers and silver cake decorations as in the photograph. Place the silver cake board edging around the sides of the cake, securing with a little icing. Pipe a shell border on the top and bottom edges of the cake to finish.

Cook's Tip

To secure the cake board edging, using a small palette knife, spread a thin layer of icing around the edge of the board. Before it dries, press on the edging.

150 | Christening Cake

Preparation time
Make 2–3 months in advance

Cooking time
3½ hours

Oven temperature
150 C, 300 F, gas 2

Makes 1 (20-cm/8-in) cake

Total calories
12300

You will need
1 (20-cm/8-in) round Rich Celebration Cake (see recipe 147)

For the icing and decoration
550 g/1¼ lb almond paste
1 (23-cm/9-in) round silver cake board
675 g/1½ lb royal icing
pink food colouring

Make the cake as directed, bake and leave to mature for 2–3 months. Cover with the almond paste, 1–2 weeks before icing.

Reserve a little of the icing for piping and colour the remainder pink. Flat ice the cake with the pink icing. Cover the silver board with a thin layer of icing and leave to dry hard. Position the cake on top.

Cut a strip of greaseproof paper the circumference and depth of the sides of the cake and draw a scalloped edge evenly all the way round. Secure onto the cake with a pin and prick through the design onto the cake. Remove the paper and pipe dots of the white icing onto the cake following the scalloped design, piping a few vertical dots between each scallop. Pipe a trellis along the bottom as shown in the photograph and a line of small dots either side. Write the child's name on top and finish with a row of stars around the edge.

Cook's Tip

To pipe a trellis on the bottom edge of the cake, pipe a series of parallel lines at an angle all around the cake, then pipe another layer of parallel lines over the top in the opposite direction.

151 | Eighteenth Birthday Cake

Preparation time
Make 2–3 months in advance

Cooking time
3½ hours

Oven temperature
150 C, 300 F, gas 2

Makes 1 (20-cm/ 8-in) cake

Total calories
12300

You will need
1 (20-cm/8-in) round Rich Celebration Cake (see recipe 147)

For the icing and decoration
550 g/1¼ lb almond paste
675 g/1½ lb royal icing
1 (23-cm/9-in) round silver cake board
green food colouring
silver key

Make the cake as directed, bake and leave to mature for 2–3 months. Cover the cake with the almond paste, 1–2 weeks before icing. Make up the icing and reserve a little white icing for piping. Colour the remainder pale green. Flat ice the cake with the green icing as shown, using a serrated scraper on the sides of the cake to give a ridged effect. Using a palette knife, cover the board with a layer of icing. Place the cake on top.

Using a greaseproof paper bag fitted with a star-shaped nozzle, pipe a shell border with the white icing around the top and bottom edges of the cake. Then using a writing nozzle, pipe CONGRATULATIONS on top of the cake. Pipe three parallel lines beside the word. When these are dry pipe another line on top of each to give a bolder design. Decorate with a silver key.

Cook's Tip

When writing with icing, have the royal icing on the soft side so that it flows smoothly and freely from the nozzle. Hold the nozzle about 2.5 cm/1 in from the surface of the cake.

152 | Twenty-first Birthday Cake

Preparation time
Make 2–3 months in advance

Cooking time
3½ hours

Oven temperature
150 C, 300 F, gas 2

Makes 1 (20-cm/ 8-in) round cake

Total calories
12300

You will need
1 (20-cm/8-in) round Rich Celebration Cake (see recipe 147)

For the icing and decoration
550 g/1¼ lb almond paste
675 g/1½ lb royal icing
1 (23-cm/9-in) round silver cake board
blue or pink food colouring

Make the cake as directed, bake and leave to mature for 2–3 months. Cover with almond paste, 1–2 weeks before icing. Flat ice the cake with two layers of royal icing, then ice the board. Make a simple top scallop template (see Cook's Tip).

Using a No 2 writing nozzle, outline the design, covering the pin marks completely. Pipe the first layer of a trellis in each scallop and leave to dry. Colour a little icing blue or pink and pipe over a second layer of trellis, using No 1 nozzle. Using a No 44 nozzle, pipe a star border around the bottom edge of the cake. Then using a No 42 nozzle, pipe similar borders around the top of the cake and along the edge of the board. Pipe forget-me-nots around the sides and join with curved stalks. Pipe 21 on the cake and overpipe with coloured icing.

Cook's Tip

To make a simple top template, cut a piece of greaseproof paper the size of the top of the cake. Fold in half three times to make a cone shape; crease the edges well. Draw the scallop on the paper, using a compass, base **of a glass or other suitable object. Prick along the line with a pin right through the paper. Open out and secure on top of the cake with pins. Use a pin to prick the outline of the design onto the cake. Remove the paper.**

153 | Ski Cake

Preparation time
Make 2–3 months in advance

Cooking time
3½ hours

Oven temperature
150 C, 300 F, gas 2

Makes 1 (18-cm/ 7-in) square cake

Total calories
12740

You will need
1 (18-cm/7-in) square Rich Celebration Cake (see recipe 147)
550 g/1¼ lb almond paste
1 (20-cm/8-in) square silver cake board
675 g/1½ lb royal icing
icing run outs
ribbon

Make the cake as directed, bake and leave to mature for 2–3 months. Cover with almond paste, 1–2 weeks before icing and place on the silver cake board. Flat ice the cake, reserving a little of the icing for the decoration. Make a mouse run-out as shown or make your own design (see Cook's Tip) and place on top of the cake, securing with a little icing.

Using a greaseproof paper bag fitted with a star-shaped nozzle, decorate the top and bottom edges of the cake with the reserved icing. Tie a ribbon around the cake to complete.

154 | Fondant-Iced Christmas Cake

Preparation time
Make 2–3 months in advance

Cooking time
3½ hours

Oven temperature
150 C, 300 F, gas 2

Makes 1 (20-cm/ 8-in) round cake

Total calories
12165

You will need
1 (20-cm/8-in) round Rich Celebration Cake (see recipe 147)

For the icing and decoration
550 g/1¼ lb almond paste
1 (23-cm/9-in) round silver cake board
350 g/12 oz icing sugar, sifted
1 egg white
1 tablespoon liquid glucose, warmed
icing sugar
egg white to brush cake
red and green food colourings
candle ribbon

Make the cake as directed, bake and leave to mature for 2–3 months. Cover with almond paste, 1–2 weeks before icing and place on the silver cake board.

To make the fondant icing, place the icing sugar, egg white and glucose in a bowl and mix, using a palette knife, until a dough is formed. Knead lightly until smooth. Roll out on a surface dusted with icing sugar. Brush the cake with egg white and cover with the icing, reserving any trimmings. Allow to dry overnight.

Colour a little of the reserved trimmings with green and some red and mould to resemble holly. Arrange in a circle on top of the cake and secure a candle in the centre. Tie a ribbon around the cake to complete.

Cook's Tip

To make an icing run-out, trace the chosen design onto greaseproof paper. Lay on a flat board and secure. Lay a piece of waxed paper on top. Pipe along the outline with royal icing and allow to dry slightly. With a slightly softer icing, flood the centre of the run out, using a cocktail stick to guide the icing. Allow to harden. Carefully lift the run-out from the paper and paint features with edible food colourings. When dry, place on the cake.

Cook's Tip

It is essential to allow the icing to dry overnight before adding the coloured decorations or their colours will run into the white icing giving a poor finish.

155 | Snow-Peaked Cake

Preparation time
Make 2–3 months in advance

Cooking time
3½ hours

Oven temperature
150 C, 300 F, gas 2

Makes 1 (20-cm/ 8-in) round cake

Total calories
12740

You will need
1 (20-cm/8-in) round Rich Celebration Cake (see recipe 147)

For the icing and decoration
550 g/1¼ lb almond paste
1 (23-cm/9-in) round silver cake board
675 g/1½ lb royal icing
Christmas cake decorations
ribbon

Make the cake as directed, bake and leave to mature for 2–3 months. Cover with almond paste, 1–2 weeks before icing and place on the silver cake board.

Flat ice the sides of the cake with the royal icing then rough ice the top. Decorate with Christmas cake decorations – a Father Christmas, snowman, robin, reindeer, snow-covered post box or angels, for example. Tie a ribbon around the cake to complete.

156 | Chocolate Log

Preparation time
30 minutes

Cooking time
12–14 minutes

Oven temperature
200 C, 400 F, gas 6

Makes 1 (20-cm/ 8-in) log

Total calories
1920

You will need

For the cake
40 g/1½ oz self-raising flour
15 g/½ oz cocoa powder
3 eggs
50 g/2 oz caster sugar

For the decoration
1 recipe Chocolate Fudge Icing (see Introduction)
1 rectangular cake board
icing sugar for dusting
holly, mistletoe and Christmas novelty decorations

Sift the flour and cocoa together twice. Whisk the eggs and sugar together in a large bowl until the whisk leaves a trail. Fold in the flour mixture. Turn into a greased and lined 20 × 30-cm/8 × 12-in Swiss roll tin. Bake for 12–14 minutes or until springy to the touch. Turn out onto lightly sugared greaseproof paper placed on a slightly damp tea towel and roll up from one short end. Leave until cold.

Unroll and spread with some of the warm fudge icing then roll up again. Leave the rest of the icing to cool.

Cut a short diagonal wedge off one end of the roll and join it to the side of the log as in the photograph. Place on a cake board. Cover with the cooled icing. Sprinkle with icing sugar and decorate with holly, mistletoe and other Christmas decorations.

Cook's Tip

To rough ice the top of the cake, cover the top completely with icing and smooth evenly. Then, using the tip of a palette knife, dip it into the icing and press the tip of the knife onto the surface of the icing and draw away to form a peak. Repeat this process until the top of the cake is covered in peaks of icing.

Cook's Tip

Mark the cooled icing with a fork to make lines that resemble the bark of a tree. The icing sugar should be dusted to look like snow.

157 | Quick Honey Christmas Cake Ring

Preparation time
25 minutes

Cooking time
2½ hours

Oven temperature
150 C, 300 F, gas 2

Makes 1 (30-cm/ 12-in) ring cake

Total calories
6530

You will need
225 g/8 oz butter or margarine
175 g/6 oz soft brown sugar
3 tablespoons creamed honey
5 eggs
100 g/4 oz chopped mixed peel
50 g/2 oz blanched almonds
100 g/4 oz glacé cherries, chopped
225 g/8 oz currants
225 g/8 oz raisins
250 g/9 oz plain flour, sifted
1 teaspoon baking powder
1 teaspoon grated nutmeg
½ teaspoon ground cinnamon
½ teaspoon ground cloves

For the icing and decoration
225 g/8 oz icing sugar
1 tablespoon lemon juice
1 tablespoon water
glacé cherries and angelica

Place all the cake ingredients in a mixing bowl and beat with a wooden spoon until well mixed, about 3 minutes. Spoon into a greased and floured 30-cm/12-in ring mould or tin. Bake for 2½ hours, leave to stand in the tin for 15 minutes, then turn out to cool on a wire rack.

Mix the icing sugar with the lemon juice and water and pour over the cake, allowing it to drizzle down the sides. Decorate with glacé cherries and angelica leaves.

Cook's Tip

The same ring idea for a cake can be used when a rich fruit cake baked in a round tin sinks in the middle. Simply cut out the sunken inner section and decorate as above – no-one will ever know!

158 | Wedding Cake

Preparation time
Make 2–3 months in advance

Cooking time
3–5 hours

Oven temperature
140 C, 275 F, gas 1

Makes 1 (23-cm/ 9-in) square cake

Total calories
18730

You will need
1 (23-cm/9-in) square Basic Fruit Cake (see Introduction)
100 g/4 oz crystallized ginger, chopped
100 g/4 oz dried apricots, chopped
2 teaspoons almond essence
1 recipe Almond Paste (see Introduction)
1 recipe Royal Icing (see Introduction)
about 50–55 white and apricot coloured piped roses
1 (25-cm/10-in) square silver cake board
silver cake board edging
few small pieces of fern

Make the cake, adding the ginger and apricots with the other dry ingredients and the almond essence with the brandy and orange juice. Bake and leave to mature for 2–3 months. Cover with the almond paste 1–2 weeks before icing. Flat ice with 4–5 layers of royal icing until completely flat.

Arrange a cluster of roses on each of the corners of the cake, trailing one or two down the sides. Ice the silver board with a thin layer of icing and allow to dry hard. Position the cake on top.

Using a greaseproof paper bag fitted with a small star-shaped nozzle, pipe the top and bottom edge of the cake. Arrange a few tiny roses on the side of the cake and three larger ones in the middle. Secure the board edging with a little icing. Position the fern last of all.

Cook's Tip

Fondant icing could be used to ice the cake if liked. You will need about 675 g/1½ lb. Colour and use any leftovers to make moulded roses for the decoration. Make up a small amount of royal icing to pipe the edgings.

159 | Mother's Day Cake

Preparation time
25 minutes

Cooking time
1¼ hours

Oven temperature
160 C, 325 F, gas 3

Makes 1 (20-cm/8-in) cake

Total calories
4675

You will need
175 g/6 oz butter or margarine
175 g/6 oz caster sugar
3 eggs
100 g/4 oz glacé cherries
50 g/2 oz crystallized ginger, chopped
50 g/2 oz crystallized pineapple, chopped
50 g/2 oz citron peel, chopped
225 g/8 oz self-raising flour

For the icing and decoration
225 g/8 oz icing sugar, sifted
2–3 tablespoons water
50 g/2 oz glacé cherries
2 tablespoons caster sugar
few pieces of angelica

Cream the butter with the sugar until light and fluffy. Gradually beat in the eggs. Wash, drain and chop the cherries. Add to the other chopped ingredients and coat thoroughly in 2 tablespoons of the flour. Sift the flour over the creamed mixture and fold in gently with a metal spoon. Gently fold in the chopped ingredients. Spoon into a greased and lined 20-cm/8-in round cake tin. Bake for 1¼ hours then turn out to cool on a wire rack.

To make the icing, mix the icing sugar with the water and spoon over the cake, allowing it to drizzle down the sides. Coat the glacé cherries in caster sugar and place small pieces of angelica on top of them to form stalks. Arrange the cherries on top of the cake.

Cook's Tip

When time is short simply decorate the top of this cake with a few fresh spring flowers or pale coloured roses. Allow the icing to set first and place the flowers on top just before serving.

160 | Easter Garland

Preparation time
20 minutes, plus 2½–3 hours to prove

Cooking time
25 minutes

Oven temperature
200 C, 400 F, gas 6

Makes 1

Total calories
2430

You will need
175 g/6 oz strong plain white flour
½ teaspoon salt
25 g/1 oz butter
25 g/1 oz plus ½ teaspoon caster sugar
5 tablespoons warm milk
2 teaspoons dried yeast
1 egg, beaten

For the filling
50 g/2 oz butter, melted
75 g/3 oz nibbed almonds
1 teaspoon ground mixed spice
grated rind of 1 lemon
1 tablespoon lemon juice
50 g/2 oz glacé cherries, chopped

For the topping
100 g/4 oz icing sugar, sifted
2 tablespoons water
15 g/½ oz nibbed almonds
few halved glacé cherries

Prepare the dough as for Selkirk Bannock (see recipe 35), but mixing the larger quantity of sugar with the dry ingredients and adding the beaten egg with the yeast mixture. Leave to prove in the same way.

Mix the filling ingredients together. Spread over and roll up the dough and cut as for Swedish Tea Ring (see recipe 47). Cover and leave to rise in the same way.

Bake for 25 minutes, then cool on a wire rack. To decorate, mix the icing sugar with the water, spoon over the top and allow to drizzle down the sides of the cake. Sprinkle with the almonds and glacé cherries. Leave to set.

Cook's Tip

I suppose this is really a large decorated version of many hot cross buns for festive Easter eating. It can be made well ahead and frozen for up to 6–8 weeks. Defrost at room temperature for 2–3 hours. Freeze un-iced.

161 | Hot Cross Buns

Preparation time
30 minutes, plus about
2–2½ hours to prove

Cooking time
20–25 minutes

Oven temperature
220 C, 425 F, gas 7

Makes 12

Calories
215 per bun

You will need
450 g / 1 lb plain flour
50 g / 2 oz caster sugar
1 tablespoon dried yeast
150 ml / ¼ pint warm milk
4 tablespoons warm water
1 teaspoon salt
1 teaspoon ground mixed spice
½ teaspoon ground cinnamon
100 g / 4 oz currants
50 g / 2 oz chopped mixed peel
50 g / 2 oz butter, melted and
    cooled

Sift 100 g / 4 oz of the flour and 1 teaspoon of the sugar into a bowl. Mix the yeast with the milk and water and stir into the flour. Leave to stand for 30 minutes.

Sift the remaining flour with the sugar, salt, spice, and cinnamon. Stir in the currants and peel. Beat the butter into the yeast mixture, then mix with the fruit mixture to make a dough. Knead for 5 minutes, cover and leave in a warm place until doubled in size, about 1–1½ hours.

Knead again for 5 minutes, divide into 12 pieces and shape each into a ball. Place well apart on greased baking trays, cover and leave to rise for 30 minutes.

Slash with a knife to form a cross in the top of each bun then bake for 20–25 minutes. Cool on a wire rack.

162 | Simnel Cake

Preparation time
Make 2–3 months in
advance

Cooking time
3½ hours

Oven temperature
150 C, 300 F, gas 2

**Makes 1 (20-cm/
8-in) round cake**

Total calories
11240

You will need
mixture for 1 (20-cm/8-in) round
    Rich Celebration Cake (see
    recipe 147)
550 g / 1¼ lb almond paste
2 tablespoons apricot jam, sieved
beaten egg white to glaze
1 tablespoon caster sugar

For the decoration
100 g / 4 oz icing sugar
1–2 tablespoons water
ribbon

Make up the cake mixture and place half in a 20-cm / 8-in round cake tin. Roll out 275 g / 10 oz of the almond paste and place on top of the cake. Cover with the remaining cake mixture and bake for 3½ hours, then allow to cool on a wire rack.

Brush the top of the cake with the jam. Roll out half of the remaining almond paste and place on top of the cake. Crimp the edges decoratively. Shape the remaining almond paste into 11 balls and place around the top edge of the cake. Brush the almond paste with the egg white. Sprinkle with caster sugar, place under a hot grill and cook until light golden. Cool.

Mix the icing sugar with the water to make a thick icing and spread in the centre of the cake. Leave to set. Tie a ribbon around the cake to complete.

Cook's Tip

Hot cross buns look especially good if given a shiny glaze after baking. Place 50 g / 2 oz granulated sugar and 3 tablespoons milk in a pan and bring slowly to the boil. Boil for 2 minutes then brush over the warm hot cross buns.

To finish the buns with paste crosses before baking, gradually stir 2 tablespoons milk and 1 teaspoon oil into 3 tablespoons plain flour. Spoon into a small piping bag fitted with a 5 mm / ¼ in plain nozzle and pipe crosses.

Cook's Tip

The cake can be further decorated for an Easter time celebration by the addition of Easter novelties such as fluffy chicks, small sweet eggs and novelty Easter rabbits if liked.

163 | *Sultana and Whisky Cake*

Preparation time
20–30 minutes

Cooking time
30 minutes

Oven temperature
180C, 350F, gas 4

Makes 1 (15-cm/ 6-in) round cake

Total calories
4250

You will need
175 g/6 oz plain flour
1 teaspoon bicarbonate of soda
1 teaspoon salt
½ teaspoon grated nutmeg
150 g/5 oz caster sugar
1 large egg, beaten
2 tablespoons whisky
1 tablespoon lemon juice
100 ml/4 fl oz corn oil
175 g/6 oz sultanas, soaked in
  boiling water for 20 minutes,
  drained and liquid reserved
75 g/3 oz hazelnuts, chopped
few whole hazelnuts to decorate

For the filling
50 g/2 oz butter
225 g/8 oz icing sugar, sifted
2 tablespoons lemon juice
2 teaspoons whisky

Sift the flour, soda, salt and nutmeg into a bowl. Stir in the sugar. Mix the egg with the whisky, lemon juice, oil and 2 tablespoons reserved sultana juice and whisk into the dry ingredients. Fold in the sultanas and nuts. Spoon into two greased and lined 15-cm/6-in sandwich tins and bake for 30 minutes. Cool on a wire rack.

Beat all the filling ingredients together and use half to sandwich the cakes together. Use the remaining icing to pipe swirls on top of the cake, then decorate with a few whole hazelnuts.

Cook's Tip

For a stronger whisky flavour the sultanas in this recipe may be soaked in warmed whisky to plump before use. Leave to stand for about 30– 40 minutes until well swollen before use.

164 | *Harvest Heart Lemon Cake*

Preparation time
20–25 minutes

Cooking time
1½ hours

Oven temperature
180C, 350F, gas 4

Makes 1 (20-cm/ 8-in) heart-shaped cake

Total calories
6200

You will need
275 g/10 oz butter or margarine
275 g/10 oz caster sugar
5 eggs, beaten
275 g/10 oz self-raising flour
grated rind of 2 lemons
15 g/½ oz angelica
25 g/1 oz glacé cherries, chopped
15 g/½ oz flaked almonds

For the filling
100 g/4 oz butter
225 g/8 oz icing sugar
2 tablespoons lemon juice

Cream the butter and sugar until light and fluffy. Beat in the eggs with the flour and lemon rind. Spoon into a greased and base-lined 20-cm/8-in heart-shaped tin.

Bake for 1½ hours until well-risen, golden and cooked. Turn out to cool on a wire rack.

To make the filling, beat the butter with the icing sugar and lemon juice until light and fluffy. Cut the cake into two layers and sandwich together again with the butter icing.

Sprinkle with the angelica, cherries and almonds to serve.

Cook's Tip

This cake will also double admirably as a Valentine's cake with its heart shape.

165 | Numeral Cake

Preparation time
about 1 hour

Cooking time
20–25 minutes

Oven temperature
180 C, 350 F, gas 4

Makes 1 numeral cake

Total calories
4730

You will need
1 recipe Victoria Sandwich mixture (see recipe 54)

For the icing and decoration
2 recipes Butter Icing (see Introduction)
food colouring
coloured sweets or chocolate buttons
candles

Make up and bake the Victoria Sandwich cake as directed. Cut out two 18-cm/7-in rounds of greaseproof paper, overlap slightly at one end and pin together. Draw the shape of the figure 3 on the two pieces of paper and mark a dotted line at the point where they overlap. Use as much of the area as possible when drawing the numeral. Unpin the pieces of paper and cut out the shapes that have been drawn. Use these as a pattern to cut out the shape from the two sandwich cakes.

Fit the cake together on a board. Colour the butter icing as wished. Reserve a quarter of the butter icing for piping and use the remainder to cover the cake. Pipe stars or scrolls around the cake with the reserved icing, decorate with the sweets and appropriate number of candles.

Cook's Tip

Using the same method as above, other numerals can be cut out from the cake. A figure 8 may be made simply by cutting out a 7.5-cm/3-in round from the middle of each cake. The ends of the cake should be cut off slightly **where they fit together. A figure 6 may be cut out of the cake which has already been sandwiched together.**

166 | Drum Cake

Preparation time
30–40 minutes

Cooking time
20–25 minutes

Oven temperature
180 C, 350 F, gas 4

Makes 1 (18-cm/ 7-in) round cake

Total calories
4075

You will need
1 (18-cm/7-in) baked Victoria Sandwich mixture (see recipe 54)
1 recipe Butter Icing (see Introduction)
red food colouring
225 g/8 oz icing sugar
2–3 tablespoons water
1 teaspoon cocoa powder
16 Smarties
2 lollipops

Sandwich the two cooked cakes together with a third of the butter icing and place on a board or serving plate. Colour the remaining butter icing a vivid red and use to coat the sides of the cake.

Mix the icing sugar with the water until smooth and spread three-quarters over the top of the cake and leave to set. Add the cocoa to the remaining icing and place in a piping bag fitted with a writing nozzle. Place 8 Smarties around the side of the cake at the top and another 8 at the bottom, midway between those at the top. Pipe diagonal lines of chocolate icing to join the Smarties top to bottom. Place lollipops on top of the cake.

Cook's Tip

With any remaining chocolate glacé icing pipe the child's name on top of the cake. Add candles for a birthday party cake.

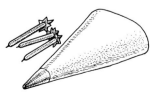

167 | Clock Cake

Preparation time
40 minutes

Cooking time
30–35 minutes

Oven temperature
180 C, 350 F, gas 4

Makes 1 (20-cm/ 8-in) clock cake

Total calories
5845

You will need
2 recipes Victoria Sandwich
   mixture (see recipe 54)
½ recipe Chocolate Butter Icing
   (see Introduction)
2 (100-g/3½-oz) packets milk
   chocolate finger biscuits
225 g/8 oz icing sugar
2–3 tablespoons water
1 teaspoon cocoa powder

Make up the cake mixture as directed and divide between two greased 20-cm/8-in sandwich tins. Bake for 30–35 minutes, then cool on a wire rack.

Sandwich the cakes together with two-thirds of the butter icing. Cover the sides with the remaining butter icing and place on a board. Trim the chocolate fingers to the height of the cake and arrange around the edge.

Mix the icing sugar with the water and spread three-quarters of this mixture over the top of the cake and leave to set. Add the cocoa to the remaining icing and place in a piping bag fitted with a writing nozzle.

Pipe a circle of dots around the top of the cake. Pipe on the clock numbers and the hands.

168 | Alphabet Stack

Preparation time
40–45 minutes

Cooking time
20–25 minutes

Oven temperature
180 C, 350 F, gas 4

Makes 16

Calories
335 per letter

You will need
1½ recipes Victoria Sandwich
   mixture (see recipe 54)

For the icing and decoration
175 g/6 oz plain chocolate
100 g/4 oz butter or margarine
225 g/8 oz icing sugar
1–2 tablespoons lemon juice
100 g/4 oz almond paste
food colourings

Make up the cake mixture as directed and place in a greased and lined 22 × 33-cm/9 × 13-in Swiss roll tin. Bake for 20–25 minutes then cool on a wire rack.

Trim the edges from the cake. Melt the chocolate and butter together. Gradually beat in the icing sugar and lemon juice and beat vigorously until soft. Spread over the top of the cake and leave until almost set. Using a sharp, wet knife cut the cake into four, both widthways and lengthways, to give 16 pieces of cake.

Roll out the almond paste thinly and cut out 16 alphabet letters, making them about 3.5–5 cm/1½–2 in. in height. Using a small artist's brush, colour the letters with various diluted food colours and leave until dry. Place on the cakes and leave until firm.

Cook's Tip

Pipe the clock hands pointing to the o'clock corresponding with the child's age if this is to be a birthday cake.

Cook's Tip

Arrange the letters in a random stack for serving, or in the name of a child if for a birthday cake.

169 | Chocolate Piggy Cake

Preparation time
40 minutes

Cooking time
20–25 minutes

Oven temperature
180C, 350F, gas 4

Makes 1 (18-cm/ 7-in) round cake

Total calories
4230

You will need
1 (18-cm/7-in) baked Victoria
  Sandwich mixture (see recipe
  54)

For the filling and decoration
3 tablespoons raspberry jam
1 recipe Butter Icing (see
  Introduction)
pink or blue food colouring
1 tablespoon cocoa powder
boiling water
225 g/8 oz almond paste
icing sugar for dusting
candles

Sandwich the cake layers together with the raspberry jam. Colour the butter icing a pale shade of either pink or blue. Mix the cocoa to a cream with a little boiling water. Knead the almond paste until pliable, then gradually knead in the cocoa cream. Roll out onto a surface dusted with icing sugar and, using a pig-shaped biscuit cutter, cut out eight pigs from the almond paste.

Cover the top and sides of the cake with some icing. Mark the top of the cake with a round-bladed knife and the sides with a serrated scraper. Using a greaseproof paper bag fitted with a star-shaped nozzle, pipe the edging on the cake as shown in the photograph. Arrange the chocolate pigs around the side of the cake and the candles on top.

170 | Igloo Cake

Preparation time
45–50 minutes

Cooking time
20–25 minutes

Oven temperature
180C, 350F, gas 4

Makes 1 igloo cake

Total calories
4445

You will need
1 recipe Victoria Sandwich mixture
  (see recipe 54)
½ Swiss roll
1 recipe Apricot Glaze (see
  Introduction)
1 recipe Fondant Icing (see
  Fondant-Iced Christmas Cake
  recipe 154)
175 g/6 oz royal icing
blue food colouring

Prepare the cake mixture and spoon into a greased and floured 900-ml/1-pint pudding basin. Bake for 1¼–1½ hours, then cool on a wire rack. Place flat side down on a board or serving plate.

Brush the cake and Swiss roll with the apricot glaze. Roll out the fondant icing thinly and use to cover the cake and Swiss roll. Place the Swiss roll in front of the cake and using the back of a knife, mark lines over the igloo and the cake to represent blocks of ice.

Colour one-quarter of the royal icing blue and with a No 2 writing nozzle, pipe on a chimney hole, outline the entrance and pipe on the child's name. Cover the plate or board with the remaining icing and lift into peaks to make snow.

Cook's Tip

You can, if liked, cut out different animals to place around the side of this cake – for example, circus animals, cats, dogs or mice! Cut out using special cutters or design using the free hand.

Cook's Tip

Decorate this cake with a few appropriate small toys or figures like penguins, seals or eskimos for a truly authentic finish.

171 | Kitten Cake

Preparation time
40 minutes

Cooking time
1¼–1½ hours

Oven temperature
180 C, 350 F, gas 4

Makes 1 kitten cake

Total calories
4795

You will need
2 recipes Victoria Sandwich
   mixture (see recipe 54)
1 recipe Chocolate Butter Icing
   (see Introduction)
3 sponge fingers
2 ice cream cones
liquorice sweets
liquorice ribbon
few short pieces spaghetti

Make up the cake mixture as directed and use to three-quarters fill a greased 600-ml/1-pint and 1.2-litre/2-pint pudding basin. Bake for 1 hour and 1¼–1½ hours respectively. Allow to cool.

Trim the small cake into a ball for the head. Trim a slice from one side of the large cake to flatten the chest. Place the large cake on a cake board or plate and fix the small one on top with a little butter icing. Position a sponge finger at the side for a tail.

Cut a 1-cm/½-in slice off the other sponge fingers. Place the sponge fingers on either side of the chest as legs; position the slices as paws. Cut the tips off the ice cream cones and use for ears. Cover the kitten with the butter icing. Shape the sweets for the eyes and nose; press into position. Tie the liquorice ribbon around the neck and use the spaghetti as whiskers.

Cook's Tip

Although the kitten in this recipe has been covered with chocolate butter icing to represent brown fur, it is possible to make a white cat with plain butter icing or even a striped or multi-coloured cat using plain and chocolate butter icing if liked – the limit is your own imagination!

172 | Merry Maypole Cake

Preparation time
40 minutes

Cooking time
20–25 minutes

Oven temperature
180 C, 350 F, gas 4

Makes 1 (18-cm/ 7-in) round cake

Total calories
3305

You will need
1 (18-cm/7-in) baked Victoria
   Sandwich (see recipe 54)

For the icing and decoration
1½ recipes Butter Icing (see
   Introduction)
pink or blue food colouring
50 g/2 oz chocolate vermicelli
coloured drinking straw
coloured ribbons
wooden figures

Sandwich the cake together with a little of the butter icing. Colour the remaining icing either pale pink or blue. Reserve one-third for piping. Spread the sides of the cake with some icing and roll in the chocolate vermicelli.

Place the cake on a board or plate and spread the top with the remaining butter icing. Place the reserved icing in a piping bag fitted with a star-shaped nozzle and pipe the edging to the cake.

Stick the straw in the middle of the cake and attach ribbons to it using a wire tie. Carefully secure the other ends to the wooden figures either with butter icing or by tying them to complete.

Cook's Tip

You can of course use edible jelly babies instead of the wooden figures to decorate the cake.

173 | Book Cake

Preparation time
40 minutes

Cooking time
20–25 minutes

Oven temperature
180 C, 350 F, gas 4

Makes 1 book cake

Total calories
4130

You will need
1½ recipes Victoria Sandwich mixture (see recipe 54)

For the icing and decoration
1 recipe Butter Icing (see Introduction)
50 g/2 oz plain chocolate, melted
1 piece of coloured ribbon

Make up the cake mixture as directed and place in a greased and lined 22 × 33-cm/9 × 13-in Swiss roll tin. Bake for 20–25 minutes then cool on a wire rack.

Cover the cake completely with butter icing, reserving about one-third for piping. Place the reserved icing in a piping bag fitted with a star-shaped nozzle and pipe edges around the cake.

Place the melted chocolate in a bag with a tiny hole cut in its point and pipe writing onto the cake to resemble a book. Arrange the ribbon down the middle of the cake to form a book-mark.

174 | Bus Cake

Preparation time
45 minutes

Cooking time
1¼–1½ hours

Oven temperature
160 C, 325 F, gas 3

Makes 1 bus cake

Total calories
5740

You will need
1 (1-kg/2-lb) baked sponge cake (see Treasure Chest recipe 175)

For the icing and decoration
1 recipe Lemon Butter Icing (see Introduction)
yellow food colouring
75 g/3 oz plain chocolate, melted
50 g/2 oz icing sugar
1 tablespoon water
Smarties
2 mini chocolate rolls
100 g/4 oz plain chocolate, grated

Make up and bake the cake as directed in Treasure Chest (see recipe 175). Cool, then cut out a piece about 2.5 × 3.5 cm/1 × 1½ in from one end to form the engine shape.

Reserve 2 tablespoons of the butter icing. Colour the remainder yellow and cover the cake completely. Cream the melted chocolate with the reserved icing. Place in a piping bag fitted with a writing nozzle and pipe the features on the bus. Mix the icing sugar with the water until smooth and pipe faces on the Smarties and place these in the windows of the bus.

Halve the mini rolls and place under the cake to form wheels. Place on a board and surround with grated chocolate.

Cook's Tip

This birthday cake idea could also double up as a cake to celebrate a confirmation, or the passing of exams or scholarship.

Cook's Tip

For a birthday cake pipe the name of the birthday boy or girl and the house name or address as the destination for the bus on the cake.

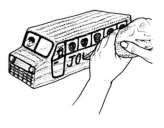

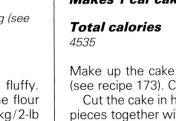

175 | Treasure Chest

Preparation time
50 minutes

Cooking time
1½ hours

Oven temperature
160 C, 325 F, gas 3

**Makes 1 (1-kg/
2-lb) loaf cake**

Total calories
4985

You will need
*175 g/6 oz butter or margarine
175 g/6 oz caster sugar
grated rind of 2 oranges
3 eggs
200 g/7 oz self-raising flour
juice of 1 orange*

For the icing and decoration
*175 g/6 oz plain chocolate
50 g/2 oz butter
½ recipe Orange Butter Icing (see
     Introduction)
variety of small sweets*

Cream the butter with the sugar until light and fluffy. Beat in the orange rind and eggs then fold in the flour and orange juice. Turn into a greased and lined 1-kg/2-lb loaf tin and bake for 1½ hours. Cool on a wire rack.

To ice and decorate the cake, melt the chocolate with the butter in a bowl over a pan of hot water. Slice off the top of the cake and reserve as the lid. Cover the whole cake thinly with chocolate; when set, place the butter icing in a piping bag fitted with a star-shaped nozzle and pipe an edge around the cake. Pipe designs around the sides and top of the cake.

Place the various sweets as 'treasure' on top, allowing some to hang over the edge. Arrange the lid, tilting slightly backwards, on the top of the cake.

176 | Cuthbert Car

Preparation time
45 minutes

Cooking time
20–25 minutes

Oven temperature
180 C, 350 F, gas 4

Makes 1 car cake

Total calories
4535

You will need
*1½ recipes Victoria Sandwich
     mixture (see recipe 54)*

For the icing and decoration
*225 g/8 oz lemon curd
1 (25-cm/10-in) square silver cake
     board
1 recipe Butter Icing (see
     Introduction)
green food colouring
Smarties
chocolate buttons*

Make up the cake mixture and bake as for Book Cake (see recipe 173). Cool on a wire rack.

Cut the cake in half widthways and sandwich the two pieces together with a little of the lemon curd. Place on the cake board. Mix the remaining lemon curd with the butter icing. Cut out a piece of greaseproof paper the same size as the cake. Draw the shape of the car on the paper, place on top of the cake and use as an outline to cut out the car. Cut out the wheels from the off-cuts.

Reserve 3 tablespoons of the icing and use the remainder to cover the cake completely. Mark the icing with a round-bladed knife. Colour the reserved icing green and pipe the features on the cake using a piping bag with a writing nozzle. Place red and yellow Smarties on the cake to represent lights and chocolate buttons for hub caps.

Cook's Tip

**It often helps to freeze a
freshly-made cake before
slicing or cutting into shapes
for decorating. The cake is
less likely to break or crumble
and a sharper edge can be
achieved. Defrost before icing
for best results.**

Cook's Tip

**If a silver cake board is not
available, a thick piece of
cardboard covered in foil may
be used.**

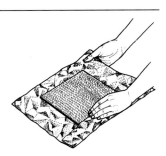

177 | Humpty Dumpty

Preparation time
50 minutes

Cooking time
40–50 minutes

Oven temperature
160 C, 325 F, gas 3

Makes 1 humpty dumpty cake

Total calories
7555

You will need
225 g/8 oz butter or margarine
225 g/8 oz caster sugar
4 eggs, lightly beaten
175 g/6 oz self-raising flour
1 teaspoon baking powder
75 g/3 oz desiccated coconut

For the icing and decoration
225 g/8 oz raspberry jam
100 g/4 oz desiccated coconut
1 recipe Butter Icing (see Introduction)
Smarties
short strip of liquorice
225 g/8 oz almond paste

Cream the butter and sugar until light and fluffy. Beat in the eggs then fold in the flour, baking powder and coconut. Two-thirds fill a greased and base-lined 600-ml/1-pint pudding basin with the mixture then spread the remainder in a greased and lined 18-cm/7-in square cake tin. Bake for 40–50 and 25–35 minutes respectively. Cool on a wire rack.

Cut the square cake in half and sandwich together with a little jam to form an oblong cake of 8.5 × 18 cm/3½ × 7 in. Coat in the jam and coconut. Cover the basin cake completely with butter icing. Use Smarties for buttons, nose and eyes and place on the wall. Cut a short piece of liquorice and use to make a mouth and eyebrows. Shape arms and legs out of almond paste and secure to the body with wooden cocktail sticks if necessary.

178 | Hedgehog Cake

Preparation time
30–40 minutes

Cooking time
25 minutes

Oven temperature
180 C, 350 F, gas 4

Makes 1 hedgehog cake

Total calories
3440

You will need
1 recipe Victoria Sandwich mixture (see recipe 54)
2 tablespoons cocoa powder
1 recipe Chocolate Butter Icing (see Introduction)
50 g/2 oz shredded almonds
3 Smarties

Make the cake mixture as directed, adding the cocoa powder with the flour and spoon into a greased and lined 20-cm/8-in sandwich tin. Bake for 25 minutes then cool on a wire rack.

Cut the cake vertically in half to make two semi-circles and sandwich together with a third of the butter icing. To form the nose, cut two diagonal slices from each side of the front of the cake and discard. Stand the flat edge on a cake board or plate and cover with the remaining butter icing. Smooth over the nose and face and fork lines from front to back over the rest of the 'hedgehog'. Stick in the almonds at random to represent prickles. Use the Smarties for the nose and eyes.

Cook's Tip

To achieve a brick wall effect for Humpty Dumpty, use a skewer to mark the coconut.

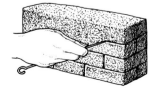

Cook's Tip

Since children's parties seem to be such busy affairs it is wise to make the party cake at least 1 week ahead and decorate in stages over the next few days.

179 | Chocolate Chuffa Cake

Preparation time
50 minutes

Cooking time
12 minutes

Oven temperature
220C, 425F, gas 7

Makes 1 train cake

Total calories
2805

You will need
3 eggs
100 g/4 oz caster sugar
65 g/2½ oz plain flour
25 g/1 oz cocoa powder
caster sugar

For the filling
½ recipe Chocolate Butter Icing (see Introduction)

For the icing and decoration
175 g/6 oz plain chocolate, melted
1 chocolate digestive biscuit
liquorice sweets

Whisk the eggs and sugar together until pale and thick. Fold in the flour and cocoa powder and spread over a greased and lined 23 × 33-cm/9 × 13-in Swiss roll tin. Bake for 12 minutes, turn onto a sheet of greaseproof paper dusted with caster sugar and roll up from one short end. Allow to cool.

Unroll the cake and spread with the butter icing then re-roll. Cut a piece approximately 10 cm/4 in long from one end and coat both pieces in melted chocolate. Place the biscuit on one end of the bigger piece and leave to set.

Turn the smaller piece up on end and place at the other end of the longer piece of cake. Arrange the sweets to form wheels and a funnel. Decorate with more sweets and with cotton wool to form smoke from the funnel.

Cook's Tip

If liked miniature chocolate-covered marshmallow biscuits can be used to form wheels on the train cake instead of the liquorice sweets.

180 | Hamburger Cake

Preparation time
45–50 minutes

Cooking time
20–25 minutes

Oven temperature
180C, 350F, gas 4

Makes 1 (18-cm/7-in) cake

Total calories
6135

You will need
1½ recipes Victoria Sandwich mixture (see recipe 54)
1 tablespoon cocoa powder
1 recipe Fondant Icing (see Fondant-Iced Christmas Cake recipe 154)
food colourings
100 g/4 oz apricot jam, sieved
100 g/4 oz marzipan
1 recipe Chocolate Butter Icing (see Introduction)
egg white to brush
15 g/½ oz crispy rice cereal

Prepare the cake mixture as directed and divide into three portions. Flavour one with the cocoa powder. Spoon into three (18-cm/7-in) sandwich tins and bake as directed. Prepare the fondant icing as directed. Divide into four portions; colour two light golden brown; one yellow and the final a vivid red.

Use the light brown icing to cover the two plain cakes brushed with apricot jam. Place one on a serving plate. Colour the marzipan green, roll out and place over the cake, crimping the edge to look like lettuce. Cover with half the butter icing and the chocolate cake. Roll out the yellow icing to a square and place on top to look like cheese. Top in turn with the rolled out red icing to represent sauce, cover with the remaining butter icing, then finally cover with the second plain cake. Brush with egg white and sprinkle with the cereal.

Cook's Tip

This really is a fun cake to make and you can vary the layers according to your own whims and likes – you might like to make an extra large double burger cake with an extra chocolate cake layer, additional fondant 'cheese' **and 'sauce' or special marzipan pickles!**

181 | Hallowe'en Pumpkin

Preparation time
50 minutes

Cooking time
1½-1¾ hours

Oven temperature
160C, 325F, gas 3

Makes 1 pumpkin cake

Total calories
6060

You will need
2 recipes Victoria Sandwich
   mixture (see recipe 54)
⅓ recipe Butter Icing (see
   Introduction)
1½ recipes Fondant Icing (see
   Fondant-Iced Christmas Cake
   recipe 154)
orange and green food colouring
liquorice allsorts

Make up the cake mixture as directed and divide between two greased and floured 1.2-litre/2-pint pudding basins. Bake for 1½-1¾ hours then cool on a wire rack.

Sandwich the flat side of each cake together with all but 1 tablespoon of the butter icing, to make a ball shape. Cut a shallow hole in the centre of the top of the cake. Mark six lines from the centre of the top and down the sides of the cake. Cut a small groove along each marked line.

Colour ⁹⁄₁₀ of the fondant icing orange and roll out thinly to completely coat the cake. Colour the remaining icing green and shape into eyebrows and jagged teeth for the pumpkin. Use liquorice allsorts for the eyes and nose. Secure with butter icing. Shape green icing into leaves and a stalk. Place in the centre of the cake.

Cook's Tip

Place the rolled-out icing onto a rolling pin and lay it over the cake. Dip your fingers in cornflour and smooth the icing over the cake, pressing it gently into the grooves. Trim away any excess with a sharp knife, smoothing out joins.

182 | Chocolate Clock Cake

Preparation time
30-40 minutes

Cooking time
20-25 minutes

Oven temperature
180C, 350F, gas 4

Makes 1 (18-cm/ 7-in) round cake

Total calories
3410

You will need
1 (18-cm/7-in) baked Victoria
   Sandwich (see recipe 54)

For the icing
50g/2oz butter or margarine
3 tablespoons milk
225g/8oz icing sugar, sifted

For the decoration
50g/2oz icing sugar
about 1 tablespoon hot water
chocolate buttons
50g/2oz plain chocolate, melted
ribbon

To make the icing, place all the ingredients in a mixing bowl and beat until smooth. Sandwich the cake together using one third of the icing, then spread the remainder over the top and sides.

To make the decoration, mix the icing sugar with the water to give a smooth icing. Place in a bag fitted with a writing nozzle and pipe the numbers 1 to 12 on the chocolate buttons and a spiral on the button to go in the centre of the cake. Place around the cake to resemble a clock with the spiral in the centre.

Draw the shape of the clock hands on greaseproof paper and carefully spread the chocolate within the outline of the drawing. Leave until set then position on the clock. Tie a ribbon around the clock to complete the cake.

Cook's Tip

It may be necessary to spoon several layers of chocolate on top of each other to achieve thick hands for the clock. Leave each layer to harden slightly before adding another layer.

183 | Tennis Cake

Preparation time
40 minutes

Cooking time
25 minutes

Oven temperature
180 C, 350 F, gas 4

**Makes 1 (28-cm/
11-in) cake**

Total calories
4260

You will need
1 recipe Victoria Sandwich mixture
(see recipe 54)
1 recipe Butter Icing (see
Introduction)
green food colouring
50 g/2 oz desiccated coconut
225 g/8 oz icing sugar
2–3 tablespoons water
ice cream wafers
toy tennis figures

Make up the cake mixture as directed and divide between two greased and lined 18 × 28-cm/7 × 11-in Swiss roll tins. Bake for 25 minutes then turn out to cool on a wire rack.

Colour the butter icing pale green and use two-thirds to sandwich the cakes together. Place on a cake board. Spread the remaining butter icing over the sides and press on coconut coloured green (see Cook's Tip).

Mix the icing sugar with the water and set aside a little. Colour the rest green and use to coat the top of the cake. Place the reserved icing in a bag fitted with a writing nozzle and pipe white lines on the cake as for a tennis court. Cut the wafers into 2.5 cm/1 in strips and place across the centre for a net. Position toy tennis figures on the court to finish.

184 | Basket Cake

Preparation time
45 minutes

Cooking time
20–25 minutes

Oven temperature
180 C, 350 F, gas 4

**Makes 1 (18-cm/
7-in) cake**

Total calories
3205

You will need
1 (18-cm/7-in) Victoria Sandwich
mixture (see recipe 54)

For the icing and decoration
1 recipe Chocolate Butter Icing
(see Introduction)
1 (20-cm/8-in) round silver cake
board
sweets

Make up the cake mixture and bake as directed. Allow to cool. Make up the chocolate butter icing. Place one of the cakes on the board and cover with a thin layer of icing. Cover with an assortment of sweets.

Fill two greaseproof paper piping bags with icing, one fitted with a plain writing nozzle and the other with a ribbon nozzle. Holding the ribbon nozzle sideways to the second cake, pipe three lines evenly spaced one above the other and all the same length. Pipe a vertical line using the writing nozzle along the edge of the basket weaving. Continue this process until the top of the cake is covered. Cover the outer edge of the lid and the base cake edge in the same way.

Arrange the lid at an angle on top of the cake to form an open basket.

Cook's Tip

To colour coconut, add a drop of food colouring to a small bowlful and stir until evenly blended.

Cook's Tip

Basket weaving with icing looks complicated but it really is quite simple if you follow the pattern in the photograph. If time is short, then simply weave the icing using the ribbon nozzle in a wavy pattern over the cake.

Special Occasion Gâteaux

Here is a purely indulgent selection of special occasion gâteaux – cakes that are laden with spices, nuts and liqueurs; cooled then split and sandwiched with creams, jams, custards and fruits; rolled or coated with chopped nuts, crushed praline, grated chocolate and whipped cream. Enjoy a slice of the good life.

185 | Walnut and Chocolate Gâteau

Preparation time
40 minutes

Cooking time
30–35 minutes

Oven temperature
190 C, 375 F, gas 5

Makes 1 (20-cm/8-in) gâteau

Total calories
3710

You will need
4 eggs
175 g/6 oz caster sugar
75 g/3 oz plain flour, sifted
100 g/4 oz walnuts, ground

For the filling and decoration
1 recipe Butter Icing (see Introduction)
2 tablespoons cocoa powder
2 tablespoons boiling water
50 g/2 oz walnuts, chopped
4 after-dinner chocolate mints, cut into triangles

Put the eggs and sugar in a bowl and whisk over a pan of hot water until thick and mousse-like. Partially fold in the flour, then add the nuts and fold in carefully. Turn into a greased and lined 20-cm/8-in deep cake tin. Bake for 30–35 minutes until firm. Cool on a wire rack.

Split the cake into three layers and sandwich with one-third of the butter icing. Blend the cocoa with the water, cool then beat into the remaining butter icing. Spread a little over the sides of the cake and roll in the walnuts. Spread more of the butter icing on top of the cake and swirl with a knife. Pipe the remaining butter icing around the edge of the cake and decorate with the after-dinner mints.

186 | Strawberry Torte

Preparation time
1 hour

Cooking time
25–30 minutes

Oven temperature
180 C, 350 F, gas 4

Makes 1 (23-cm/9-in) gâteau

Total calories
6215

You will need
1½ recipes Victoria Sandwich mixture (see recipe 54)
1 kg/2 lb strawberries, hulled
600 ml/1 pint double cream, whipped
6 tablespoons sweet or medium sherry
3 tablespoons granulated sugar
1¼ teaspoons cornflour
2 tablespoons water
1 teaspoon lemon juice
100 g/4 oz toasted flaked almonds

Divide the cake mixture between three greased and lined 23-cm/9-in sandwich tins. Bake for 25–30 minutes then turn out to cool on a wire rack.

Purée 225 g/8 oz of the strawberries and slice a further 225 g/8 oz. Sieve the puréed strawberries and fold into 450 ml/¾ pint whipped cream with the sliced strawberries. Sprinkle the cake layers with the sherry then sandwich together with the prepared cream.

Purée 175 g/6 oz of the remaining strawberries, sieve and place in a pan with the sugar, cornflour and water. Cook for 1–2 minutes until thickened. Stir in the lemon juice and cool. Halve the remaining strawberries and place, cut sides down, on top of the cake. Brush with the glaze to coat. Brush the sides of the cake with the glaze and coat with the almonds. Pipe the edge of the cake with the remaining whipped cream.

187 | Raspberry and Peach Torte

Preparation time
50 minutes

Cooking time
20 minutes

Oven temperature
190 C, 375 F, gas 5

Makes 1 large rectangular gâteau

Total calories
4160

You will need
275 g/10 oz plain flour
175 g/6 oz butter
100 g/4 oz caster sugar
2 large egg yolks, beaten
chocolate leaves to decorate

For the filling
1 (425-g/15-oz) can peach slices, drained
300 ml/½ pint whipping cream
225 g/8 oz raspberries, hulled

Sift the flour into a bowl, rub in the butter then stir in the sugar. Add the egg yolks and bind to a dough. Knead lightly then divide in half and roll each piece out to a 30 × 13-cm/12 × 5-in rectangle. Place on greased baking trays and bake for 20 minutes. Cool on a wire rack.

Reserve about 15 peach slices and chop the remainder. Whip the cream and fold the chopped peaches into half of the cream with 100 g/4 oz of the raspberries. Use to sandwich the cake layers together.

Arrange the peach slices down the centre of the torte. Place the remaining cream in a piping bag and pipe swirls of cream down each side of the peaches. Top each swirl with a raspberry and decorate with chocolate leaves.

Cook's Tip

To make chocolate leaves, spread melted chocolate thinly onto greaseproof paper. When firm but not brittle, cut out leaf shapes using a sharp knife. Alternatively, dip in melted chocolate the underside of washed and very lightly oiled rose leaves. Leave to harden then peel away the leaf from the chocolate.

188 | Raspberry Summer Gâteau

Preparation time
45 minutes

Cooking time
15–20 minutes

Oven temperature
180 C, 350 F, gas 4

Makes 1 (20-cm/8-in) gâteau

Total calories
3265

You will need
4 eggs
100 g/4 oz caster sugar
100 g/4 oz self-raising flour
pinch of salt
50 g/2 oz ground almonds
50 g/2 oz butter, melted and cooled
icing sugar to dust

For the filling
300 ml/½ pint double cream
1 tablespoon icing sugar
2 tablespoons Kirsch
450 g/1 lb raspberries, hulled

Whisk the eggs with the sugar until very thick and creamy. Sift the flour with the salt and almonds and fold into the mixture with the melted butter. Pour into two greased, floured and lined 20-cm/8-in sandwich tins and bake for 15–20 minutes or until firm to the touch. Cool on wire racks.

Whip the cream with the icing sugar and Kirsch until thick, then fold in three-quarters of the raspberries.

Cut one cake layer into eight equal wedges. Pile three-quarters of the raspberry cream onto the uncut cake layer and top with four alternate cake wedges. Dust the remaining cake wedges with icing sugar and return to the cake in the same position as they were originally, spaced alternately between the plain cake wedges. Pile the remaining cream mixture into the centre and decorate with the remaining raspberries.

Cook's Tip

If whisking the cake mixture by hand rather than with an electric beater, do this in a bowl set over a pan of hot water. This will help to encourage the mixture to thicken slightly and trap air so producing a light mixture.

189 | Brandy Orange Ring

Preparation time
45 minutes

Cooking time
30–35 minutes

Oven temperature
190 C, 375 F, gas 5

Makes 1 (20-cm/ 8-in) gâteau

Total calories
3550

You will need
3 eggs, separated
75 g/3 oz caster sugar
4 tablespoons milk
175 g/6 oz self-raising flour, sifted
50 g/2 oz butter, melted

For the syrup
225 g/8 oz sugar
150 ml/$\frac{1}{4}$ pint brandy
150 ml/$\frac{1}{4}$ pint orange juice

For the decoration
150 ml/$\frac{1}{4}$ pint double cream, whipped
2 oranges, segmented
orange rind shreds

Whisk the egg yolks and sugar together until pale and frothy. Whisk in the milk, then fold in the flour and butter. Whisk the egg whites until stiff and fold into the batter. Pour into a well-greased and floured 20-cm/8-in savarin or ring mould. Bake for 30–35 minutes. Leave in the tin.

To make the syrup, place the sugar, brandy and orange juice in a pan. Heat until dissolved then boil for 2–3 minutes until thick and syrupy.

Turn out the cake onto a deep serving plate and pour over the hot syrup. Leave for 2–3 hours to cool.

Decorate with whipped cream, orange segments and orange rind shreds.

Cook's Tip

To make orange rind shreds for flavouring or decoration pare the rind away from an orange with a canelle knife. Alternatively, pare away with a vegetable peeler or sharp knife then cut into thin julienne strips.

190 | Citrus Mousse Gâteau

Preparation time
40 minutes, plus chilling time

Cooking time
15 minutes

Oven temperature
180 C, 350 F, gas 4

Makes 1 (20-cm/ 8-in) gâteau

Total calories
4080

You will need
100 g/4 oz self-raising flour
1 tablespoon cornflour
2 teaspoons baking powder
25 g/1 oz butter
4 tablespoons water
3 eggs
200 g/7 oz caster sugar

For the filling and decoration
1 (135-g/4$\frac{3}{4}$-oz) packet lemon jelly
150 ml/$\frac{1}{4}$ pint boiling water
150 g/5 oz lemon or citrus yogurt
450 ml/$\frac{3}{4}$ pint double cream
lemon rind shreds

To make the cake, sift the flour, cornflour and baking powder together. Melt the butter with the water. Whisk the eggs and sugar until pale and very thick. Fold the flour into the egg mixture. Bring the water mixture to the boil and fold into the cake mixture. Pour into two greased, floured and lined 20-cm/8-in sandwich tins. Bake for 15 minutes then turn out to cool on wire racks.

Dissolve the jelly in the water. Cool slightly then whisk in the yogurt. Chill until beginning to thicken.

Whip two-thirds of the cream to soft peaks then whisk into the jelly mixture and leave to set. Sandwich the cake layers together with half of this mixture and use the remainder to cover the top. Pipe the remaining whipped cream in swirls over the top edge of the cake and decorate with lemon rind shreds.

Cook's Tip

The filling for this gâteau can be varied slightly by using different flavoured yogurts and jellies. Always use the same or complementary flavours for best effect.

191 | Chocolate Mallow Gâteau

Preparation time
20 minutes

Cooking time
15–20 minutes

Oven temperature
180 C, 350 F, gas 4

**Makes 1 (20-cm/
8-in) gâteau**

Total calories
3375

You will need
5 eggs, separated
175 g/6 oz caster sugar
175 g/6 oz plain chocolate, melted
2 tablespoons very hot water

For the filling and decoration
300 ml/½ pint double cream
icing sugar

Beat the egg yolks with the sugar until pale and creamy. Whisk in the chocolate, then the water. Whisk the egg whites until stiff and fold gently into the egg yolk mixture. Turn into two greased and lined 20-cm/8-in sandwich tins. Bake for 15–20 minutes, until firm to the touch. Leave the cakes to cool in their tins.

Whip the cream until it stands in stiff peaks then use to sandwich the cake layers together. Dust with icing sugar to finish.

192 | Brandy Torte

Preparation time
30 minutes

Cooking time
1–1¼ hours

Oven temperature
160 C, 325 F, gas 3

**Makes 1 (23-cm/
9-in) gâteau**

Total calories
3895

You will need
5 eggs, separated
200 g/7 oz caster sugar
4 tablespoons grated chocolate
2 teaspoons ground cinnamon
finely grated rind and juice of 1
  lemon
100 g/4 oz ground almonds
4 tablespoons brandy
100 g/4 oz dried breadcrumbs
2 teaspoons baking powder

For the decoration
300 ml/½ pint double cream
grated chocolate
chocolate leaves

Beat the egg yolks with the sugar until light and creamy. Stir in the chocolate, cinnamon, lemon rind and juice, almonds and brandy. Whisk the egg whites until stiff and fold into the mixture. Mix the breadcrumbs with the baking powder and fold into the mixture. Turn into a greased 23-cm/9-in loose-bottomed cake tin and bake for 1–1¼ hours until firm. Cool on a wire rack.

Whip the cream until thick. Spread the top and sides of the cake thinly with cream. Press chocolate over the sides. Pipe any remaining cream on top and decorate with chocolate leaves.

Cook's Tip

The cakes will sink a little in their tins during cooling and the tops may crack – don't worry if this happens to yours – both results are characteristic of the gâteau.

Cook's Tip

Dry the breadcrumbs for this recipe in a cool oven – they will take up to 1 hour depending upon temperature. For economy, dry whilst cooking another dish at a low temperature. Freeze for up to 3 months if liked.

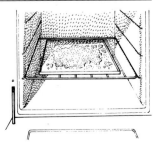

193 | Chocolate Chestnut Layer

Preparation time
45 minutes

Cooking time
20–25 minutes

Oven temperature
190 C, 375 F, gas 5

Makes 1 (20-cm/ 8-in) long gâteau

Total calories
2780

You will need
1 recipe Chocolate Whisked Sponge mixture (see Introduction)
1 (227-g/8-oz) can unsweetened chestnut purée
1 tablespoon clear honey
175 ml/6 fl oz double cream
2 tablespoons Cointreau
100 g/4 oz chocolate curls
chocolate leaves

Turn the whisked sponge mixture into a greased and lined 20 × 30-cm/8 × 12-in Swiss roll tin and bake for 20–25 minutes. Cool on a wire rack.

Place the chestnut purée, honey and 2 tablespoons of the cream in a bowl and whip thoroughly. Whip the remaining cream until stiff then whisk in half the chestnut purée mixture and the Cointreau.

Cut the cake into three 20-cm/8-in long pieces and sandwich together with one third of the cream mixture. Cover the sides with more cream and coat with chocolate curls. Spread the remaining cream mixture over the top of the cake and draw lines across with a palette knife. Pipe the remaining chestnut purée mixture around the edge of the cake and decorate with chocolate leaves.

Cook's Tip

To make chocolate curls for the sides of this cake, use a potato peeler to scrape curls directly from the block of chocolate. Make sure the chocolate is not too cold or the curls will not form properly and will break.

194 | Gâteau Ganache

Preparation time
40 minutes

Cooking time
1–1½ hours

Oven temperature
140 C, 275 F, gas 1

Makes 1 (20-cm/ 8-in) gâteau

Total calories
3625

You will need
4 egg whites
225 g/8 oz caster sugar
few drops of vanilla essence
1 teaspoon vinegar
100 g/4 oz hazelnuts, toasted and ground

For the chocolate sauce
175 g/6 oz plain chocolate
150 ml/¼ pint water
50 g/2 oz sugar

For the filling and decoration
250 ml/8 fl oz cream
icing sugar
chocolate shapes

Whisk the egg whites until stiff then gradually whisk in the sugar. Fold in the vanilla, vinegar and hazelnuts. Spread the mixture into two 20-cm/8-in rounds on baking trays lined with silicone paper. Bake for 1–1½ hours until crisp. Cool on wire racks then peel off the paper.

To make the chocolate sauce, heat the chocolate, water and sugar in a pan until dissolved, then boil for 10 minutes and allow to cool.

Add 4 tablespoons of the chocolate sauce to the cream then whip until thick. Sandwich the meringues together with three-quarters of the cream and dust the top with icing sugar. Pipe the remaining cream in rosettes on top and decorate with chocolate shapes. Serve with the remaining chocolate sauce.

Cook's Tip

After preparing chocolate shapes (follow the directions in Cook's Tip 98 for making chocolate triangles, but use a pastry cutter to make small rounds, as in the photograph, if you wish), leave to dry in a cool place, but not in the refrigerator or they will set with a dull finish. They may be stored in an airtight container layered with greaseproof paper for several weeks.

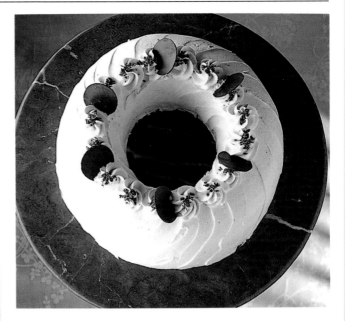

195 | *Gâteau Diane*

Preparation time
30 minutes

Cooking time
1½–2 hours

Oven temperature
140 C, 275 F, gas 1

Makes 1 (20-cm/8-in) gâteau

Total calories
2845

You will need
4 egg whites
225 g/8 oz caster sugar

For the filling and decoration
1 recipe Chocolate Butter Icing
    (see Introduction)
50 g/2 oz flaked almonds, toasted
25 g/1 oz plain chocolate, melted

Whisk the egg whites until stiff, then add 2 tablespoons of the sugar and continue whisking until the mixture is very stiff. Carefully fold in the remaining sugar. Spoon into mounds or pipe into two 20-cm/8-in rounds on baking trays lined with silicone paper. Bake for 1½–2 hours until crisp. Peel off the lining paper and cool on a wire rack.

Sandwich the meringue rounds together with one-third of the chocolate butter icing. Spread the remaining butter icing on top of the meringue and around the sides. Sprinkle almonds over the top. Put the melted chocolate in a greaseproof paper piping bag, snip off the end and drizzle lines of chocolate over the nuts.

196 | *Mocha Brandy Ring*

Preparation time
45 minutes

Cooking time
35–40 minutes

Oven temperature
160 C, 325 F, gas 3

Makes 1 (23-cm/9-in) gâteau

Total calories
3575

You will need
100 g/4 oz plain chocolate
1 tablespoon instant coffee
    powder
5 tablespoons water
100 g/4 oz self-raising flour
4 tablespoons corn oil
3 eggs, separated
2 tablespoons sugar
½ recipe Sugar Syrup (see
    Chocolate Brandy Gâteau recipe
    198), flavoured with 1 tablespoon
    instant coffee powder and 3
    tablespoons brandy
300 ml/½ pint double cream
grated chocolate
chocolate shapes (see Cook's Tip
    98)

Place the chocolate, coffee and water in a small pan and heat gently until melted. Leave until cool.

Sift the flour into a bowl, make a well in the centre and add the oil, egg yolks and chocolate mixture. Beat until very smooth. Whisk the egg whites until stiff, then whisk in the sugar; fold into the cake mixture then turn into a greased 23-cm/9-in ring mould. Bake for 35–40 minutes then leave in the tin.

Make up the sugar syrup and flavour as above. Spoon over the hot cake and leave until cool. Turn out onto a serving dish, cover with whipped cream and mark into swirls with a palette knife. Pipe rosettes on top and decorate with grated chocolate and chocolate shapes.

Cook's Tip

If you have a microwave then you can melt the chocolate in its paper piping bag. Simply place the broken chocolate pieces in the bag and cook on Medium (50%) power for 1½–2¼ minutes until melted. Snip off the end and pipe.

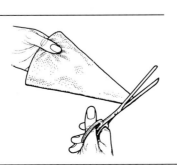

Cook's Tip

To whip cream, make sure the whisk and bowl are clean and really cold, particularly in hot weather when cream tends to overwhip. Choose a bowl or basin with a round or curved inside base and one which has a capacity at least four *times that of the unwhipped cream. Whip with a balloon or spiral whisk; or use an electric beater. Cream will be at the ideal stage for spreading or piping when it stands in soft or just stiff peaks.*

197 | Rich Chocolate Gâteau

Preparation time
30 minutes

Cooking time
35–40 minutes

Oven temperature
190 C, 375 F, gas 5

Makes 1 (23-cm/ 9-in) gâteau

Total calories
2700

You will need
1 (23-cm/9-in) Chocolate Whisked Sponge Cake (see Introduction)

For the chocolate meringue butter icing
2 egg whites
100 g/4 oz icing sugar, sifted
100 g/4 oz unsalted butter
50 g/2 oz plain chocolate, melted
75 g/3 oz chocolate caraque (see Cook's Tip)

Split the cooked sponge cake in half. To make the meringue butter icing, place the egg whites and icing sugar in a bowl over a saucepan of simmering water and whisk until the mixture holds its shape. Cool slightly. Cream the butter until soft and light then beat into the meringue mixture with the melted chocolate.

Sandwich the cakes together with some of the meringue butter icing and use the rest to cover the cake. Decorate with the chocolate caraque.

198 | Chocolate Brandy Gâteau

Preparation time
30 minutes plus overnight standing time

Cooking time
45 minutes

Oven temperature
180 C, 350 F, gas 4

Makes 1 (20-cm/ 8-in) gâteau

Total calories
3945

You will need
150 g/5 oz plain flour
25 g/1 oz cocoa powder
2 teaspoons baking powder
pinch of salt
150 g/5 oz soft brown sugar
2 eggs, separated
6 tablespoons oil
6 tablespoons milk
½ teaspoon vanilla essence
300 ml/½ pint double cream
grated chocolate

For the sugar syrup
100 g/4 oz granulated sugar
150 ml/¼ pint water
2 tablespoons brandy

Sift the flour, cocoa, baking powder and salt together into a large bowl. Stir in the sugar. Beat the egg yolks, oil, milk and vanilla together. Pour into the dry ingredients and beat until smooth. Whisk the egg whites until stiff and fold into the cake mixture. Pour into a greased and lined 20-cm/8-in deep round cake tin and bake for 45 minutes until firm. Leave in the tin.

To make the syrup, put the sugar and water in a pan and heat to dissolve. Bring to a rolling boil and boil for 1 minute. Remove from the heat, cool slightly then add the brandy. Spoon over the hot cake and leave overnight.

Turn out onto a serving plate and completely cover with three-quarters of the whipped cream. Pipe the remainder around the edges and top with the chocolate.

Cook's Tip

To make chocolate caraque, pour a thin layer of chocolate onto a marble slab or cold surface and cool until it begins to set and go cloudy. Using a sharp, thin-bladed knife at a slight angle, push it across the chocolate with a **slight sawing movement, scraping off a thin layer to form a long scroll.**

Cook's Tip

The sugar syrup above is sufficient to soak any 20–23-cm/8–9-in cake. Flavour with any liqueur or spirit to whatever strength required, but add the liqueur or spirit after the syrup has cooled a little.

199 | Strawberry Choux Ring

Preparation time
40 minutes

Cooking time
35–40 minutes

Oven temperature
220C, 425F, gas 7

Makes 1 (25-cm/10-in) gâteau

Total calories
4365

You will need
1 recipe Choux Pastry (see Introduction)
50 g/2 oz flaked almonds
3 tablespoons strawberry jam
300 ml/½ pint double cream, whipped with the finely grated rind and juice of 1 small orange
450 g/1 lb strawberries, halved

For the icing
225 g/8 oz icing sugar
1–2 tablespoons orange juice

Spoon or pipe the choux pastry mixture onto a dampened baking tray to form a 25-cm/10-in ring, with sides about 2.5 cm/1 in high. Sprinkle with almonds. Bake for 35–40 minutes, split in half horizontally and leave to cool.

Spread the jam inside the bottom of the choux ring. Fill with the cream and strawberries, then replace the top half of the ring.

Mix the icing sugar with enough orange juice to make a coating consistency and drizzle over the ring. Allow to set.

200 | Pineapple Blitz Torte

Preparation time
30–40 minutes

Cooking time
30–35 minutes

Oven temperature
180C, 350F, gas 4

Makes 1 (20-cm/8-in) gâteau

Total calories
3505

You will need
100 g/4 oz plain flour
2 teaspoons baking powder
75 g/3 oz butter
225 g/8 oz caster sugar
3 eggs, separated
½ teaspoon vanilla essence
6 tablespoons milk
100 g/4 oz flaked almonds (optional)

For the filling
150 ml/¼ pint double cream, whipped
1 (227-g/8-oz) can pineapple pieces, drained

Sift the flour with the baking powder. Cream the butter and half of the sugar until light and fluffy. Beat in the egg yolks then the vanilla essence. Fold in the flour mixture with the milk and divide between two greased and floured 20-cm/8-in sandwich tins.

Whisk the egg whites until stiff, then whisk in the remaining sugar, a tablespoon at a time, until stiff. Spoon into a piping bag fitted with a large star-shaped nozzle and pipe a layer of stars over each sponge. Sprinkle with almonds, if using, and bake for 30–35 minutes. Leave in the tins for 10 minutes.

Place one cake, meringue side up, on a serving plate. Cover with the whipped cream and pineapple then top with the second cake layer, meringue side up.

Cook's Tip

You can use any kind of soft berry fruit to make this gâteau – try replacing the strawberries with raspberries, redcurrants, blackcurrants, loganberries or blackberries if liked.

Cook's Tip

It is necessary to drain the pineapple pieces thoroughly for this recipe or the cream will separate or curdle and the cake layers will become soggy. Drain well and dry slightly on absorbent kitchen paper.

201 | Apricot Cream Shortcake

Preparation time
40 minutes

Cooking time
25 minutes

Oven temperature
180 C, 350 F, gas 4

Makes 1 (23-cm/ 9-in) shortcake

Total calories
3420

You will need
75 g/3 oz butter
50 g/2 oz caster sugar
1 egg
175 g/6 oz plain flour, sifted
225 g/8 oz dried apricots
75 g/3 oz soft brown sugar
juice of 1 lemon
300 ml/½ pint water
25 g/1 oz cornflour, blended with 2 tablespoons water
150 ml/¼ pint double cream, whipped
2–3 tablespoons apricot jam, warmed and sieved
75 g/3 oz flaked almonds, toasted

Cream the butter with the sugar then beat in the egg. Stir in the flour and mix well. Knead lightly, divide in half and roll each piece into a 23-cm/9-in circle. Place on baking trays and prick with a fork. Chill.

To prepare the filling, place the apricots, brown sugar, lemon juice and water in a pan. Simmer for 25 minutes. Stir in the cornflour and simmer for 3 minutes then allow to cool.

Meanwhile, bake the shortcake for 15–20 minutes, leave to cool slightly then cool on a wire rack.

Place a shortcake round on a serving plate and cover with the apricot filling. Spread with the cream and top with the second round. Brush with the apricot jam and sprinkle with the almonds.

Cook's Tip

This is a good make-ahead cake – make the shortcake rounds and store in an airtight container for 2–3 days. Alternatively, freeze for up to 3 months. Defrost for 1–2 hours at room temperature then fill as above.

202 | Flaky Honey and Walnut Layer

Preparation time
30 minutes

Cooking time
about 10 minutes

Makes 1 (20-cm/ 8-in) gâteau

Total calories
3385

You will need
1 (215-g/7½-oz) packet frozen puff pastry, defrosted
oil for shallow frying
6 tablespoons clear honey
100 g/4 oz walnut halves, sliced
300 ml/½ pint double cream, whipped
icing sugar for dusting

Divide the pastry into three pieces and roll each out thinly on a floured surface to a 20-cm/8-in round.

Pour oil into a large frying pan to a depth of about 5 mm/¼ in and heat gently until just beginning to smoke. Carefully add a pastry circle and fry for 1–2 minutes on each side until golden and very puffy. Remove and drain very well on absorbent kitchen paper. Allow to cool.

Place one round on a serving plate and drizzle over half of the honey. Scatter with half the sliced walnuts and cover with half of the cream. Repeat the layers and finish with a pastry round. Sprinkle thickly with icing sugar and mark with a skewer in a pattern (see Cook's Tip).

Cook's Tip

To pattern the top of the gâteau, heat a metal skewer over a gas flame or an electric ring until red hot. Hold it carefully with an oven glove; as the hot end of the skewer makes contact with the sugar it will sizzle to caramelize.

203 | Blackcurrant Shortcake

Preparation time
30 minutes, plus chilling time

Cooking time
20 minutes

Oven temperature
200 C, 400 F, gas 6

Makes 1 (20-cm/ 8-in) shortcake

Total calories
3930

You will need
225 g/8 oz butter
75 g/3 oz soft brown sugar
225 g/8 oz plain flour, sifted
75 g/3 oz hazelnuts, toasted and chopped

For the filling and decoration
1 (397-g/14-oz) can blackcurrant pie filling
150 ml/¼ pint double cream, whipped

Beat the butter until soft then beat in the sugar. Stir in the flour until well mixed then stir in the hazelnuts. Mix to a firm dough, knead lightly, divide in half and roll each piece into a 20-cm/8-in circle. Place on greased baking trays, prick all over with a fork, cover and chill for 30 minutes.

Bake for about 20 minutes until golden. Leave on the trays for 5 minutes then carefully transfer to a wire rack. Cut one of the rounds into eight sections while still warm.

Place the whole round on a serving plate and spread with the pie filling. Pipe 8 large cream rosettes on top, then place the shortcake sections on top to serve.

Cook's Tip

To pipe cream, whip it until it stands in soft peaks – it will get slightly stiffer as it is pushed through the nozzle. Spoon into a piping bag fitted with a star or plain nozzle. Twist the top of the bag once or twice to press the cream *down into the nozzle and remove any air pockets. Press from the top of the bag and pipe small amounts at a time.*

204 | Tipsy Cinnamon Flake

Preparation time
35 minutes

Cooking time
8 – 12 minutes

Oven temperature
190 C, 375 F, gas 5

Makes 1 (23-cm/ 9-in) gâteau

Total calories
5340

You will need
175 g/6 oz butter or margarine
225 g/8 oz caster sugar
1 large egg, beaten
150 g/5 oz plain flour
1 tablespoon ground cinnamon

For the filling
300 ml/½ pint double cream
150 ml/¼ pint single cream
40 g/1½ oz cocoa powder
2 – 3 tablespoons brandy
6 – 8 tablespoons redcurrant jelly or damson jam
75 g/3 oz plain chocolate, grated to decorate

Cream the butter and sugar together until light and fluffy. Beat in the egg. Sift in the flour and cinnamon and stir to make a soft dough. Draw a 23-cm/9-in circle on five pieces of greaseproof paper and place each on a dampened baking tray. Spread about 3 tablespoons of the prepared dough in a thin layer on each prepared baking tray. Bake for 8 – 12 minutes, until just golden round the edge. Leave to stand for 5 minutes then transfer on the paper to a wire rack.

To make the filling, whip the creams with the cocoa and brandy. Place one pastry round on a serving plate, spread with a little of the jelly or jam, cover with some of the cream and top with a pastry round. Repeat the layers finishing with a layer of cream. Sprinkle with grated chocolate to serve.

Cook's Tip

Do not assemble the cake layers with their filling until about 30 minutes before serving or they will become too limp and soggy.

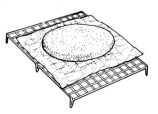

205 | Hazelnut Gâteau

Preparation time
50 minutes

Cooking time
20 minutes

Oven temperature
200 C, 400 F, gas 6

**Makes 1 (20-cm/
8-in) gâteau**

Total calories
3660

You will need
50 g/2 oz ground almonds
40 g/1½ oz hazelnuts, finely
   chopped
75 g/3 oz caster sugar
3 egg whites
100 g/4 oz plain chocolate
25 g/1 oz unsalted butter
100 ml/4 fl oz double cream

For the orange cream
100 g/4 oz unsalted butter
150 ml/¼ pint double cream
25 g/1 oz caster sugar
finely grated rind of ½ orange

For the decoration
50 g/2 oz hazelnuts, chopped
icing sugar to dust

Mix the almonds with the hazelnuts and half of the sugar. Stiffly whisk the egg whites, whisk in the remaining sugar and fold in the nut mixture. Spread into a greased and lined 20 × 30-cm/8 × 12-in Swiss roll tin. Bake for 20 minutes and leave to cool in the tin.

Melt the chocolate in a bowl over a pan of hot water. Add the butter and melt, cool slightly then fold in the whipped cream. For the orange cream, beat the butter. Whip the cream with the sugar, then add to the butter, a little at a time, mixing gently. Stir in the orange rind.

Cut the sponge into three 20-cm/8-in long pieces. Spread one with the chocolate cream. Top with another and chill to set. Spread with half the orange cream and top with the final sponge. Cover with the orange cream and coat with hazelnuts. Dust with the icing sugar.

Cook's Tip

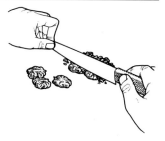

If liked, this gâteau can be coated with chopped walnuts instead of hazelnuts. The cream can also be flavoured with grated lemon rind instead of the orange.

206 | Gâteau Mount Pleasant

Preparation time
45 minutes

Cooking time
35 minutes

Oven temperature
200 C, 400 F, gas 6

**Makes 1 (20-cm/
8-in) gâteau**

Total calories
3360

You will need
100 g/4 oz caster sugar
4 eggs
100 g/4 oz plain flour
100 g/4 oz butter, melted
675 g/1½ lb cooking apples,
   peeled, cored and sliced
½ teaspoon ground cinnamon
2 tablespoons Calvados

For the topping
2 dessert apples
1 tablespoon sugar
juice of ½ lemon
3 tablespoons apricot jam
300 ml/½ pint whipping cream
½ teaspoon ground cinnamon

Whisk the sugar and eggs until thick over a pan of hot water. Remove from the heat and fold in the flour and butter. Pour into a greased and floured 20-cm/8-in deep round cake tin and bake for 35 minutes. Cool on a wire rack. Meanwhile, cook the apples with the cinnamon and about 2 tablespoons water to form a thick purée. Cool. Slice the cake into three layers and sprinkle the bottom and middle layer with the Calvados. Sandwich together with the cooled apple purée.

Core, slice and poach the apples in a little water with the sugar and lemon juice until softened but still firm in shape. Drain, cool then place on top of the cake. Warm the apricot jam and brush over the apple. Whip the cream with the cinnamon until thick then pipe around the cake.

Cook's Tip

Calvados is a liqueur made from apples that is especially popular in Normandy. It is also sometimes known as Apple Jack.

207 | Aladdin's Cave Gâteau

Preparation time
30 minutes

Cooking time
15 minutes

Oven temperature
190 C, 375 F, gas 5

**Makes 1
rectangular
gâteau**

Total calories
2600

You will need
4 eggs
100 g/4 oz caster sugar
100 g/4 oz self-raising flour
¼ teaspoon salt

For the filling
300 ml/½ pint double cream,
  whipped
2 teaspoons caster sugar
350 g/12 oz prepared soft fruits
25 g/1 oz icing sugar, sifted
a few fruits with stems for
  decoration (optional)

Place the eggs and sugar in a bowl set over a pan of hot water and whisk until thick. Sift the flour with the salt, remove the bowl from the heat and fold in the flour. Pour into a greased and floured 35 × 20-cm/14 × 8-in rectangular cake tin and bake for 15 minutes. Cool on a wire rack.

Carefully cut the sponge vertically in half and spread the bottom layer with whipped cream. Sprinkle with the caster sugar. Carefully position the second sponge layer on top of the cream at an angle so that its edge rests on the side of the plate and looks like an open jewellery box. Fill the open sponge and cream centre with the prepared fruit, allowing it to spill over the edge of the cake. Chill lightly before serving. Decorate as shown, if liked.

Cook's Tip

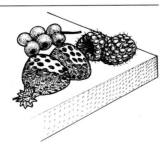

*Hulled raspberries,
strawberries and blackberries
along with topped and tailed
red and blackcurrants make
the ideal filling for this cake.*

208 | Tia Maria Torte

Preparation time
30 minutes, plus about
20 minutes standing
time

Cooking time
15–20 minutes

Oven temperature
200 C, 400 F, gas 6

**Makes 1 (23-cm/
9-in) gâteau**

Total calories
5805

You will need
75 g/3 oz self-raising flour
3 tablespoons cocoa powder
4 eggs
75 g/3 oz caster sugar

For the filling and decoration
1 recipe Sugar Syrup (see
  Chocolate Brandy Gâteau recipe
  198) flavoured with 2
  tablespoons Tia Maria
1 recipe Butter Icing (see
  Introduction)
few drops of coffee essence
25 g/1 oz chocolate vermicelli
12 small Florentines (see recipe
  239)

Sift the flour with the cocoa twice. Whisk the eggs with the sugar until thick then fold in the flour mixture. Spoon into two greased and lined 23-cm/9-in cake tins and bake for 15–20 minutes. Cool on a wire rack.

Place one cake on a board and drizzle over less than half of the syrup. Leave for about 10 minutes until absorbed. Flavour the butter icing with coffee essence to taste. Spread one-third over the soaked sponge. Cover with the second sponge and drizzle over the remaining syrup; leave for 10 minutes.

Reserve 3 tablespoons of the butter icing and use the rest to coat the top and sides of the cake. Coat the sides with chocolate vermicelli. Lightly mark the top with a fork, then score into 12 sections. Pipe a butter icing rosette on each portion and top with a Florentine.

Cook's Tip

Many good cooks shy away from making a gâteau because of the seemingly complicated decorations required to make them look good. Many can however be bought ready-made and look every bit as good as home-made. Try using shop-bought Florentines for the above cake or use wafer-thin mints, whole or cut into triangles, or other small biscuits, like chocolate fingers, miniature brandy snaps or even chocolate mint sticks.

209 | Cinnamon, Apple and Lemon Torte

Preparation time
30 minutes

Cooking time
50 minutes

Oven temperature
180 C, 350 F, gas 4

Makes 1 (19-cm/7½-in) gâteau

Total calories
3540

You will need
175 g/6 oz butter or margarine
175 g/6 oz soft light brown sugar
75 g/3 oz oat flakes
1 teaspoon ground cinnamon
450 g/1 lb cooking apples, peeled, cored and sliced
grated rind and juice of 1 lemon
2 eggs, beaten
100 g/4 oz self-raising flour
1 teaspoon ground mixed spice
150 ml/¼ pint whipping cream, whipped
3 tablespoons apricot jam, warmed

Melt 50 g/2 oz of the butter and fry 50 g/2 oz of the sugar with the oats and cinnamon until golden. Spoon into a greased and lined 19-cm/7½-in deep round cake tin and level the top.

Mix the apple with the lemon rind and juice. Cream the remaining butter and sugar together until light and fluffy, then gradually beat in the eggs. Sift the flour with the spice and fold into the egg mixture. Fold in the prepared apple. Spoon on top of the oat mixture and level the top. Bake for about 50 minutes then turn out onto a serving dish and allow to cool.

To serve, top the torte with the whipped cream and spoon or pipe lines of jam across the top. Swirl through the cream if liked.

210 | Gâteau St Honoré

Preparation time
50 minutes

Cooking time
15–20 minutes

Oven temperature
200 C, 400 F, gas 6

Makes 1 (15-cm/6-in) gâteau

Total calories
4815

You will need
100 g/4 oz plain flour
pinch of salt
75 g/3 oz butter
1 recipe Choux Pastry (see Introduction)
12 sugar cubes
½ recipe Confectioner's Custard (see Cook's Tip)
450 ml/¾ pint whipping cream
50 g/2 oz vanilla sugar
glacé cherries, angelica and crystallized violets to decorate

Mix the flour with the salt, rub in the butter then bind together with 2–3 tablespoons water. Roll out to a 15-cm/6-in circle and place on a greased baking tray.

Place the choux pastry in a piping bag fitted with a small plain nozzle and pipe small buns around the edge of the pastry circle, about 2.5 cm/1 in. in from the edge. Pipe the remaining choux pastry into buns of the same size onto a second greased baking tray. Bake both trays for 15–20 minutes then allow to cool.

Heat the sugar cubes with 2 tablespoons water to dissolve. Boil briskly to make a golden caramel. Dip the separate choux buns in the caramel and position on top of the choux buns on the pastry. Spoon the custard into the centre. Whip the cream with the vanilla sugar and spoon on top. Decorate with cherries, angelica and violets.

Cook's Tip

If liked, the jam can be drawn across the cream in a feather pattern. Pipe the jam across the cream in parallel lines. Draw the pointed end of a knife across the jam and cream alternately in opposite directions.

Cook's Tip

To make confectioner's custard, mix 2 egg yolks with 20 g/¾ oz sugar, 20 g/¾ oz flour, 15 g/½ oz cornflour and a little milk from 300 ml/½ pint milk. Boil the remaining milk, pour onto the egg mixture and beat well. Return to the pan and cook until smooth and thickened. Allow to cool. Whisk 1 egg white until stiff with 40 g/1½ oz caster sugar, fold into the cooled mixture and use as required.

211 | Ice Cream Coffee Gâteau

Preparation time
30 minutes, plus 6 hours freezing time

Makes 1 (15-cm/ 6-in) gâteau

Total calories
1560

You will need
2 tablespoons apricot jam
10 sponge fingers, halved
2 eggs, separated
2 tablespoons coffee essence
1 tablespoon medium dry sherry
4 tablespoons icing sugar
150 ml/$\frac{1}{4}$ pint double cream
melted chocolate and whipped cream to decorate

Gently heat the jam and brush the edges of the sponge fingers. Use to line the sides of a 15-cm/6-in round cake tin lined with greaseproof paper. Stand the biscuits around the edge, sugared sides facing out, pressing the biscuits close together.

Beat the egg yolks with the coffee essence and sherry. Whisk the egg whites until stiff. Gradually whisk in the icing sugar and whisk until thick and glossy. Fold into the coffee mixture. Whip the cream and fold in. Pour into the prepared tin and freeze until firm, about 6 hours.

To serve, turn out of the tin and decorate with drizzled melted chocolate and whipped cream.

Cook's Tip

Remove the gâteau from the freezer to the refrigerator about 30 minutes before serving to allow the ice cream to soften slightly for easy cutting.

212 | Sachertorte

Preparation time
50 minutes

Cooking time
50–60 minutes

Oven temperature
180 C, 350 F, gas 4

Makes 1 (23-cm/ 9-in) gâteau

Total calories
6590

You will need
100 g/4 oz butter
175 g/6 oz caster sugar
175 g/6 oz plain chocolate, melted
1 teaspoon vanilla essence
6 egg yolks
75 g/3 oz plain flour
8 egg whites
6 tablespoons apricot jam, warmed

For the chocolate icing
225 g/8 oz plain chocolate
100 ml/4 fl oz double cream
350 g/12 oz icing sugar, sifted
whipped cream and chocolate curls to decorate

Cream the butter with the sugar until light and fluffy. Beat in the melted chocolate and vanilla. Gradually add the egg yolks and fold in the flour. Whisk the egg whites until stiff and fold in. Spoon into a greased and floured 23-cm/9-in loose-bottomed cake tin and bake for 50–60 minutes. Leave to cool in the tin for 30 minutes then turn out onto a wire rack.

Slice the cake horizontally and sandwich together with the warmed apricot jam.

Melt the chocolate in a bowl over hot water, then beat in the cream and icing sugar. Allow to cool for 10 minutes then spread over the top and sides of the cake. Leave to set for 30 minutes then decorate with swirls of cream and chocolate curls.

Cook's Tip

A smooth finish to the icing can be achieved if a wet palette knife is smoothed across the surface after spreading.

213 | Mocha Brandy Gâteau

Preparation time
30 minutes

Cooking time
45 minutes

Oven temperature
180 C, 350 F, gas 4

Makes 1 (20-cm/8-in) gâteau

Total calories
4140

You will need
175 g/6 oz plain flour
2 teaspoons baking powder
½ teaspoon salt
150 g/5 oz soft brown sugar
2 eggs, separated
6 tablespoons corn oil
4 tablespoons milk
1 tablespoon cocoa powder
1 tablespoon coffee essence

For the glaze
100 g/4 oz granulated sugar
5 tablespoons strong black coffee
1 tablespoon cocoa powder
2 tablespoons brandy
300 ml/½ pint double cream
25 g/1 oz toasted flaked almonds

Sift the flour, baking powder and salt together. Mix in the sugar. Add the egg yolks, oil, milk, cocoa and coffee essence and beat well. Whisk the egg whites until stiff and fold in. Pour into a greased and floured 20-cm/8-in shallow cake tin and bake for 45 minutes. Allow to cool slightly in the tin then turn out onto a wire rack to cool.

To make the glaze, heat the sugar, black coffee, cocoa and 4 tablespoons water to dissolve. Bring to the boil and simmer for 5 minutes. Remove from the heat and add the brandy. Prick the surface of the cake with a skewer and return to the tin. Pour over the hot glaze and leave to soak. To serve, place on a plate and top with whipped cream and almonds.

Cook's Tip

If liked, the cake can be soaked with a rum-flavoured glaze. Simply use 2 tablespoons dark rum instead of the brandy.

214 | Loganberry Gâteau

Preparation time
50 minutes

Cooking time
30–35 minutes

Oven temperature
190 C, 375 F, gas 5

Makes 1 (20-cm/8-in) square gâteau

Total calories
3465

You will need
4 eggs
100 g/4 oz caster sugar
grated rind of ½ lemon
75 g/3 oz plain flour
25 g/1 oz cornflour
25 g/1 oz butter, melted

For the filling and decoration
450 g/1 lb loganberries
6 tablespoons sherry
450 ml/¾ pint double cream, whipped
finely grated chocolate

Place the eggs, sugar and lemon rind in a bowl and whisk over a pan of hot water until thick. Fold in the flour, cornflour and butter then pour into a greased and base-lined 20-cm/8-in square cake tin. Bake for 30–35 minutes then turn out to cool on a wire rack.

Reserve half of the loganberries for decoration. Cut the cake into three layers, sprinkle the bottom layer with a little sherry and spread with some whipped cream and a portion of loganberries. Repeat the layers once more then top with the final sponge layer. Cover the sides with cream and coat with grated chocolate.

Cover the top with a layer of cream and pipe a border around the edge. Fill the centre with the reserved loganberries.

Cook's Tip

When available, decorate the top of the cake with a few loganberry, raspberry or mint leaves to add yet more colour.

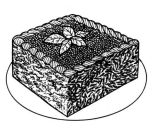

215 | Autumn Gâteau

Preparation time
40 minutes

Cooking time
1¾ hours

Oven temperature
160 C, 325 F, gas 3

**Makes 1 (18-cm/
7-in) square
gâteau**

Total calories
5170

You will need
175 g/6 oz butter or margarine
175 g/6 oz caster sugar
3 eggs
2 medium cooking apples, peeled,
cored and grated
200 g/7 oz self-raising flour
75 g/3 oz desiccated coconut

For the filling and decoration
2 tablespoons cornflour
2 tablespoons clear honey
250 ml/8 fl oz apple juice
1 large red dessert apple
juice of ½ lemon
300 ml/½ pint double cream
shredded coconut

Cream the butter with the sugar until pale and fluffy. Gradually beat in the eggs and stir in the grated apples. Fold in the flour with the coconut and turn into a greased and base-lined 18-cm/7-in square cake tin. Bake for 1¾ hours then cool on a wire rack.

Blend the cornflour with the honey and a little apple juice. Heat the remaining juice until warm then stir in the cornflour mixture. Return to the pan, bring to the boil, stirring constantly, and cook for 3–4 minutes. Cool.

Core and slice the apple and sprinkle with the lemon juice. Cut the cake in half. Whip the cream and reserve a little for piping. Gradually add the cornflour mixture to the cream and chill. Spread the base with some of this mixture, cover with the second layer and spread with the remaining mixture. Sprinkle the cake with shredded coconut, pipe the cream and decorate as shown.

Cook's Tip

*If preferred you could use
150 ml/¼ pint double cream
and 150 ml/¼ pint whipping
cream for this recipe. This
mixture will still whip and
holds its shape and will be a
little less expensive.*

216 | Gâteau Pithiviers

Preparation time
25 minutes

Cooking time
30–45 minutes

Oven temperature
230 C, 450 F, gas 8
200 C, 400 F, gas 6

**Makes 1 (23-cm/
9-in) gâteau**

Total calories
3335

You will need
1 (398-g/14-oz) packet frozen puff
pastry, defrosted
100 g/4 oz ground almonds
100 g/4 oz caster sugar
40 g/1½ oz unsalted butter, melted
2 egg yolks
2 tablespoons double cream
2 tablespoons dark rum
beaten egg to glaze
1 tablespoon icing sugar, sifted

Roll out the pastry on a floured surface to make two 23-cm/9-in circles. Line a 20-cm/8-in pie plate with one.

Cream the almonds with the sugar, butter, egg yolks, cream and rum and spoon into the pie plate. Brush the pastry rim with water then top with the second pastry circle. Seal and crimp the edges and push up to make petal shapes. Decorate the top with any pastry trimmings. Glaze with beaten egg and bake at the higher temperature for 10–15 minutes. Reduce the oven temperature and cook for a further 20–30 minutes, or until golden and cooked through.

Remove from the oven, dust with icing sugar and place under a hot grill to caramelize the sugar.

Cook's Tip

*This is a delicious gâteau to
serve with single cream or
natural yogurt or even a
scoop of ice cream.*

217 | Almond Gâteau

Preparation time
40 minutes

Cooking time
50–55 minutes

Oven temperature
160 C, 325 F, gas 3

**Makes 1 (20-cm/
8-in) gâteau**

Total calories
5015

You will need
3 eggs
200 g/7 oz golden syrup
75 g/3 oz self-raising flour
100 g/4 oz ground almonds
½ teaspoon almond essence

For the filling and topping
225 g/8 oz cream cheese
150 ml/¼ pint soured cream
3 tablespoons golden syrup
grated rind and juice of 1 lemon
few drops of almond essence
1½ teaspoons powdered gelatine
1 tablespoon hot water
300 ml/½ pint double cream
100 g/4 oz flaked almonds, toasted
few blanched almonds, toasted
few lemon slices, quartered

Whisk the eggs with the golden syrup until creamy. Fold in the flour, ground almonds and almond essence. Turn into a greased and base-lined 20-cm/8-in round cake tin. Bake for 50–55 minutes and turn out to cool on a wire rack, removing the greaseproof paper while still hot.

To make the filling, beat together the first five ingredients. Dissolve the gelatine in the hot water. Whisk into the cheese mixture and chill until almost set. Slice the cake and spoon the filling over the base. Top with the remaining half.

Whip the cream and spread a little over the sides of the cake. Coat the sides with the flaked almonds. Cover the top with cream and pipe swirls around the edge. Decorate with whole almonds and quartered lemon slices.

Cook's Tip

Press the almonds onto the cream-coated sides of the cake using a palette knife.

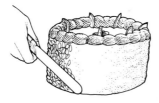

218 | Austrian Coffee Gâteau

Preparation time
30 minutes

Cooking time
40–50 minutes

Oven temperature
160 C, 325 F, gas 3

**Makes 1 (20-cm/
8-in) ring cake**

Total calories
3280

You will need
100 g/4 oz butter or margarine
100 g/4 oz caster sugar
2 eggs
100 g/4 oz self-raising flour
2 tablespoons coffee essence
grated rind of 1 lemon

For the syrup
150 ml/¼ pint black coffee
50 g/2 oz caster sugar
1 tablespoon brandy

For the decoration
300 ml/½ pint double cream
chocolate curls

Cream the butter with the sugar until light and fluffy. Add the eggs, one at a time, adding a little flour with the second egg. Beat in the coffee essence, then fold in the remaining flour with the lemon rind. Turn into a greased 20-cm/8-in ring tin and bake for 40–50 minutes. Turn out to cool on a wire rack.

To make the syrup, heat the coffee with the sugar until dissolved. Add the brandy and simmer for 5 minutes. Cool. Prick the cake with a skewer and pour over the syrup, a little at a time, until it is all absorbed.

Whip the cream and spread a little all over the cake. Pipe the remainder around the edge and decorate with chocolate curls.

Cook's Tip

Place the cake on a wire rack with a large plate underneath to catch the syrup. This can be saved and poured over the cake again until all is absorbed.

219 | Tipsy Ring

Preparation time
25 minutes

Cooking time
40–50 minutes

Oven temperature
160 C, 325 F, gas 3

Makes 1 (23-cm/ 9-in) ring cake

Total calories
3785

You will need
100 g/4 oz butter or margarine
100 g/4 oz caster sugar
5 tablespoons ginger wine
2 eggs
100 g/4 oz self-raising flour
25 g/1 oz cocoa powder

For the icing and decoration
175 g/6 oz plain chocolate
50 g/2 oz butter
150 ml/¼ pint double cream
few pieces of cystallized ginger

Cream the butter with the sugar and 2 tablespoons of the ginger wine until fluffy. Gradually beat in the eggs then fold in the flour sifted with the cocoa. Turn into a greased 23-cm/9-in ring tin and bake for 40–50 minutes. Turn out to cool on a wire rack. Whilst the cake is still warm drizzle the remaining ginger wine over it.

Melt the chocolate with the butter. Allow to cool slightly then drizzle over the cake. Whip the cream until stiff and pipe around the top edge of the cake. Decorate with crystallized ginger.

220 | Praline Gâteau

Preparation time
45 minutes

Cooking time
15–20 minutes

Oven temperature
180 C, 350 F, gas 4

Makes 1 (20-cm/ 8-in) gâteau

Total calories
3690

You will need
100 g/4 oz caster sugar
3 eggs
75 g/3 oz plain flour
40 g/1½ oz butter or margarine, melted
grated rind of 1 lemon

For the praline
100 g/4 oz split almonds
150 g/5 oz caster sugar

For the filling and decoration
300 ml/½ pint double cream

Whisk the sugar and eggs in a bowl over a pan of hot water until thick. Fold in the flour, butter and lemon rind and divide between two greased and base-lined 20-cm/ 8-in sandwich tins. Bake for 15–20 minutes. Allow to cool slightly then turn out onto a wire rack.

Place the almonds and sugar in a pan and heat to melt the sugar. Cook until the sugar caramelizes and turns golden. Pour onto an oiled tin and allow to set. Crush finely.

Whip the cream and mix some with a little of the praline to sandwich the cake layers together. Spread the sides with more cream and coat with the praline. Spread the remaining cream on top and pipe around the cake edge with rosettes. Sprinkle with any remaining praline.

Cook's Tip

Use 1 tablespoon coffee essence instead of the cocoa powder and rum instead of ginger wine if liked. Soak the cake in rum instead of ginger wine but ice and decorate as above.

Cook's Tip

The praline is best crushed in a polythene bag with a rolling pin. Prepared praline can be kept for a good few weeks in an airtight tin.

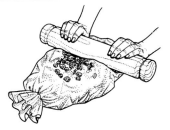

221 | Chocolate Brandy Snap Gâteau

Preparation time
45 minutes

Cooking time
25–30 minutes

Oven temperature
180 C, 350 F, gas 4

**Makes 1 (20-cm/
8-in) gâteau**

Total calories
2720

You will need
3 eggs
75 g/3 oz caster sugar
65 g/2½ oz plain flour
15 g/½ oz cocoa powder
½ teaspoon baking powder

For the filling and decoration
300 ml/½ pint double cream
1 (100-g/3½-oz) packet brandy
   snaps
ribbon
25 g/1 oz plain chocolate, melted

Whisk the eggs and sugar in a bowl over a pan of hot water until thick. Sift the flour with the cocoa powder and baking powder and fold into the egg mixture. Divide between two greased and base-lined 20-cm/8-in sandwich tins and bake for 25–30 minutes. Turn out to cool on a wire rack.

Whip the cream and use a little to sandwich the cake layers together. Spread a little round the sides and press on the brandy snaps. Tie a ribbon around the cake to keep the brandy snaps secure until serving. Spread the remaining cream over the top of the cake. Place the chocolate in a piping bag fitted with a writing nozzle and drizzle over the cream. Swirl with a skewer.

Cook's Tip

To slice the cake, release the ribbon, and cut with a sawing action using a serrated knife.

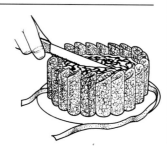

222 | Brandied Chestnut Roll

Preparation time
35–40 minutes

Cooking time
10–12 minutes

Oven temperature
220 C, 425 F, gas 7

**Makes 1 (23-cm/
9-in) roll**

Total calories
4105

You will need
3 eggs
100 g/4 oz caster sugar
100 g/4 oz plain flour
2 tablespoons brandy
caster sugar to dust

For the filling and decoration
300 ml/½ pint double cream
1 tablespoon caster sugar
1 (250-g/8¾-oz) can chestnut
   spread
175 g/6 oz plain chocolate
15 g/½ oz butter
2 tablespoons brandy
few marrons glacés (optional)

Whisk the eggs with the sugar until pale and thick. Fold in the flour and brandy and pour into a greased and lined 23 × 33-cm/9 × 13-in Swiss roll tin. Bake for 10–12 minutes. Turn out onto a sheet of greaseproof paper dusted with caster sugar placed on a damp teatowel. Trim the edges from the cake then roll up to enclose the paper and towel. Cool on a wire rack.

Whip the cream with the sugar until stiff, then stir half the cream into the chestnut spread and mix until smooth. Carefully unroll the cake, remove the paper and teatowel and spread with the chestnut cream. Re-roll.

Melt the chocolate with the butter and brandy. Cool then use to cover the cake completely. Mark with a fork when half set. Decorate with the reserved cream and marrons glacés if liked.

Cook's Tip

Chestnut spread can be bought from specialist shops and delicatessens. It is usually imported from France and is called Crème de Marrons.

223 | *Fresh Lime Gâteau*

Preparation time
40 minutes

Cooking time
8–10 minutes

Oven temperature
200 C, 400 F, gas 6

Makes 1 (18-cm/ 7-in) roll

Total calories
1870

You will need
2 eggs
50 g/2 oz caster sugar
50 g/2 oz plain flour
grated rind of 1 lime
caster sugar for dusting

For the filling and decoration
300 ml/½ pint double cream
juice of ½ lime
slices of fresh lime

Whisk the eggs with the sugar over a pan of hot water until very thick. Fold in the flour with the grated lime rind and spoon into a greased and lined 18 × 28-cm/7 × 11-in Swiss roll tin. Bake for 8–10 minutes. Turn out onto a sheet of greaseproof paper dusted with caster sugar placed on a damp teatowel. Trim the edges from the cake then roll up to enclose the paper and towel. Cool on a wire rack.

Whip the cream with the lime juice. Carefully unroll the cake, remove the paper and teatowel and spread with some of the cream. Re-roll and place on a plate. Cover with the remaining cream and pipe rosettes along the bottom edge. Decorate with lime slices.

224 | *Black Forest Gâteau*

Preparation time
50 minutes

Cooking time
35–40 minutes

Oven temperature
190 C, 375 F, gas 5

Makes 1 (20-cm/ 8-in) gâteau

Total calories
2660

You will need
3 eggs
100 g/4 oz caster sugar
75 g/3 oz plain flour
15 g/½ oz cocoa powder

For the filling
1 (425-g/15-oz) can stoned black cherries
1 tablespoon arrowroot powder
Kirsch
300 ml/½ pint double cream
grated chocolate to decorate

Whisk the eggs with the sugar in a bowl over a pan of hot water until thick. Sift the flour with the cocoa and fold into the egg mixture. Pour into a greased and lined 20-cm/8-in deep, round cake tin and bake for 35–40 minutes. Turn out to cool on a wire rack.

Drain the juice from the cherries and mix with the arrowroot. Return to the pan and cook until clear and thickened, stirring constantly. Stir in the cherries; cool.

Cut the cake in half and sprinkle with a little Kirsch. Whip the cream and pipe a circle around the outside edge of the base. Fill the centre with half of the cherry mixture. Place the sponge layer on top. Coat the sides with cream and grated chocolate. Pipe swirls of cream on top and fill the centre with the remaining cherries. Sprinkle the cream swirls with chocolate to finish.

Cook's Tip

To make a St Clement's Gâteau, simply use the grated rind of 1 small orange instead of the lime in the recipe above; use the juice of ½ lemon for the cream instead of lime juice; and decorate with orange and lemon slices.

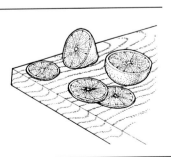

Cook's Tip

If liked, chocolate-flavoured cake covering may be used to make the grated chocolate decoration for this gâteau.

225 | Hazelnut Meringue Gâteau

Preparation time
40 minutes

Cooking time
2½–3 hours

Oven temperature
110C, 225F, gas ¼

**Makes 1 (20-cm/
8-in) gâteau**

Total calories
3830

You will need
6 egg whites
350 g/12 oz caster sugar
2 teaspoons lemon juice
175 g/6 oz ground hazelnuts
25 g/1 oz hazelnuts, finely
  chopped

For the filling
100 g/4 oz plain chocolate
150 ml/¼ pint soured cream
150 ml/¼ pint double cream,
  whipped
1 tablespoon brandy
chopped mixed nuts and chocolate
  curls to decorate

Whisk the egg whites until stiff. Gradually whisk in half of the sugar and the lemon juice until thick and glossy. Fold in the remaining sugar and ground nuts. Spread over three baking trays lined with rice paper marked into 20-cm/8-in circles. Sprinkle one with the chopped nuts (this will be the top). Bake for 2½–3 hours until crisp and dry. Cool on a wire rack and trim away any rice paper from the edges.

Melt the chocolate and stir in the soured cream. Fold in the whipped cream and brandy and chill lightly.

Pipe or spoon the filling onto the bottom and middle layers of the gâteau, reserving a little for the decoration, and sandwich together. Decorate the top with the reserved filling piped into swirls, chopped nuts and chocolate curls. Allow to stand for 1 hour before serving.

Cook's Tip

**To make your own substitute
soured cream, simply stir 2–3
teaspoons lemon juice into
150 ml/¼ pint double cream.**

226 | Chocolate Roulade

Preparation time
35 minutes, plus
overnight cooling

Cooking time
25–30 minutes

Oven temperature
180C, 350F, gas 4

**Makes 1 (20-cm/
8-in) roll**

Total calories
3065

You will need
150 g/5 oz plain chocolate, broken
  into pieces
3 tablespoons water
4 eggs, separated
150 g/5 oz caster sugar

For the filling and decoration
icing sugar for dusting
300 ml/½ pint double cream,
  whipped
chocolate rose leaves (see Cook's
  Tip 187)

Melt the chocolate with the water in a pan. Whisk the egg yolks with half the sugar until thick, then whisk in the chocolate mixture. Whisk the egg whites until stiff, then whisk in the remaining sugar. Fold into the chocolate mixture. Turn into a greased and lined 20 × 30-cm/ 8 × 12-in Swiss roll tin and bake for 25–30 minutes, until firm. Leave to cool for 5 minutes, then cover with a clean, damp teatowel and place in the refrigerator overnight.

Remove the cloth and turn onto a sheet of greaseproof paper dusted thickly with icing sugar. Peel off the paper.

Spread three-quarters of the cream evenly over the roulade and roll up like a Swiss roll. Pipe the remaining cream along the top and decorate with chocolate leaves.

Cook's Tip

**In the depths of winter if you
cannot find rose leaves to
make the chocolate leaves,
try using holly leaves instead.**

227 | Nougatine Meringue

Preparation time
50 minutes

Cooking time
40 minutes

Oven temperature
160 C, 325 F, gas 3

**Makes 1 (30-cm/
12-in) slice**

Total calories
5785

You will need
200 g/7 oz stoned dates
225 g/8 oz sponge fingers
200 g/7 oz walnuts
1 teaspoon baking powder
8 egg whites
400 g/14 oz caster sugar

For the decoration
300 ml/½ pint double cream
150 ml/¼ pint single cream
glacé cherries, halved

Roughly chop the dates, sponge fingers and walnuts into 1-cm/½-in pieces. Toss with the baking powder. Whisk the egg whites until stiff. Fold in the sugar and whisk in again until soft peaks form. Fold in the date mixture and spread into a 20 × 30-cm/8 × 12-in Swiss roll tin lined with silicone paper. Bake for about 40 minutes until lightly browned. Cool in the tin.

Turn onto a wire rack, remove the paper and cut in half lengthways. Slide one half onto a plate.

Whip the creams together. Spread half on one meringue slice, then top with the second slice. Pipe or spread the remaining cream over the top and decorate with glacé cherries.

Cook's Tip

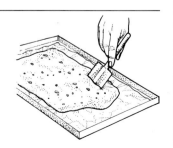

**Remember to leave a 1-cm/
½-in border around the sides
when placing the meringue
mixture in the Swiss roll tin –
this will allow the meringue
mixture to swell evenly
during cooking.**

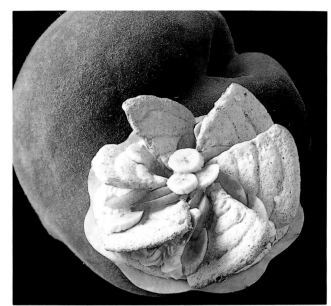

228 | Banana Peach Vacherin

Preparation time
45 minutes

Cooking time
30–40 minutes

Oven temperature
190 C, 375 F, gas 5

**Makes 1 (23–
25-cm/9–10-in)
gâteau**

Total calories
2760

You will need
3 egg whites
175 g/6 oz caster sugar
75 g/3 oz ground walnuts

For the filling
2 peaches
1 tablespoon icing sugar
2 bananas, peeled, sliced and
    tossed in 1 tablespoon lemon
    juice
300 ml/½ pint double cream,
    whipped

Line two baking trays with rice paper and mark a 20-cm/8-in circle on each. Mark one circle into six segments.

Whisk the egg whites until stiff. Gradually whisk in the sugar until thick and glossy. Fold in the walnuts. Spoon into a piping bag fitted with a 1-cm/½-in plain nozzle and pipe concentric circles of the meringue towards the centre of the full marked round. Pipe the remaining meringue to form six wedge shapes, leaving in both cases room for the meringue to spread slightly. Bake for 30–40 minutes until crisp; cool on a wire rack.

Peel and slice one of the peaches. Fold the icing sugar, bananas (reserving a few slices) and the sliced peach into the whipped cream and pile onto the meringue base. Top with the six wedges positioned at an angle. Decorate with peach and banana slices.

Cook's Tip

**Fill the vacherin at least 1
hour before serving to ensure
neat portioning of the
wedges. However, do not fill
more than 4 hours before
serving for best results.**

229 | Chestnut Vacherin

Preparation time
40 minutes

Cooking time
35–40 minutes

Oven temperature
180C, 350F, gas 4

Makes 1 (20-cm/8-in) gâteau

Total calories
3200

You will need
4 egg whites
225 g/8 oz caster sugar
½ teaspoon vanilla essence
100 g/4 oz hazelnuts, finely ground

For the filling
225 g/8 oz canned chestnut purée
50 g/2 oz icing sugar, sifted
2 tablespoons dark rum
150 ml/¼ pint double cream

For the decoration
150 ml/¼ pint double cream, whipped
a few whole hazelnuts
25 g/1 oz plain chocolate, grated

Whisk the egg whites until stiff, gradually beat in the sugar until thick and glossy. Add the vanilla essence and fold in the hazelnuts. Divide the mixture between two greased 20-cm/8-in sandwich tins, lined with non-stick paper. Bake for 35–40 minutes. Cool on a wire rack.

Whisk the chestnut purée with the icing sugar and rum. Whip the cream and fold into the chestnut mixture. Use half of this filling to sandwich the cake layers together. Spread the remaining filling over the top of the cake and swirl attractively.

Decorate the cake with rosettes of whipped cream and whole hazelnuts. Fill the centre with grated chocolate. Slice to serve.

230 | Ritz Meringue

Preparation time
20 minutes

Cooking time
30 minutes

Oven temperature
180C, 350F, gas 4

Makes 1 (23-cm/9-in) gâteau

Total calories
3980

You will need
3 egg whites
½ teaspoon baking powder
225 g/8 oz sugar
16 Ritz biscuits, crushed
25 g/1 oz flaked almonds, crushed
50 g/2 oz walnuts, coarsely ground
300 ml/½ pint double cream, whipped
200 g/7 oz chocolate caraque (see Cook's Tip 197)

Whisk the egg whites until stiff, then sift in the baking powder. Whisk in the sugar, a tablespoon at a time, until the meringue stands in peaks. Fold in the biscuit crumbs and nuts and pour into a greased and lined 23-cm/9-in loose-bottomed cake tin. Bake for 30 minutes, then cool in the tin.

Place on a serving plate and cover with the whipped cream. Arrange the chocolate caraque around the edge and all over the top.

Cook's Tip

This is the perfect tea time gâteau to serve at any time of the year. In winter try it with lemon tea, in summer with iced coffee or tea.

Cook's Tip

This tasty gâteau can also be made using other slightly salted cracker biscuits similar to Ritz. Remember to crush the biscuits and not to use any type that is too salty or distinctive for this sweet recipe.

231 | Hummingbird Pavlova

Preparation time
40 minutes

Cooking time
1 hour

Oven temperature
150 C, 300 F, gas 2

Makes 1 (23-cm/9-in) gâteau

Total calories
2265

You will need
4 egg whites
pinch of salt
225 g/8 oz caster sugar
1 teaspoon white wine vinegar or lemon juice
2 teaspoons cornflour
50 g/2 oz walnuts, chopped

For the decoration
300 ml/½ pint double cream, whipped
1 (227-g/8-oz) can pineapple slices, drained
2–3 bananas
1 tablespoon lemon juice
3 kiwi fruit

Whisk the egg whites and salt together until stiff, then gradually whisk in the sugar until the mixture stands in stiff peaks. Lightly whisk in the vinegar or lemon juice. Sift the cornflour over the meringue and fold in with the walnuts. Pile onto a baking tray lined with silicone paper and spread into a 23-cm/9-in round. Hollow out the centre slightly.

Bake for 1 hour. Cool on a wire rack, then peel off the paper and place on a serving plate.

Spread the cream in a layer over the pavlova. Cut the pineapple into neat slices. Slice the bananas and toss in the lemon juice. Peel and slice the kiwi fruit. Arrange all the fruit over the cream to serve.

Cook's Tip

The vinegar or lemon juice is an essential part of the pavlova meringue recipe since it ensures that the centre stays soft and marshmallow-like in texture whilst the outside is crisp, so don't be tempted to omit it.

232 | Walnut Brandy Meringue

Preparation time
40 minutes

Cooking time
1–1½ hours

Oven temperature
140 C, 275 F, gas 1

Makes 1 (23-cm/9-in) gâteau

Total calories
3975

You will need
4 egg whites
225 g/8 oz caster sugar
50 g/2 oz walnuts, finely chopped

For the filling
50 g/2 oz plain chocolate, broken into pieces
2 tablespoons brandy
4 egg yolks, beaten
25 g/1 oz caster sugar
450 ml/¾ pint double cream, whipped
Maltesers

Whisk the egg whites until stiff then whisk in the sugar until thick and glossy. Fold in the walnuts and spread into two 23-cm/9-in rounds on baking trays lined with silicone paper. Bake for 1–1½ hours until crisp. Cool on a wire rack, then peel off the paper.

Put the chocolate, brandy, egg yolks and sugar in a bowl over a pan of simmering water. Cook until the chocolate melts and the custard coats the back of a spoon. Leave until cold.

Fold two-thirds of the whipped cream into the chocolate mixture and use to sandwich the meringue rounds together. Place on a serving plate.

Pipe the remaining whipped cream around the edge and decorate with Maltesers.

Cook's Tip

This meringue can also be decorated with candied coffee beans, small pieces of chocolate flake or chocolate-coated whole nuts, instead of the Maltesers if liked.

Biscuits and Cookies

A dip into this treasure trove of recipes will bring a barrel, tin or boxful of tempting biscuits and cookies to satisfy the most particular of tastes. There are recipes for homely and crumbly biscuits, for rolled out, shaped, piped, cut or stamped out crisp treats and for cookies to make in a roll then cut and bake.

233 | Chocolate Caramel Slices

Preparation time
20–25 minutes

Cooking time
about 35–40 minutes

Oven temperature
180 C, 350 F, gas 4

Makes 14

Calories
275 per slice

You will need
100 g/4 oz butter
50 g/2 oz caster sugar
175 g/6 oz plain flour, sifted

For the filling
100 g/4 oz butter
50 g/2 oz caster sugar
2 tablespoons golden syrup
1 (196-g/6.1-oz) can condensed milk

For the topping
100 g/4 oz plain chocolate
15 g/½ oz butter

Cream the butter and sugar until light and fluffy. Add the flour and stir until the mixture binds together. Knead until smooth. Roll out on a floured surface to line a greased 20-cm/8-in shallow, square tin and prick well. Bake for 25–30 minutes then allow to cool in the tin.

Place the filling ingredients in a saucepan and stir until dissolved. Bring slowly to the boil, then cook, stirring, for 5–7 minutes. Cool slightly, then pour over the cold biscuit mixture and leave to set.

To make the topping, melt the chocolate with the butter in a bowl over a pan of simmering water and spread over the filling. Leave until set then cut into slices.

234 | Chocolate Chip Biscuits

Preparation time
10–15 minutes

Cooking time
15–20 minutes

Oven temperature
180 C, 350 F, gas 4

Makes about 30

Calories
80 per biscuit

You will need
100 g/4 oz butter or margarine
50 g/2 oz caster sugar
1 egg, beaten
150 g/5 oz self-raising flour, sifted
175 g/6 oz plain chocolate, chopped

Cream the butter and the sugar together until light and fluffy. Add the egg and beat well. Fold in the flour and chocolate.

Place teaspoons of the mixture, a little apart, on greased baking trays. Bake for 15–20 minutes then transfer to a wire rack to cool.

Cook's Tip

You will find that the chocolate will melt faster and with little risk of scorching if you grate it before melting with the butter.

Cook's Tip

You can use 175 g/6 oz plain or milk chocolate polka dots, instead of ordinary chocolate in this recipe, dispensing with the need to chop the chocolate.

235 | Ginger Biscuits

Preparation time
10–15 minutes

Cooking time
20 minutes

Oven temperature
190 C, 375 F, gas 5

Makes 12–14

Calories
180–155 per biscuit

You will need
225 g/8 oz plain flour
1 teaspoon ground ginger
100 g/4 oz butter or margarine
100 g/4 oz molasses sugar
100 g/4 oz cane syrup

Sift the flour with the ginger. Cream the butter with the sugar until light and fluffy. Add the flour mixture with the cane syrup and knead until smooth.

Roll out on a floured surface and stamp out rounds using a 7.5-cm/3-in cutter. Place on greased baking trays.

Bake for 20 minutes, then transfer to a wire rack to cool.

236 | Digestive Biscuits

Preparation time
15 minutes

Cooking time
15–20 minutes

Oven temperature
190 C, 375 F, gas 5

Makes about 22

Calories
65 per biscuit

You will need
175 g/6 oz wholemeal flour
25 g/1 oz medium oatmeal
½ teaspoon salt
1 teaspoon baking powder
75 g/3 oz butter or margarine
40 g/1½ oz soft brown sugar
2–3 tablespoons milk

Mix the flour and oatmeal together, then sift in the salt and baking powder. Rub in the butter, then stir in the sugar. Add the milk and mix to a stiff dough. Roll out thinly on a floured surface, prick well and cut into 6-cm/2½-in rounds with a plain cutter. Place on greased baking trays.

Bake for 15–20 minutes then cool on a wire rack.

Cook's Tip

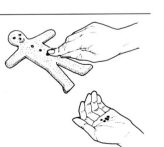

This mixture can also be used to make 6–7 gingerbread men. Use a cutter and make buttons or eyes and mouths, from raisins and slivers of glacé cherries.

Cook's Tip

These digestives may be coated with a little melted chocolate after cooling. You will need about 150 g/5 oz melted chocolate to spread on one side of the biscuits.

237 | Tollhouse Rockies

Preparation time
10–15 minutes

Cooking time
20 minutes

Oven temperature
200C, 400F, gas 6

Makes 12

Calories
195 per cookie

You will need
225 g/8 oz plain flour
2 teaspoons baking powder
$\frac{1}{4}$ teaspoon salt
100 g/4 oz butter or margarine
100 g/4 oz sugar
grated rind of 1 orange
75 g/3 oz plain chocolate chips or
    polka dots
1 egg, beaten

Sift the flour, baking powder and salt into a bowl. Rub in the butter until the mixture resembles fine bread-crumbs. Stir in the sugar, orange rind and chocolate chips, mixing well. Add the egg and mix to a firm dough.

Divide the dough into 12 portions and place in irregular heaps on greased baking trays, allowing plenty of space between each to spread.

Bake for about 20 minutes or until well risen and golden brown. Cool on a wire rack. Eat within 2–3 days.

238 | Chocolate Flake Fingers

Preparation Time
15 minutes

Cooking time
40 minutes

Oven temperature
160C, 325F, gas 3

Makes 10

Calories
410 per finger

You will need

For the base
225 g/8 oz butter
100 g/4 oz icing sugar, sifted
grated rind of $\frac{1}{2}$ lemon
grated rind of $\frac{1}{2}$ orange
225 g/8 oz plain flour
100 g/4 oz cornflour
$\frac{1}{4}$ teaspoon salt

For the topping
100 g/4 oz plain dessert chocolate
1 tablespoon golden syrup
5 chocolate flake bars
4 tablespoons finely chopped
    mixed nuts

Cream the butter with the icing sugar, lemon rind and orange rind until light and fluffy. Sift the flour with the cornflour and salt and gradually add to the butter mixture, mixing well. Press into a floured 18-cm/7-in square baking tin.

Bake for 40 minutes, allow to cool slightly, then cut into 10 fingers. Allow to cool on a wire rack.

Melt the chocolate with the golden syrup in a bowl over a pan of hot water. Cut the flake bars in half crossways and place half a bar on top of each short-bread finger. Dip both ends of the fingers in the melted chocolate mixture, sprinkle with the nuts and leave to set on greaseproof paper.

Cook's Tip

Tollhouse Rockies are typical American cookies – but when does a biscuit become a cookie and vice versa? No one really knows except that the British tend to call their crunchy nibbles biscuits, like the French – meaning twice baked – and the Americans opt for the word cookie to describe their range of crunchy or chewy, plain or fancy, crisp and crumbly sweet offerings.

Cook's Tip

These biscuits can be made with a currant shortbread mixture. Simply prepare the base as above, adding 40 g/ $1\frac{1}{2}$ oz currants to the butter mixture.

239 | Ginger Florentines

Preparation time
20–30 minutes

Cooking time
10 minutes

Oven temperature
180 C, 350 F, gas 4

Makes 12

Calories
230 per Florentine

You will need
90 g/3½ oz butter
100 g/4 oz caster sugar
100 g/4 oz flaked almonds,
    coarsely chopped
25 g/1 oz sultanas
15 g/½ oz crystallized ginger, finely
    chopped
25 g/1 oz glacé cherries, chopped
15 g/½ oz chopped mixed peel
1 tablespoon single cream
175 g/6 oz plain dessert chocolate

Melt the butter in a pan and stir in the sugar until dissolved. Boil for 1 minute, remove from the heat and stir in the almonds, sultanas, ginger, cherries, peel and cream, mixing well.

Drop spoonfuls onto baking trays lined with greaseproof paper, spreading them very well apart. Bake for 10 minutes or until golden brown. While still hot, trim with a sharp knife into even round shapes. Allow to cool on a wire rack.

Melt the chocolate in a bowl over a pan of hot water. Spread over the florentines and leave to set.

240 | Chocolate and Orange Chequerboards

Preparation time
25 minutes, plus 1 hour
chilling time

Cooking time
15 minutes

Oven temperature
190 C, 375 F, gas 5

Makes 24

Calories
135 per chequerboard

You will need
200 g/7 oz soft margarine
100 g/4 oz caster sugar
300 g/11 oz plain flour, sifted
1 tablespoon cocoa powder,
    dissolved in 1 tablespoon water
finely grated rind of 1 orange
yellow and red food colouring
    (optional)
beaten egg white
50-75 g/2-3 oz mixed chopped
    nuts

Cream the margarine with the sugar until light and fluffy then add the flour and mix to a dough. Mix the cocoa mixture with two-thirds of the dough and knead to blend. Add the orange rind and food colourings, if used, to the remaining dough.

Halve the chocolate dough. Divide one piece of chocolate dough and the orange dough into 12 pieces and roll into 1 × 15-cm/½ × 6-in fingers. Divide into two piles, each with 3 chocolate and 3 orange fingers. Assemble in a chequerboard pattern as illustrated. Brush with beaten egg white, then surround with the remaining rolled out chocolate dough. Roll in the nuts. Cut each block into 12 slices and place on greased baking trays. Bake for 15 minutes then cool on a wire rack.

Cook's Tip

To achieve a decorative ridged effect in the chocolate topping to the Florentines, mark with the prongs of a fork in a wavy pattern before the chocolate sets.

Cook's Tip

These biscuits should be stored in an airtight tin where they will keep for a maximum of 3 weeks.

241 | Oat Crunchies

Preparation time
10 minutes, plus 1 hour standing time

Cooking time
15–20 minutes

Oven temperature
160 C, 325 F, gas 3

Makes about 30

Calories
70 per biscuit

You will need
100 g/4 oz rolled oats
50 g/2 oz medium oatmeal
150 g/5 oz soft brown sugar
100 ml/4 fl oz oil
1 egg
½ teaspoon almond essence

Place the oats, oatmeal, sugar and oil in a bowl, mix well and leave to stand for 1 hour.

Add the egg and almond essence and beat together thoroughly. Place teaspoons of the mixture well apart on greased baking trays and press flat with a damp fork.

Bake for 15–20 minutes until golden. Leave to cool for 2 minutes then transfer to a wire rack to cool.

242 | Peanut Cookies

Preparation time
10–15 minutes

Cooking time
10–12 minutes

Oven temperature
180 C, 350 F, gas 4

Makes 12–15

Calories
90–70 per cookie

You will need
50 g/2 oz butter or margarine
50 g/2 oz soft brown sugar
50 g/2 oz salted peanuts, coarsely
  chopped
grated rind of 1 orange
75 g/3 oz self-raising flour
1 tablespoon orange juice

Cream the butter with the sugar until light and fluffy. Mix in all the remaining ingredients to form a smooth dough.

Take small pieces of the dough, about the size of a walnut, and roll into a ball. Place well apart on greased baking trays. Flatten with a fork and bake for 10–12 minutes. Cool on a wire rack.

Cook's Tip

Use a plain unflavoured cooking oil like corn, safflower, sunflower or groundnut oil for making these biscuits. Olive and other nut oils like walnut or hazelnut will have too distinctive a flavour.

Cook's Tip

When working with a sticky mixture such as this, it is often easier to achieve the required ball shapes by using wet hands.

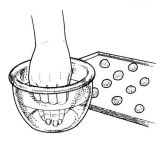

243 | Flapjacks

Preparation time
5–10 minutes

Cooking time
25–30 minutes

Oven temperature
180C, 350F, gas 4

Makes 16

Calories
140 per flapjack

You will need
100 g/4 oz butter or margarine
100 g/4 oz soft brown sugar
3 tablespoons golden syrup
225 g/8 oz rolled oats

Melt the butter with the sugar and syrup in a large pan. Stir in the rolled oats and mix thoroughly. Turn into a greased 20-cm/8-in shallow, square tin and smooth the top with a palette knife.

Bake for 25–30 minutes until golden brown. Cut into slices while still warm, then cool completely before removing from the tin.

244 | Spiced Peanut Bars

Preparation time
20 minutes

Cooking time
25–30 minutes

Oven temperature
180C, 350F, gas 4

Makes 32

Calories
120 per biscuit

You will need
100 g/4 oz golden syrup
100 g/4 oz butter or margarine
225 g/8 oz unsalted peanuts, chopped
2 eggs
175 g/6 oz self-raising flour
$\frac{1}{2}$ teaspoon ground allspice
$\frac{1}{2}$ teaspoon ground cinnamon
generous pinch of grated nutmeg
pinch of salt
grated rind of 1 orange

For the topping
2 tablespoons golden syrup
50 g/2 oz peanut butter
50 g/2 oz unsalted peanuts, chopped
generous pinch of ground cinnamon
2 tablespoons orange juice

Melt the golden syrup with the butter, add the peanuts and allow to cool slightly then beat in the eggs. Sift the flour with the spices and salt then beat into the peanut mixture together with the orange rind. Spread evenly into a greased and base-lined 25-cm/10-in shallow, square cake tin. Bake for 25–30 minutes.

Meanwhile mix together all the ingredients for the topping and warm over a gentle heat. Spread the topping over the cake immediately it comes out of the oven then allow to cool in the tin. Cut into bars when cold.

Cook's Tip

These flapjacks may be coated with a sesame topping if liked. Mix 50 g/2 oz sesame seeds with 2 tablespoons thick honey and warm to a spreading consistency. Spread over the flapjack mixture after baking, return to the oven and cook for a further 5–10 minutes.

Cook's Tip

Children will enjoy these biscuits as an extra for the luncheon box as they are very filling and nutritious.

245 | Jam Faces

Preparation time
20 minutes

Cooking time
15 minutes

Oven temperature
190C, 375F, gas 5

Makes about 20

Calories
210 per biscuit

You will need
225 g/8 oz butter or margarine
225 g/8 oz caster sugar
2 eggs, beaten
few drops of vanilla essence
450 g/1 lb plain flour, sifted
jam for spreading

Cream the butter with the sugar, then gradually beat in the eggs and vanilla essence. Stir in the flour and mix to a fairly soft dough. Turn onto a floured surface and knead gently. Roll out to 3 mm/⅛ in thickness and cut into rounds with a 6-cm/2½-in cutter. From half of these, remove two rounds to represent eyes, using a 1-cm/½-in cutter, then make a slit for the mouth.

Place all the biscuits on greased baking trays.

Bake for about 15 minutes or until golden. Leave on the baking trays for a few minutes, then transfer to a wire rack to cool.

When cold, spread the plain biscuits with jam and put the faces on top.

Cook's Tip

These are popular biscuits with children and make a welcome addition to any birthday party menu. Children will especially enjoy cutting out the faces – vary the shapes of the eyes and mouths for extra fun.

246 | Fruity Oatcakes

Preparation time
15–20 minutes

Cooking time
10–15 minutes

Oven temperature
180C, 350F, gas 4

Makes 20–24

Calories
115–95 per oatcake

You will need
100 g/4 oz butter or margarine
100 g/4 oz soft brown sugar
grated rind of 1 orange
grated rind of 1 lemon
50 g/2 oz plain flour
175 g/6 oz pinhead oatmeal
50 g/2 oz rolled oats
pinch of bicarbonate of soda
pinch of salt
1 egg yolk

Cream the butter with the sugar until light and fluffy. Stir together the remaining dry ingredients. Beat the egg yolk into the creamed mixture then gradually stir in the dry ingredients to form a soft dough. Knead lightly then roll out thinly. Use a 5-cm/2-in cutter to cut out the biscuits, re-rolling as necessary. Place well apart on greased baking trays.

Bake for 10-15 minutes, allow to cool slightly on the baking trays, then transfer to a wire rack to cool.

Cook's Tip

To make traditional oatcakes, omit the sugar and grated fruit rinds from the recipe. The butter should then be rubbed into the dry ingredients and mixed to a dough with the egg yolk. Bake for 15–20 minutes.

247 | Almond Macaroons

Preparation time
15 minutes

Cooking time
15–20 minutes

Oven temperature
160 C, 325 F, gas 3

Makes 20–22

Calories
50–45 per macaroon

You will need
2 egg whites
100 g/4 oz caster sugar
100 g/4 oz ground almonds
1 teaspoon ground rice
few drops of almond essence
halved almonds

Whisk the egg whites until stiff. Gradually whisk in the sugar and continue whisking until the mixture is thick and glossy. Stir in the ground almonds, ground rice and a few drops of almond essence

Place the mixture in a piping bag fitted with a large plain nozzle. Pipe small circles of the mixture onto baking trays lined with rice paper. Place an almond on top of each.

Bake for 15–20 minutes. Carefully remove as much rice paper from around the macaroons as possible and cool on a wire rack.

248 | Shortbread

Preparation time
15 minutes, plus 1
hour chilling time

Cooking time
40 minutes

Oven temperature
160 C, 325 F, gas 3

Makes 8

Calories
195 per biscuit

You will need
150 g/5 oz plain flour
pinch of salt
1 teaspoon ground cinnamon
25 g/1 oz ground rice
50 g/2 oz caster sugar
100 g/4 oz butter
caster sugar to dust

Sift the flour, salt, cinnamon and rice into a bowl and stir in the sugar. Rub in the butter then knead until smooth but not sticky. Wrap in clingfilm and chill for 30 minutes.

Press the dough out to an 18-cm/7-in round and place on a greased baking tray. Flute the edge and prick all over with a fork. Mark into 8 portions and chill for 30 minutes.

Bake for about 40 minutes or until pale golden. Leave on the baking tray for 10 minutes, then transfer to a wire rack to cool. Dust with sugar to serve.

Cook's Tip

To pipe out the mixture, hold the piping bag at a right angle to the baking tray and squeeze gently for the required amount of mixture. Pull away quickly to break the mixture or cut away with a knife for a clean break.

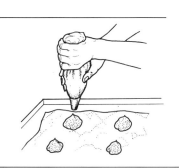

Cook's Tip

If liked the mixture can be pressed into a decorative shortbread mould. If this is liberally dusted with caster sugar before the mixture is added it will help the release properties when unmoulding onto the baking tray.

249 | Walnut Coffee Trumpets

Preparation time
15 minutes

Cooking time
about 30 minutes

Oven temperature
180C, 350F, gas 4

Makes 20

Calories
125 per biscuit

You will need
50 g/2 oz butter or margarine
25 g/1 oz golden syrup
50 g/2 oz soft brown sugar
50 g/2 oz walnuts, chopped
40 g/1½ oz plain flour

For the filling
300 ml/½ pint double cream
2 tablespoons golden syrup
1 tablespoon coffee essence

Place the butter, syrup and sugar in a saucepan and stir over a gentle heat until melted and well mixed. Stir in the nuts and flour. Place teaspoonfuls of this mixture onto greased baking trays.

Bake, in batches, for 8–10 minutes, until well spread, bubbling and a dark golden colour. Allow to cool on the trays for a minute then carefully remove with a palette knife and wrap around greased cream horn tins. Leave to cool on a wire rack then carefully remove the tins.

To make the filling, whip the cream with the syrup until thick then stir in the coffee essence. Spoon or pipe the cream into the horns and serve at once.

250 | Cinnamon Rings

Preparation time
15 minutes

Cooking time
10–15 minutes

Oven temperature
180C, 350F, gas 4

Makes 24

Calories
105 per biscuit

You will need
175 g/6 oz plain flour
100 g/4 oz butter or margarine
50 g/2 oz caster sugar
½ teaspoon ground cinnamon
grated rind of 1 orange
1 egg yolk

For the decoration
225 g/8 oz icing sugar, sifted
2–3 tablespoons orange juice
coarsely grated orange rind

Sift the flour into a bowl and rub in the butter. Add the sugar, cinnamon, orange rind and egg yolk and mix to a smooth dough. Knead lightly then roll out thinly. Use a 6-cm/2½-in cutter to cut out 24 biscuits. Cut the middle out of each biscuit using a 2.5-cm/1-in fluted cutter. Place on greased baking trays.

Bake for 10–15 minutes until golden then cool on a wire rack.

To decorate the rings, mix the icing sugar with the orange juice until smooth. Carefully coat the top of the biscuits with the icing and sprinkle with the orange rind. Leave to set.

Cook's Tip

These biscuits may be stored unfilled for 2–3 weeks in an airtight container and make an ideal accompaniment to cold desserts.

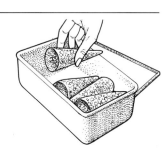

Cook's Tip

Any leftover centres of the rings that cannot be re-rolled to make more biscuits can be baked separately as small biscuits for children or small appetites.

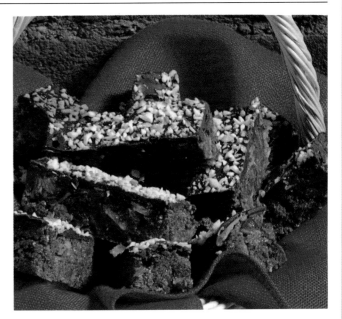

251 | Date Fingers

Preparation time
30 minutes

Cooking time
1 hour 10–1 hour 20 minutes

Oven temperature
160 C, 325 F, gas 3
190 C, 375 F, gas 5

Makes 18

Calories
210 per biscuit

You will need
100 g/4 oz butter or margarine
50 g/2 oz caster sugar
1 egg yolk
100 g/4 oz self-raising flour
100 g/4 oz ground almonds
4 bananas
juice of 1 lemon
225 g/8 oz dates, stoned and
  halved
50 g/2 oz blanched almonds,
  halved
3 tablespoons soft brown sugar

For the topping
1 egg
50 g/2 oz soft brown sugar
25 g/1 oz plain flour
50 g/2 oz ground almonds
icing sugar to dust

Cream the butter with the sugar until light and fluffy. Beat in the egg yolk and stir in the flour and ground almonds to make a very soft dough. Press into the base of a greased 18 × 28-cm/7 × 11-in Swiss roll tin and prick with a fork. Bake 'blind' at the lower temperature for 30–40 minutes. Cool slightly. Slice the bananas and sprinkle with the lemon juice. Add the remaining ingredients, stir well and spread over the base.

Whisk the egg with the sugar until creamy. Sift over the flour and fold in with the ground almonds. Spread thinly over the banana mixture. Increase the oven temperature and bake for 40 minutes until golden. Cool in the tin, cut into fingers then dust with icing sugar.

Cook's Tip

**Use 4 medium-sized bananas
for the filling for these
biscuits. If you only have large
or small ones then remember
this is about 675 g/1½ lb
unpeeled weight of bananas.**

252 | Fruity Bran Fingers

Preparation time
15 minutes, plus
overnight standing

Makes 16

Calories
165 per finger

You will need
grated rind and juice of 2 oranges
grated rind of 1 lemon
50 g/2 oz clear honey
2 tablespoons sherry
50 g/2 oz butter, melted
100 g/4 oz All-Bran cereal
100 g/4 oz dried figs, chopped
100 g/4 oz sultanas
50 g/2 oz flaked almonds
50 g/2 oz glacé cherries, chopped

For the icing and decoration
75 g/3 oz plain chocolate, melted
25 g/1 oz butter, melted
50 g/2 oz blanched almonds,
  chopped

Mix together the fruit rinds and juice, honey, sherry and butter. Combine the All-Bran, figs, sultanas, almonds and cherries then pour over the wet ingredients and mix together thoroughly. Press into a greased 15 × 24-cm/6 × 9½-in shallow, oblong tin.

To ice and decorate, mix the melted chocolate with the melted butter and spread evenly over the top of the fruit mixture. Sprinkle with the chopped almonds and leave overnight in a cool place until quite firm.

Cut into fingers and carefully remove from the tin.

Cook's Tip

**For an exciting addition to
children's parties, cut the un-
iced mixture into cubes. Put
on the end of cocktail sticks
and dip into melted
chocolate. Stick into an
orange or grapefruit.**

253 | Brandy Snap Creams

Preparation time
20 minutes

Cooking time
about 30 minutes

Oven temperature
180 C, 350 F, gas 4

Makes about 20

Calories
115 per brandy snap

You will need
50 g/2 oz butter or margarine
1 tablespoon golden syrup
50 g/2 oz soft brown sugar
1 teaspoon lemon juice
50 g/2 oz plain flour
1 teaspoon ground ginger
½ teaspoon ground mixed spice
300 ml/½ pint double cream
25 g/1 oz stem ginger, very finely
    chopped
1 teaspoon brandy or ginger wine
    (optional)
2 tablespoons chopped mixed nuts

Melt the butter in a pan with the golden syrup and sugar. When bubbling, add the lemon juice, flour, ginger and mixed spice, mixing well. Place teaspoonfuls onto a greased baking tray, allowing room to spread.

Bake, in batches, for 6–8 minutes. Cool slightly, lift with a spatula and while hot, mould around the greased handles of wooden spoons. Cool then remove.

Whip the cream with the stem ginger and brandy or ginger wine if used. Fill the brandy snaps with the cream and dip the ends into nuts to coat. Chill lightly before serving.

254 | Chocolate Chews

Preparation time
5–10 minutes

Cooking time
15–20 minutes

Oven temperature
180 C, 350 F, gas 4

Makes about 12

Calories
105 per chew

You will need
2 egg whites
75 g/3 oz caster sugar
150 g/5 oz desiccated coconut
2 tablespoons cocoa powder,
    sifted

Whisk the egg whites until stiff, then whisk in the sugar. Carefully fold in the coconut and cocoa powder. Place small mounds of the mixture on a baking tray lined with silicone paper.

Bake for 15–20 minutes, until lightly browned – the mixture will still feel soft but will crisp as it cools. Carefully remove from the paper with a palette knife when cool.

Cook's Tip

The cooked brandy snaps can also be moulded around cream horn tins for a special occasion. The cream can then be piped or spooned into the open end and dipped in nuts for serving.

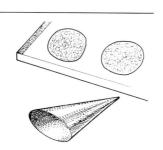

Cook's Tip

Give these chews a mocha flavour by replacing 2 teaspoons of the cocoa powder with coffee powder if liked.

255 | Chocolate Macaroon Fingers

Preparation time
20 minutes

Cooking time
15 minutes

Oven temperature
180 C, 350 F, gas 4

Makes about 18

Calories
115 per finger

You will need
175 g/6 oz caster sugar
150 g/5 oz ground almonds
2 tablespoons ground rice
2 egg whites
½ teaspoon almond essence
75 g/3 oz plain chocolate, melted

Mix the sugar, almonds and ground rice together. Beat the egg whites lightly, add the dry ingredients and almond essence and beat to a smooth, firm consistency.

Leave the mixture to stand for 5 minutes, then place in a piping bag fitted with a 2-cm/¾-in plain nozzle. Pipe 7.5-cm/3-in lengths on baking trays lined with silicone paper.

Bake for 15 minutes. leave to cool on the baking trays then remove from the silicone paper.

Dip each end of the macaroons in melted chocolate, then place on a piece of greaseproof paper to set.

Cook's Tip

For a different flavour occasionally why not dip the fingers in a coffee, orange or mint flavoured chocolate.

256 | Coconut Macaroons

Preparation time
10 minutes, plus cooling time

Cooking time
20 minutes

Oven temperature
180 C, 350 F, gas 4

Makes 18

Calories
145 per macaroon

You will need
225 g/8 oz desiccated coconut
275 g/10 oz sugar
5 egg whites
glacé cherries, halved, to decorate

Mix the coconut, sugar and egg whites together in a saucepan. Heat gently, stirring carefully with a wooden spoon until the mixture is warm but not hot – about 60 C/140 F. Remove from the heat and leave until cold.

Divide the mixture into 18 mounds, setting them down on greased and floured baking trays. Top each mound with a half glacé cherry.

Bake for 20 minutes until pale golden brown. Cool on a wire rack.

Cook's Tip

These macaroons can be topped with coloured glacé cherries for a children's party – try green and yellow as well as red.

257 | Garibaldi Biscuits

Preparation time
20–25 minutes

Cooking time
10–12 minutes

Oven temperature
200 C, 400 F, gas 6

Makes 24

Calories
35 per biscuit

You will need
100 g/4 oz self-raising flour
pinch of salt
40 g/1½ oz butter or margarine
25 g/1 oz caster sugar
3 tablespoons milk
50 g/2 oz currants
beaten egg to glaze

Sift the flour with the salt, rub in the butter then add the sugar, mixing well. Add 2 tablespoons of the milk and mix to a firm dough. Knead until smooth, about 2–3 minutes.

Roll out to a 23-cm/9-in square, cut in half and brush one half with the remaining milk. Sprinkle evenly with the currants, then cover with the remaining piece of dough. Press down lightly to seal, then roll out with a floured rolling pin to a 25 × 20-cm/10 × 8-in rectangle. Cut into 24 neat fingers and place on greased baking trays. Glaze with beaten egg.

Bake for 10–12 minutes or until golden. Cool slightly on the trays then on a wire rack.

Cook's Tip

These biscuits will keep for up to 1 week if stored in an airtight tin.

258 | Sesame Flapjacks

Preparation time
15 minutes

Cooking time
20 minutes

Oven temperature
180 C, 350 F, gas 4

Makes 12

Calories
255 per flapjack

You will need
100 g/4 oz thick honey
50 g/2 oz golden syrup
100 g/4 oz butter or margarine
grated rind of 1 orange
100 g/4 oz stoned dates, chopped
50 g/2 oz sesame seeds
225 g/8 oz rolled oats

For the topping
50 g/2 oz sesame seeds
2 tablespoons thick honey

Melt the honey, syrup and butter together. Add the orange rind, dates, sesame seeds and oats and stir well. Press into a 24 × 15-cm/9½ × 6-in shallow, oblong tin lined with rice paper. Bake for 20 minutes.

To make the topping, mix the sesame seeds with the honey and warm over a saucepan of hot water until soft enough to spread easily. Remove the flapjack from the oven, spread with the sesame and honey mixture, return to the oven and cook for a further 10–15 minutes, until golden. Allow to cool in the tin then cut into 12 slices while still warm.

Cook's Tip

If when you reach for your honey jar you find that the contents have crystallized, then place the jar in a pan of warm water and heat gently until the mixture revitalizes and becomes runny again.

259 | Cheesy Digestive Biscuits

Preparation time
20 minutes

Cooking time
25–30 minutes

Oven temperature
180 C, 350 F, gas 4

Makes about 20

Calories
80 per biscuit

You will need
175 g/6 oz wholemeal flour
25 g/1 oz medium oatmeal
¼ teaspoon salt
75 g/3 oz lard
1 tablespoon demerara sugar
40 g/1½ oz Cotswold cheese with chives, finely grated
1 egg, beaten
2 tablespoons water

Sift the flour, oatmeal and salt into a bowl and discard any bran that remains in the sieve. Rub in the lard, stir in the sugar and cheese, mixing well. Add two-thirds of the egg and water and mix to a firm dough. Roll out on a floured surface and cut out about 20 rounds with a 7.5-cm/3-in cutter. Place on greased baking trays and prick with a fork. Brush with the remaining egg.

Bake for 25–30 minutes or until lightly golden. Cool on a wire rack. Serve with cheese and pickles or as a savoury snack.

260 | Cheese and Chive Shortbread

Preparation time
15–20 minutes

Cooking time
1 hour

Oven temperature
150 C, 300 F, gas 2

Makes 8

Calories
220 per slice

You will need
150 g/5 oz plain flour
25 g/1 oz ground rice
¼ teaspoon grated nutmeg
⅛ teaspoon mustard powder
pinch of salt
100 g/4 oz butter or margarine
100 g/4 oz Cheddar cheese, finely grated
2 teaspoons snipped chives
1 tablespoon single cream

Sift the flour, ground rice, nutmeg, mustard and salt into a bowl. Rub in the butter, stir in the cheese and chives, mixing well. Bind together with the cream to make a firm dough.

Press evenly into a floured 18-cm/7-in loose-bottomed flan tin. Make a decorative edge by pressing around with the prongs of a fork. Prick thoroughly.

Bake for about 1 hour or until golden brown and crisp. Cut into eight segments while still hot, then leave to cool in the tin.

Cook's Tip

For a special savoury topping sprinkle the biscuits with a little sea salt after glazing and before baking.

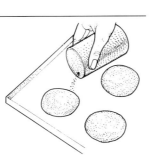

Cook's Tip

This shortbread is good served instead of bread or biscuits with cheese, soups and salads.

Cheesecakes

Rich and crumbly, smooth and creamy, baked and palate-sticking, or chilled and light – there is a cheesecake in this chapter to suit your taste. Whether you prefer the firmer, richer baked cheesecake or lighter, more delicate, unbaked cheesecake, remember to make serving slices small. When time and pocket allow, try ringing the changes with favourite recipes by using a different type of biscuit crumb base – muesli, ginger nut, chocolate chip and walnut biscuits all make good substitutes for plain digestives – and top with imaginative decorations, from sliced fruit, chopped nuts and drizzled chocolate to piped cream and sprinkled spices.

261 | Summerfruit Ring

Preparation time
20 minutes, plus chilling time

Cooking time
30 minutes

Oven temperature
180 C, 350 F, gas 4

Serves 6–8

Calories
605–455 per portion

You will need
225 g/8 oz curd cheese
225 g/8 oz cream cheese
100 g/4 oz caster sugar
2 large eggs

For the base
100 g/4 oz digestive biscuits, crushed
50 g/2 oz butter, melted

For the decoration
225 g/8 oz redcurrants, topped and tailed
225 g/8 oz raspberries, hulled
150 ml/¼ pint double cream

Beat the cheeses together until smooth, then beat in the sugar and eggs, one at a time. Pour into a lightly oiled 20-cm/8-in ring tin and bake for 30 minutes.

Meanwhile, mix the crushed biscuits with melted butter. Press over the top of the cooked cheesecake and chill until firm.

Carefully loosen the edge of the cheesecake and dip the bottom of the tin into very hot water for 30 seconds. Invert onto a serving plate and chill until required.

To serve, fill the centre of the ring with the fruit and decorate with whipped cream.

262 | Creamy New York Cheesecake

Preparation time
30 minutes, plus chilling time

Cooking time
45 minutes

Oven temperature
230 C, 450 F, gas 8
180 C, 350 F, gas 4

Serves 8–10

Calories
745–595 per portion

You will need
175 g/6 oz digestive biscuits
75 g/3 oz butter, melted

For the filling
450 g/1 lb cream cheese
450 g/1 lb cottage cheese, sieved
275 g/10 oz caster sugar
2 teaspoons vanilla essence
pinch of salt
5 eggs, separated
1 (170-g/6-oz) can evaporated milk
100 ml/4 fl oz double cream
3 tablespoons plain flour
1 tablespoon lemon juice

Mix the biscuit crumbs with the butter and press onto the base of a lightly greased 23-cm/9-in loose-bottomed, spring-release cake tin. Chill until firm, 15–20 minutes.

Meanwhile, beat the cheeses with the sugar, vanilla essence, salt and egg yolks until smooth and creamy. Add the evaporated milk, cream and flour. Whisk the egg whites until stiff then fold into the cheesecake mixture with the lemon juice. Turn into the prepared tin.

Place in the oven preheated to the higher temperature then immediately reduce to the lower temperature. Bake for 45 minutes, then turn off the oven. Allow the cheesecake to cool in the oven with the door slightly ajar. Chill before serving.

Cook's Tip

The easiest way to crush biscuits for cheesecakes is to place them in a polythene bag and crush with a rolling pin.

Cook's Tip

This cheesecake can be made with a variety of biscuit crumbs to ring the changes. Why not try chocolate digestive biscuits, ginger cookies or muesli biscuits for example.

263 | Blackcurrant and Ginger Cheesecake

Preparation time
20 minutes, plus chilling time

Serves 6–8

Calories
950–710 per portion

You will need
100 g/4 oz butter, melted
225 g/8 oz gingernut biscuits, crushed

For the filling
450 g/1 lb cream cheese
50 g/2 oz caster sugar
6 tablespoons single cream
550 g/1¼ lb blackcurrants, topped and tailed
15 g/½ oz powdered gelatine

For the topping
300 ml/½ pint double cream
1 egg white, stiffly whisked

Mix the butter with the gingernut crumbs and use to line the base of a lightly greased 23-cm/9-in loose-bottomed cake tin. Chill to firm, about 10–15 minutes.

Beat the cream cheese and sugar together until smooth and creamy. Stir in the cream and 450 g/1 lb of the blackcurrants. Dissolve the gelatine in 2 tablespoons of boiling water and stir into the blackcurrant mixture. Spoon over the chilled cheesecake crust and chill until set, about 1 hour.

Meanwhile, whip the cream until stiff, then fold in the egg white. Swirl over the top of the cheesecake. Top with the remaining blackcurrants. Chill for about 15 minutes before serving.

Cook's Tip

The cream cheese will mix better if it is at room temperature, so remove from the refrigerator about 2 hours before using. Alternatively, if you have a microwave then soften for 1–2 minutes on Medium (50%) power.

264 | Easy Prune and Apricot Cheesecake

Preparation time
25 minutes

Cooking time
40 minutes

Oven temperature
180 C, 350 F, gas 4

Serves 6

Calories
400 per portion

You will need
175 g/6 oz digestive biscuits, crushed
75 g/3 oz butter, melted

For the topping
2 eggs, beaten
25 g/1 oz caster sugar
grated rind of 1 lemon
juice of ½ lemon
100 g/4 oz cottage cheese, sieved
150 ml/¼ pint soured cream
15 g/½ oz plain flour
1 (213-g/7½-oz) can apricot halves, drained, dried and chopped
1 (213-g/7½-oz) can prunes, drained, stoned, dried and chopped
icing sugar to dust

Mix the biscuit crumbs with the butter and use to line the base of a lightly greased 18-cm/7-in shallow, loose-bottomed cake tin. Chill until firm.

Mix the eggs with the sugar, lemon rind, lemon juice, cottage cheese, soured cream and flour. Fold in the apricots and prunes. Spoon over the biscuit base.

Bake for 40 minutes. Turn the oven off and leave the cheesecake to cool in the oven.

Unmould, dust with icing sugar and cut into wedges to serve.

Cook's Tip

Sieve the cottage cheese twice to ensure that the cheesecake is smooth and creamy. Press through a metal or nylon sieve or purée in a blender or food processor until smooth.

265 | Orange Raisin Cheesecake

Preparation time
25 minutes

Cooking time
50 minutes

Oven temperature
220 C, 425 F, gas 7
190 C, 375 F, gas 5

Serves 8–10

Calories
475–380 per portion

You will need
1 (368-g/13-oz) packet frozen puff
  pastry, defrosted
75 g/3 oz butter
75 g/3 oz caster sugar
2 eggs, beaten
225 g/8 oz curd cheese
50 g/2 oz ground almonds
finely grated rind of 1 orange
2 tablespoons frozen concentrated
  orange juice, defrosted
2 tablespoons lemon juice
75 g/3 oz glacé cherries, quartered
75 g/3 oz raisins
4 tablespoons orange curd

Roll out two-thirds of the pastry and use to line a 20-cm/8-in loose-bottomed flan tin.

Cream the butter with the sugar until light and fluffy. Beat in the eggs alternately with the curd cheese. Add the almonds, orange rind, orange and lemon juices and mix well. Fold in the cherries and raisins. Spoon into the pastry case and smooth the top.

Roll out the remaining dough and cut into 10 (1-cm/½-in) strips. Lay on top of the cheesecake in a lattice design. Place the cheesecake on a heated baking tray and bake at the higher temperature for 15 minutes.

Reduce the oven temperature and bake for a further 35 minutes. Remove from the oven and carefully remove the flan tin. Brush the top and sides with the orange curd and leave to cool. Serve cold.

Cook's Tip

The orange curd will brush easily if warmed slightly before use. Either heat in a small pan or stand the jar of curd in a bowl of warm water.

266 | Petite Cheesecakes

Preparation time
25 minutes

Cooking time
25 minutes

Oven temperature
190 C, 375 F, gas 5

Makes 24

Calories
115 per cheesecake

You will need
1 recipe shortcrust pastry (see
  Introduction)

For the filling
150 ml/¼ pint soured cream
2 eggs, separated
75 g/3 oz caster sugar
grated rind of 1 lemon
2 teaspoons lemon juice
225 g/8 oz cottage cheese
1 tablespoon plain flour
50 g/2 oz icing sugar, sifted

Roll out the pastry on a lightly floured surface and cut out 24 (7.5-cm/3-in) rounds. Use to line greased patty tins. Chill while preparing the filling.

Place the soured cream, egg yolks, caster sugar, lemon rind, half of the lemon juice, the cottage cheese and flour in a blender or liquidiser and mix until smooth. Alternatively, mix together then pass through a fine sieve. Whisk the egg whites until stiff and fold into the mixture with a metal spoon. Divide the mixture between the pastry cases.

Bake for about 25 minutes then turn out to cool on a wire rack.

Mix the icing sugar with the emaining lemon juice to make a thin glacé icing. Brush over the cheesecakes before serving.

Cook's Tip

If liked these cheesecakes can be made with an orange filling. Use the grated rind of 1 small orange and 2 teaspoons orange juice instead of the lemon rind and lemon juice.

267 | *Hazelnut Cheesecake*

Preparation time
30 minutes

Cooking time
1 hour 10 minutes

Oven temperature
200 C, 400 F, gas 6
160 C, 325 F, gas 3

Serves 8

Calories
475 per portion

You will need
75 g/3 oz plain flour
25 g/1 oz hazelnuts, ground
50 g/2 oz sugar
50 g/2 oz butter

For the filling
275 g/10 oz cream cheese
150 g/5 oz sugar
50 g/2 oz plain flour
1 teaspoon vanilla essence
4 eggs
150 ml/$\frac{1}{4}$ pint natural yogurt
100 g/4 oz plain chocolate, melted

To make the base, stir the flour, hazelnuts and sugar together in a bowl. Rub in the butter and knead lightly to a dough. Press onto the base of a greased 20-cm/8-in loose-bottomed cake tin. Bake at the higher temperature for 10 minutes.

Beat the cream cheese with the sugar. Stir in the flour and vanilla essence, then gradually beat in the eggs. Beat in the yogurt and pour half this filling over the biscuit base. Stir the chocolate into the remaining filling and drop spoonfuls into the tin. Lightly swirl the two mixtures together.

Reduce the oven temperature and bake for 1 hour. Turn off the oven and leave the cheesecake in the oven for another hour to cool.

Cook's Tip

Swirl the two mixtures together by inserting the tip of a knife or skewer into the cheesecake and stir lightly, taking care not to disturb the base.

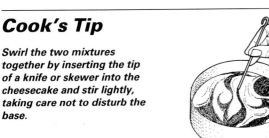

268 | *Chocolate Cheesecake*

Preparation time
20 minutes, plus chilling time

Serves 6

Calories
725 per portion

You will need
100 g/4 oz chocolate digestive biscuits, crushed
50 g/2 oz butter, melted

For the filling
225 g/8 oz cream cheese
100 g/4 oz caster sugar
2 eggs, separated
100 g/4 oz plain chocolate, melted
2 teaspoons powdered gelatine
150 ml/$\frac{1}{4}$ pint double cream, whipped

For the decoration
150 ml/$\frac{1}{4}$ pint double cream
chocolate curls
icing sugar

Mix the biscuit crumbs with the melted butter and press onto the base of an 18-cm/7-in spring form tin. Chill until firm, about 10–15 minutes.

To make the filling, beat the cream cheese until smooth. Add the sugar, egg yolks and melted chocolate. Dissolve the gelatine in 2 tablespoons of hot water and add to the cheesecake mixture. Whisk the egg whites until stiff and fold in with a metal spoon. Finally fold in the cream. Pour into the tin and chill to set.

Unmould the cheesecake onto a serving plate. Whip the cream and pipe a border around the top edge of the cheesecake. Decorate the centre with chocolate curls and sprinkle with icing sugar.

Cook's Tip

Powdered gelatine can be dissolved in boiling water if stirred briskly to mix. Alternatively, sprinkle the gelatine over the stated quantity of cold water, leave until spongy then place in a pan of hot water and leave **until clear and dissolved, about 5–10 minutes.**

269 | Baked Cherry Cheesecake

Preparation time
25–30 minutes

Cooking time
1 hour 5–1 hour 10 minutes

Oven temperature
200 C, 400 F, gas 6
180 C, 350 F, gas 4

Serves 6–8

Calories
525–390 per portion

You will need
½ recipe rich shortcrust pastry (see Introduction)

For the filling
4 eggs
4 tablespoons caster sugar
finely grated rind and juice of 1 lemon
225 g/8 oz cottage cheese, sieved
300 ml/½ pint soured cream
1 tablespoon plain flour

For the decoration
1 (397-g/14-oz) can cherry pie filling
150 ml/¼ pint double cream

Roll out the pastry on a lightly floured surface and use to line a 20-cm/8-in deep, loose-bottomed cake tin. Bake 'blind' at the higher temperature for 20 minutes, removing the paper and beans after 15 minutes.

To make the filling, beat the eggs with the sugar until light and fluffy, then beat in the remaining filling ingredients. Pour into the pastry case.

Reduce the oven temperature and bake for 45–50 minutes. Turn off the oven and leave the cheesecake in the oven to cool.

To serve, remove from the tin and place on a serving plate. Top with the cherry pie filling and decorate with whipped cream.

Cook's Tip

This baked cheesecake can be topped with any number of different flavoured pie fillings. Try blackcurrant, redcurrant or blackberry and apple for example.

270 | Lemon Sponge Cheesecake

Preparation time
25 minutes

Cooking time
1½ hours

Oven temperature
160 C, 325 F, gas 3

Serves 6

Calories
540 per portion

You will need
50 g/2 oz butter or margarine
50 g/2 oz caster sugar
1 egg, beaten
50 g/2 oz self-raising flour

For the filling
350 g/12 oz cottage cheese, sieved
150 ml/¼ pint double cream
25 g/1 oz plain flour
50 g/2 oz caster sugar
3 eggs, beaten
finely grated rind of 2 lemons
juice of 1 lemon

For the topping
100 g/4 oz sugar
2 lemons, peeled and sliced
50 g/2 oz butter
25 g/1 oz flaked almonds

Beat the first four ingredients until smooth. Pour into a greased and lined 18-cm/7-in cake tin. Bake for 15 minutes. Mix the filling ingredients together and pour over the sponge. Return to the oven and cook for 1¼ hours. Turn off and leave the cheesecake in the oven for a further 30 minutes to cool. Remove and cool.

Place the sugar in a pan and heat until caramelized. Dip in the lemon slices then cool on a wire rack. Add the butter and almonds to the pan and cook until the mixture thickens. Turn onto waxed paper and leave to set, then crumble over the cheesecake with the lemon slices.

Cook's Tip

To line a deep cake tin, cut a piece of greaseproof paper long enough to go around the inside of the tin and about 5 cm/2 in taller than the height of the tin. Fold up about 2.5 cm/1 in of the strip, creasing it well and snip the folded edge at regular intervals. Cut 2 rounds to line the base of the tin. Place one round on the base of the tin. Position the strip around the tin, then cover and secure in place with the second round base paper.

271 | Sugar and Spice Cheesecake

Preparation time
20 minutes

Cooking time
35 minutes

Oven temperature
180 C, 350 F, gas 4

Serves 8

Calories
545 per portion

You will need
175 g/6 oz digestive biscuits, crushed
1 tablespoon soft brown sugar
75 g/3 oz butter, melted

For the filling
350 g/12 oz cream cheese
2 eggs, beaten
100 g/4 oz sugar
$\frac{1}{2}$ teaspoon vanilla essence

For the topping
3 tablespoons soft brown sugar
1 teaspoon ground cinnamon
150 ml/$\frac{1}{4}$ pint double cream

Mix the biscuit crumbs with the sugar and butter and press onto the base and sides of a 23-cm/9-in loose-bottomed flan tin. Chill to firm.

Beat the cream cheese with the eggs, sugar and vanilla essence until smooth. Pour into the crumb case then bake for 20 minutes.

Meanwhile, mix the sugar with the cinnamon. Sprinkle over the cheesecake and cook for a further 15 minutes or until the filling has set. Leave in the tin until cold.

To serve, transfer to a serving plate and decorate with whipped cream.

Cook's Tip

Try not to remove the cheesecake from the oven to sprinkle with the sugar and cinnamon mixture or the mixture may fall and produce a sticky, close-textured cheesecake.

272 | Walnut and Cherry Cheesecake

Preparation time
15–20 minutes

Cooking time
1 hour

Oven temperature
180 C, 350 F, gas 4

Serves 8

Calories
792 per portion

You will need
150 g/5 oz digestive biscuits, crushed
50 g/2 oz walnuts, chopped
1 tablespoon soft brown sugar
65 g/$2\frac{1}{2}$ oz butter, melted

For the filling
450 g/1 lb cream cheese
225 g/8 oz caster sugar
4 eggs
300 ml/$\frac{1}{2}$ pint soured cream
4 tablespoons cornflour
1 tablespoon lemon juice

For the decoration
150 ml/$\frac{1}{4}$ pint double cream
1 (425-g/15-oz) can black cherries

Mix the biscuit crumbs with the walnuts, sugar and butter and press onto the base of a deep 20-cm/8-in loose-bottomed cake tin.

Beat the cream cheese with the sugar until smooth, then gradually beat in the eggs, soured cream, cornflour and lemon juice. Pour over the crumb base and bake for 1 hour. Turn off the oven but leave the cheesecake in the oven for 30 minutes to cool. Remove from the oven but leave in the tin until cool, then chill until firm.

Carefully transfer the cheesecake to a serving plate and decorate with piped, whipped cream and stoned cherries.

Cook's Tip

This cheesecake can also be made with hazelnuts or brazil nuts if liked. The cherries can also be replaced with sliced canned peaches or apricots if liked.

Index